W9-CBB-115

The COMPLETE ILLUSTRATED *Guide to*

Furniture & Cabinet
Construction

The COMPLETE ILLUSTRATED *Guide to*

Furniture & Cabinet
Construction

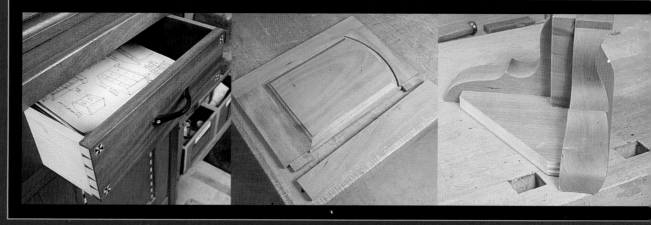

ANDY RAE

The Taunton Press

Text © 2001 by Andy Rae
Photographs © 2001 by Andy Rae (except where noted)
Illustrations © 2001 by The Taunton Press, Inc.

All rights reserved.

The Taunton Press, Inc., 63 South Main Street, PO Box 5506, Newtown, CT 06470-5506
e-mail: tp@taunton.com

DESIGN: Lori Wendin
LAYOUT: Steve Hughes, Suzie Yannes
PHOTOGRAPHER: Andy Rae (except where noted)
ILLUSTRATOR: Melanie Powell

LIBRARY OF CONGRESS CATALOGING-IN-PUBLICATION DATA:
Rae, Andy.
    The complete illustrated guide to furniture & cabinet construction / Andy Rae.
        p. cm.
    Includes index.
    ISBN-13: 978-1-56158-402-4
    ISBN-10: 1-56158-402-9
    1. Furniture making--Amateurs' manuals. 2. Cabinetwork--Amateurs' manuals. I. Title.
TT195 .R34 2001
684.1'04--dc21   2001033100

Printed in China
15 14 13

About Your Safety: Working with wood is inherently dangerous. Using hand or power tools improperly or ignoring safety practices can lead to permanent injury or even death. Don't try to perform operations you learn about here (or elsewhere) unless you're certain they are safe for you. If something about an operation doesn't feel right, don't do it. Look for another way. We want you to enjoy the craft, so please keep safety foremost in your mind whenever you're in the shop.

To Paul McClure, head chief and happy woodworking hero who bridged all barriers, social to scientific. May we reap the fruit of the wisdom he left behind on his beloved mother, the Earth.

Acknowledgments

FIRST, MY HUMBLE APPRECIATION to my editors at The Taunton Press. I was lucky to have three: Helen Albert, associate publisher, whose eagle vision lifted an idea that, at the outset, appeared too heavy to fly, and Jennifer Renjilian and Tom Clark, for their support, steadfastness—and swift solutions.

For excellent photographic services, I credit the folks at Commercial Color in Allentown, Pennsylvania, and at Iris Photography in Asheville, North Carolina. And special thanks to John Hamel, photographer, for short- and long-distance mentoring, plus some pretty fine photos over the years.

I've had the curious luck to know many fellow woodworkers and writers on a personal level. My deepest gratitude goes to my woodworking and writing teachers, past and present, who have knowingly and unknowingly inspired and taught: My creative mother, Johanna Weir, and my two artistic fathers, Jud Rae and Walter Weir, all three for their unique interest in making things; brother Gurnee Barrett, who demonstrated it was worth doing right; George Nakashima, for his unspoken commands, Frank Klausz, for his outspoken commands, and Toshio Odate, for speaking the unspoken; Dave Cann and Paul Connor, whose metalworking hands have saved mine many times; the crazy woodworking folks at Arcosanti, including Kerry Gordon, Michael Christ, and Chris Fraznick; Fred Matlack, who never says it can't be done; Sue Taylor, for asking elucidative questions; Dave Sellers, for his anarchy with heart; Jim Cummins, for huge excitement in small things; Rich Wedler, whose woodworking is music to my ears; Jonathan Frank, for trusting woodworkers; Palmer Sharpless, for his wisdom on woodworking—even in the dark without electricity; "Old" Jim, Michael Burns,

Jim Budlong, and David Welter, for teaching from afar; William Draper, who gave me the freedom to explore—and paid me for it; Tim Snyder, whose insights always point the way; Mira Nakashima, for bridging the old and the new; Lonnie Bird, who's quiet approach bespeaks fierce skill; Edward Schoen, for showing me how to problem solve my way out of anything; Kitty Mace, for challenging everything; Pat Edwards, for hosting itinerant woodworkers; Ned Brown, who unwittingly inspired me to excel; Simon Watts, for being the gent of all gentleman woodworkers; Steve and Susan Blenk, for persistence and tall goodwill; Tom Brown, who patiently taught a young man the art of installation; Leonard Lee, a bona-fide tool nut and enthusiast; Kevin Ireland, my first editor (you never forget your first); David Sloan, for curiously encouraging curiosity; Frank Pollaro, for adventure and bravado; Mike Dresdner, who's always there when there's nowhere else to go; Eric Stang, for enthusiasm and artistic inspiration; Paul Anthony, whose feedback keeps my feet on the ground; Janet Lasley, for helping me to stay alive in the business of woodworking; Steve "Pimo" Metz and John Yarnall, who both demonstrate that patience and planning always win the day; Ellis Walentine, for clever solutions and unexpected detours; Mike Callihan, for last-minute woodworking; the folks at the Lehigh Valley (Pennsylvania) Guild, for their sometimes embarrassing encouragement; Ric Hanisch, for having the courage to design from the heart; Peter Kauzman, for staying up late; and Manny Pagan and Yeung Chan, both exemplifying what true woodworking passion is all about.

Last, I thank my family, Lee, Zy, and Shade—especially my wife, Lee Speed—for enduring my "one year leave of absence" for writing this book. I love you guys and always will.

Contents

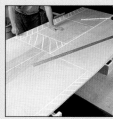

PART THREE Doors · 130

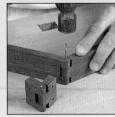

PART FOUR Bases, Feet, and Stands · 176

PART FIVE Frame Construction · 212

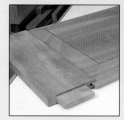

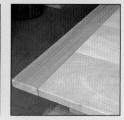

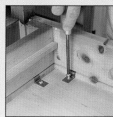

Introduction

MAKING FURNITURE is one of the most satisfying ways to pass time: The *schiiick* of a plane iron on wood; the dizzying aroma of freshly sawn sugar pine or East Indian rosewood; the endless array of color, texture, and feel of woods from around the world; the tense but joyful final assembly, when all work and toil come together in a conclusive burst of completion. What excitement! This is the fine—and fun—art of woodworking. The reward is beautiful furniture.

To experience this excitement, you'll need to have a degree of control over your work and your tools, command a working knowledge of your materials, and understand some basic design principles. Unlike most other crafts, furniture making and cabinetmaking demand vast knowledge—and attentiveness. You must know what tools and techniques to use and how to arrange the correct sequence, or order, of events when using them. You should listen with attentive ears and eyes to the material you're working and choose wood wisely, allowing for its eccentricities. With its countless pieces and parts, cabinetmaking involves a high level of organization, and organizing your work and your shop space are part and parcel of the craft. By combining all your skills, you can make any type of furniture your dreams conjure up. You're limited only by your imagination. I hope this book will provide you with a starting point for these skills. With practice, many small joys are waiting for you. They're worth seeking.

Above all, be patient. It takes time to master some of the smallest things. There are tricks and shortcuts, of course. They come with experience, and many are shown in the pages ahead. More important is the awareness that comes from trying many approaches and finding one that works for you. In a very real sense, woodworking is a personal journey. That's because there is no right or wrong way of making furniture. What counts is what works. After 20 plus years of practicing the craft, I still search daily for new ways of working. Once you discover something that works, call it your own, and stand by it. You'll have found something that will make your woodworking more pleasurable. And your fine furniture will reflect the results.

How to Use This Book

IRST OF ALL, this book is meant to be used, not put on a shelf to gather dust. It's meant to be pulled out and opened on your bench when you need to do a new or unfamiliar technique. So the first way to use this book is to make sure it's near where you do woodworking.

In the pages that follow you'll find a wide variety of methods that cover the important processes of this area of woodworking. Just as in many other practical areas, in woodworking there are often many ways to get to the same result. Why you choose one method over another depends on several factors:

Time. Are you in a hurry or do you have the leisure to enjoy the quiet that comes with hand tools?

Your tooling. Do you have the kind of shop that's the envy of every woodworker or a modest collection of the usual hand and power tools?

Your skill level. Do you prefer simpler methods because you're starting out or are you always looking to challenge yourself and expand your skills?

The project. Is the piece you're making utilitarian or an opportunity to show off your best work?

In this book, we've included a wide variety of techniques to fit these needs.

To find your way around the book, you first need to ask yourself two questions: What result am I trying to achieve? What tools do I want to use to accomplish it?

In some cases, there are many ways and many tools that will accomplish the same result. In others, there are only one or two sensible ways to do it. In all cases, however, we've taken a practical approach; so you may not find your favorite exotic method for doing a particular process. We have included every reasonable method and then a few just to flex your woodworking muscles.

To organize the material, we've broken the subject down to two levels. "Parts" are major divisions of this class of techniques. "Sections" contain related techniques. Within sections, techniques and procedures that create a similar result are grouped together, usually organized from the most common way to do it to methods requiring specialized tools or a larger degree of skill. In some cases, the progression starts with the method requiring the most basic technology and then moves on to alternative methods using other common shop tools and finally to specialized tools.

The first thing you'll see in a part is a group of photos keyed to a page number. Think of this as an illustrated table of contents. Here you'll see a photo representing each section in that part, along with the page on which each section starts.

Each section begins with a similar "visual map," with photos that represent major groupings of techniques or individual techniques. Under each grouping is a list of the step-by-step essays that explain how to do the methods, including the pages on which they can be found.

Sections begin with an "overview," or brief introduction to the methods described therein. Here's where you'll find important general information on this group of techniques, including any safety issues. You'll also read about specific tools needed for the operations that follow and how to build jigs or fixtures needed for them.

The step-by-step essays are the heart of this book. Here a group of photos represents the key steps in the process. The accompanying text describes the process and guides you through it, referring you back to the photos. Depending on how you learn best, either read the text first or look at the photos and drawings; but remember, they are meant to work together. In cases where there is an

The "VISUAL MAP" tells you where to locate the essay that details the operation you wish to do.

A "SECTION" groups related processes together.

The "OVERVIEW" gives you important general information about the group of techniques, tells you how to build jigs and fixtures, and provides advice on tooling and safety.

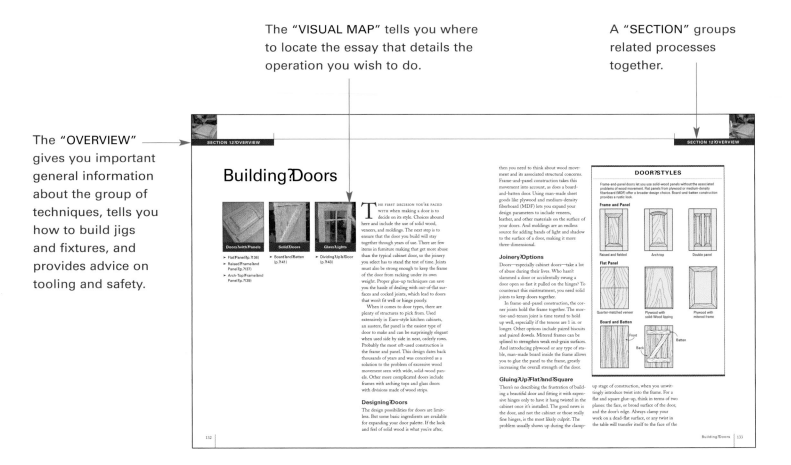

alternative step, it's called out in the text and the visual material as a "variation."

For efficiency, we've cross-referenced redundant processes or steps described in another related process. You'll see yellow "cross-references" called out frequently in the overviews and step-by-step essays.

When you see this symbol ⚠, make sure you read what follows. The importance of these safety warnings cannot be overemphasized. Always work safely and use safety devices, including eye and hearing protection. If you feel uncomfortable with a technique, don't do it, try another way.

At the back of the book is an index to help you find what you're looking for in a pinch. There's also list of further reading to help you brush up on how to use tools and keep them sharp, as well as some general references on design.

Finally, remember to use this book whenever you need to refresh your memory or to learn something new. It's been designed to be an essential reference to help you become a better woodworker. The only way it can do this is if you make it as familiar a workshop tool as your favorite bench chisels.

—The editors

"CROSS-REFERENCES" tell you where to find a related process or the detailed description of a process in another essay.

"STEP-BY-STEP ESSAYS" contain photos, drawings, and instructions on how to do the technique.

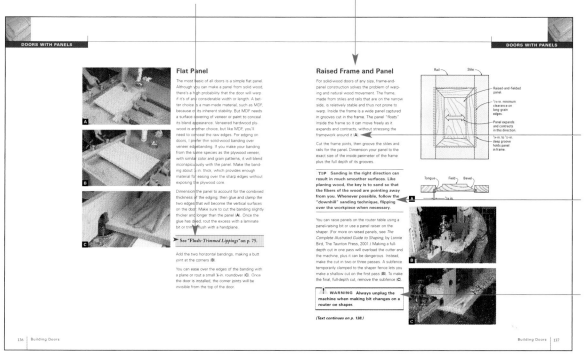

The "TEXT" contains keys to the photos and drawings.

"TIPS" show short-cuts and smart ways to work.

"WARNINGS" tell you specific safety concerns for this process and how to address them.

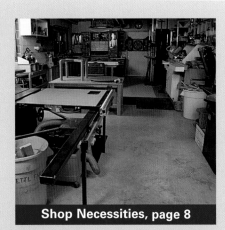
Shop Necessities, page 8

Woodworking Machines and Tools, page 13

Working Wood, page 22

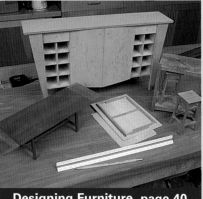
Designing Furniture, page 40

PART ONE

Tools and Materials

BUILDING FINE FURNITURE hinges on three critical components: an understanding of the material, the proper tools, and old-fashioned know-how. Without a thorough knowledge of woodworking, you'd be hard-pressed to follow even some of the simplest of woodworking plans. Yet a workshop without basic woodworking tools and the right materials faces the same dilemma. Some woodworkers start out by equipping their shops with a full complement of the best tools that money can buy, expecting good tools will make up for a lack of skill. On the other hand, first-rate work in the hands of a skilled craftsman can be enhanced by the right tools.

My advice is to buy the best tools and supplies you can afford, *as you need them.* In the interim, your skills will grow. Fine woodworking does not happen overnight. As your skills progress, you'll become more astute in your purchasing prowess, your desire will be greater, and you can buy the right tools when you know you really need them.

Shop Necessities

BUILDING FURNITURE AND CABINETS brings immense satisfaction. But frustration often blocks our aims. I remember the aggravation I encountered starting out, working in a cramped studio space with very few tools. My first attempts at building furniture were clouded with problems. Attempts at making an accurate cut often ended up in less-than-satisfactory results, due to a combination of poor light, confined space, and tools pushed far beyond their capacities. Looking back, I think there's a better way.

The following paragraphs are written with the intention of steering you clear of the frustrations I faced as a fledgling furniture maker. I'll talk about some essential gear you'll need for years of satisfying woodworking. But by no means should you consider these items sacred. I mention them as a guide only. Some gear I consider essential for constructing cabinets and furniture, such as a table saw and good light. Other "necessities" are handy to have, but you can always make do with less.

The fact is, almost all the woodworking operations and techniques that I describe in this book can be accomplished with a variety of tools, not just the ones I show. If you don't own a jointer, try jointing with a handplane. Or use a handsaw if you can't get to a motorized version. The point is to make do with what you have. We all start woodworking this way. As you learn the craft, you'll build up not only your tool collection but your hard-won skills.

Shop Space and Fixtures

Certain items for the woodworking shop are necessary, and for the most part they're easy to come by. Good light is essential. If you can't get natural light, use a combination of incandescent and fluorescent. Incandescent clamp-on spotlights, or task lights, are cheap and allow you to position the light right where you need it. Overhead fluorescent fixtures can brighten a room considerably.

[TIP] **You can buy lamps with magnets on their bases from many woodworking suppliers. The magnet clamps to any ferrous metal surface, making it possible to position a light on a woodworking machine, such as a bandsaw, for a better view of the cutting action.**

When laying out your work space, make sure you allocate enough room for assembly. Cabinets, with their multitude of parts and pieces, can quickly overcome a small room. One answer is to make your machines and fixtures moveable, so your can clear a space when necessary.

See *"Mobilize Your Workshop"* on p. 11.

Another is to group core machines together in a central hub, such as the table saw, jointer, and planer. And don't overlook heating your work space. Not only will you and your hands be comfortable but most finishes and glues can't survive temperatures below 65°F.

For me, the workbench is the heart of my shop, where some of the most important action takes place. Scrimp on or skip this tool at your own peril. A workbench should be solid, sturdy, and stout. The top should be flat, so you can reference your work on it, and the top and base should be heavy, to resist the pounding, pushing, and pulling that takes place on it.

Plywood clamped to sawhorses can make a bench, but it won't compare to the sheer mass and work-holding capacity of a European-style joiner's bench. Its broad, heavy top is ideal for joinery and layout tasks. This style of bench has a tail vise and a series of angled holes in the vise and along the top of the bench into which you place a pair of *bench dogs* made from wood or metal. By placing a workpiece between two dogs and tightening the vise, you can pull the work flat to the benchtop. This is useful for carving and cutting operations and is especially well suited for handplaning.

Another effective means of clamping work tight to your benchtop is to drill a hole right through the top, and pound a holdfast over your workpiece. Be sure to use some scrap stock to prevent the holdfast from marring your work. I had a metal-working friend make my holdfast, but they're commonly available from woodworking catalogs.

At the far end of the bench, the shoulder vise is ideal for holding long boards on edge or for grasping tapered or irregular work-

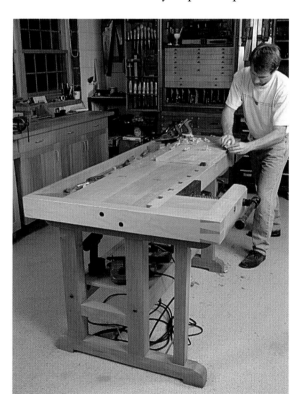

Pinching the workpiece between bench dogs helps pull it flat to the benchtop, especially useful when handplaning.

A holdfast uses a wedging action through the benchtop to keep a piece in position for handwork, especially for carving or chopping tasks.

The open jaws of a shoulder vise allow larger workpieces to pass right through for easy clamping. The vise has a swiveling jaw to provide even pressure onto tapered workpieces.

A low work table for assembly, clamping, and sanding will help save your back.

ASSEMBLY TABLE

Plywood or MDF, 1 in. thick, edged with hardwood

60 in.

40 in.

3/4-in. plywood spine

Wooden runners guide bins.

This side open for storing large items.

Plastic bin for screws.

25 in.

3 in.

3 in.

3/4-in. plywood

Make rails from 2-in.-thick hardwood.

pieces, since the jaw pivots to accommodate angles. Best of all, there are no obstructions or hardware between the jaws, so long work can pass right through the vise. You can build your own bench, as I did and as many other woodworkers do (see *The Workbench Book*, by Scott Landis, The Taunton Press), or buy a commercial bench from a woodworking catalog or store.

An assembly table does well to complement the workbench, as shown at left. Its low working surface lets you work on large assemblies with good control and comfort. And it works overtime as a glue-up table or a platform for applying finishes. You can also make good use of the space below for storing screws, hardware, clamping devices, and other tools.

Keeping your tools organized will make them accessible; a tool cabinet serves this purpose, especially if you keep it near your workbench. I recommend building your own so you can lay out the interior to fit specific tools. It's a good idea to construct lots of shallow drawers and cubbyholes or to hang tools from box-type doors, dedicating specific spots for their storage. This way, you can get to a tool in an instant—and see when it's missing. (For more ideas and information on building your own toolbox, see *The Toolbox Book*, Jim Tolpin, The Taunton Press.)

As you read through this book, you'll notice plenty of smaller jigs and fixtures. Shopmade jigs complement a tool or a procedure, making construction easier or more accurate—or a combination of the two. The more furniture you build, the more jigs you'll acquire. You'll even—I hope—devise a few jigs yourself for some of the woodworking procedures shown in this book. Write notes

Running cleats along an open wall provides room to store your collection of jigs and fixtures.

directly on your jigs; then the next time you use them, you'll have all the set-up information at your fingertips.

Keep some basic materials on hand for making jigs. Medium-density fiberboard (MDF) and Baltic birch (multi-ply) plywood are great; and pneumatic (air-driven) staples or brads and glue afford a quick way of putting jigs together. Build them fast, but make sure they're accurately constructed, so they work with precision. Don't fuss too much over a jig's aesthetics. Remember that jigs are only aids to the more important stuff, the actual furniture you make. When your shop starts to overflow with jigs and fixtures, keep them organized where you can get at them. A wall is handy spot.

Mobilize Your Workshop

One of the most efficient moves I ever made in outfitting my shop was to put wheels on almost all of my major machines and fixtures. Mobilizing your tools makes it easy to reorganize areas when needed, say for creating a large, open space to build a complex or

MAKING A FEATHERBOARD

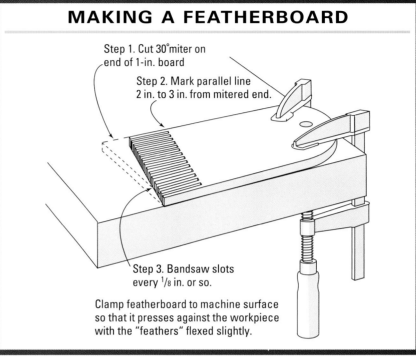

Step 1. Cut 30° miter on end of 1-in. board

Step 2. Mark parallel line 2 in. to 3 in. from mitered end.

Step 3. Bandsaw slots every 1/8 in. or so.

Clamp featherboard to machine surface so that it presses against the workpiece with the "feathers" flexed slightly.

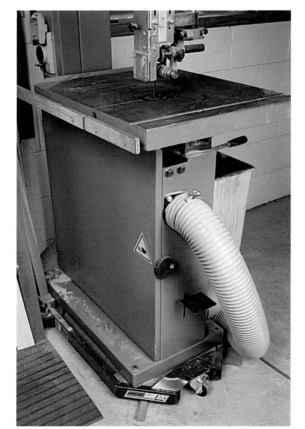

A mobile base allows you to move heavy machines and equipment easily. Make sure power runs through extra-long wires.

SHOPMADE DOLLY

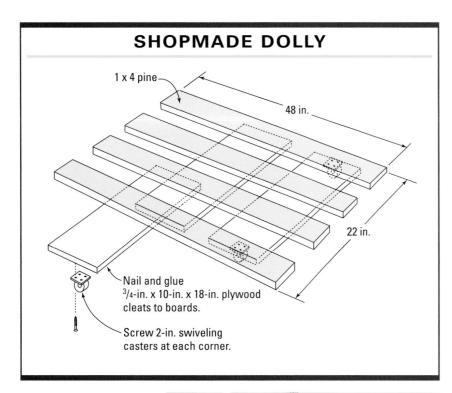

1 x 4 pine

48 in.

22 in.

Nail and glue
3/4-in. x 10-in. x 18-in. plywood
cleats to boards.

Screw 2-in. swiveling
casters at each corner.

Large casters under shop tables and cabinets create mobile work centers.

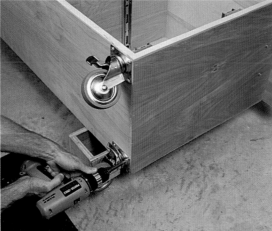

Handmade dollies help keep work safe, because they provide an easy way to move finished pieces out of harm's way.

good-size cabinet. You can mount large machinery on commercial mobile bases. My big 20-in. bandsaw sits on a mobile base with wheels, and I place small wedges underneath when it needs to be stationary. By pulling out the wedges and unlocking the rear wheels, even a small person can move this 500-lb. behemoth with ease.

Even shop tables and cabinets can benefit from mobility, which you can provide by attaching heavy-duty locking casters to the bottoms of legs and cases. Dual-locking, swiveling casters are best: The brake lever locks not only the wheel but also the swiveling plate, for maximum rigidity when the cabinet is stationary.

To move your work in progress around the shop or to rotate pieces while you're applying a finish, build wooden dollies from scrap pine and plywood, as shown at top left. These dollies are highly maneuverable, lightweight, and stowable, yet they support considerable weight.

Woodworking Machines and Tools

WHILE IT WOULD BE GREAT to own every conceivable woodworking machine and tool—plus the room to accommodate them—the reality is that we often get by with very little. However, I do believe that certain machines belong in the shop of a furniture maker or cabinetmaker, whether amateur or professional. The table saw tops the list.

The *table saw* is the foremost tool in the shop of a cabinetmaker, and it's a versatile one at that. While it can rip and crosscut stock to width and length, it's also adept at cutting all sorts of joints, from tapers and coves to moldings and other nonlinear shapes, when equipped with the right jigs and accessories. For handling large panels or long planks, you should outfit your saw with side and outfeed support, either in the form of rollers or dedicated tables. Keep in mind that the table saw is a space hog. Ideally, you'll want 16 ft. before and after the blade and 10 ft. or more to one side of the blade. A contractor-style table saw will work fine for furniture making, although a 3-hp to 5-hp cabinet-style saw will provide more accuracy and muscle to slice through thick hardwoods.

Invest in good sawblades for your saw. For general crosscutting and ripping, an all-purpose alternate-top bevel (ATB) blade with 40 teeth will suffice. For heavy ripping in thick hardwoods, you'll get smooth cuts with a flat-top (FT) rip blade with about 24 teeth. A stacked dado blade will cut flat-bottomed grooves and rabbets.

For safety, always guide work against the rip fence or with the miter gauge, or use a jig that references one of these two areas. Never hold the work freehand. Although a standard miter gauge works great for precise crosscuts in all sorts of work, things get a little hairy as the stock gets bigger. A miter gauge simply can't handle large work accurately or safely. To overcome these inadequacies, I use what

The table saw is the primary machine in any shop. You can increase its capacity by building a heavy-duty crosscut jig for handling wide or long boards.

is essentially an oversize miter gauge with two steel runners that ride in the miter gauge groove. Like a miter gauge, this crosscutting jig is great for small parts, yet beefy enough to handle long or wide stock. For really big work, you can use a clamp to secure the work to the jig, then push the assembly past the sawblade.

[TIP] **Clean and protect your machines' working surfaces by coating them regularly with paste wax. Use the furniture-variety wax, not the automotive kind, which has abrasives. Apply a generous coat with a rag, then buff it off by rubbing hard with a clean cloth. The slick surface that results fights rust buildup and provides good control when pushing work over the surface.**

BOTTOMLESS CROSSCUT JIG

30 in.

$1/4$-20 x $1^1/2$-in. bolt

Steel runner, $3/8$ in. x $3/4$ in. x 24 in.

Glue three pieces of $3/4$-in. plywood to fence.

$3^3/4$ in.

2 in.

Countersink 1 in. dia. for accessing bolt head with socket wrench.

Drill and countersink for fence-attachment screw.

Drill and tap for bolts.

#8 x 2-in. screw

After the table saw and its associated accessories and jigs, try to acquire the following machines as your resources or budget allows. Often a good bargain can be had by searching the Internet or local auctions for used machines. Just be sure to inspect the tool thoroughly before buying. I've listed the machines in order of my personal preference.

The *jointer* is used for flattening and truing faces and edges. Jointers are measured by their table width; 6-in. and 8-in. jointers are common. Bigger is better for flattening wide stock, such as tabletops or panels. For safety, never joint stock shorter than 12 in., and use push blocks or sticks to move the work over the cutterhead.

The *thickness planer* is used after the jointer for smoothing and thicknessing stock to a uniform thickness, particularly face-jointed boards. It is *not* designed to flatten work (although it's possible to do this with specialty jigs). Like the jointer, bigger is better, and 12-in. to 15-in. models are common. The 12-in. and 13-in. benchtop planers are particularly inexpensive, and their high-rotations-per-minute (rpm) universal motors spin the knives at an incredible pace, resulting in a smooth surface on difficult or gnarly woods. Big cast-iron planers, with their sturdy frames and powerful induction motors, take a bigger bite per pass, making them better suited for production work.

The *bandsaw* is a wonderfully resourceful tool, and it really shines when it comes to all sorts of curved cuts. But the bandsaw also excels at joinery and straight cuts, particularly when set up with a wide (½ in. or more) blade and a rip fence. For ripping rough stock and sawing really thick timber, such as resawing boards into veneer, the bandsaw can't be beat for accuracy, ease, and safety.

Bandsaws are measured by their throat, or the distance from the blade guide to the post, indicating the maximum *width* they can handle. *Height* capacity is measured under the blade guides, and higher is better. Most 14-in. saws can be fitted with riser blocks to increase the post height. European-style bandsaws, typically 16 in. and up, are becoming more common, and outperform the smaller saws. Their stiff frames, big motors, and superior blade-guide systems let you saw big, thick stuff all day long without a whimper.

The *miter saw,* or *chop saw,* has virtually replaced the radial-arm saw for accurate miter cuts and general crosscutting. A sliding miter saw has even more capacity, crosscutting stock as wide as 12 in. Power miter saws work best if you incorporate them into a workstation with support tables on either side of the blade. Also, it's worth building a flip-up stop system for cutting multiples without having to reach for a tape measure.

The *router table* will increase your router's capacity and can be used as a small-scale shaper. With the router mounted upside down, you can take advantage of shaping small stock, cut a host of joints, and more conveniently rout small pieces with more control and safety. You can make your own router table and fence, buy one, or cobble one together from commercial components. In a pinch, simply mount your router upside down in a vise. Important features to look for are a flat top and a rigid, straight fence. Remember that spinning large bits (1½ in. and up) means lowering the rpm, so look

for a variable-speed router for big router table work.

The *drill press* is more accurate and safer than using a hand drill for many drilling operations, especially when spinning big bits. Plus it adapts itself well to all sorts of drilling jigs and fixtures. You can even cut mortises on the drill press with a mortising attachment. Benchtop models are great if you can spare a benchtop, and they cost less. Floor models have the advantage of drilling into long or tall work.

The *wood lathe* is just the ticket if bowls or spindle turning is on your woodworking agenda. For average spindle work, a bench-top lathe with 32 in. to 36 in. between centers will accommodate most spindles, including table legs. Columns or bedposts necessitate a longer bed length, and big bowls need more height capacity, or *swing,* between the bed and the headstock and tailstock. If big turnings are what you seek, look for the mass and heft of a large floor-model lathe.

Basic Handheld Power Tools

To supplement your big machines, you'll want a few portable power tools. In fact, in a pinch, many of these smaller tools can supplant their bigger cousins. A basic power tool kit includes a jigsaw, for cutting curves and making inside or stabbing cuts; a biscuit joiner, for quick yet strong and accurate plate joinery; a random-orbit sander and a belt sander, for smoothing or flattening small and large surfaces; a circular saw, to trim large panels into manageable size; a big, 3-hp variable-speed plunge router, for mortising and grooving and spinning large bits;

Important portable power tools include (clockwise from lower left): jigsaw, plate joiner, random-orbit sander, belt sander, plunge router, fixed-base router, and driver drill.

a medium-size fixed-base router, for all those other topside routing tasks where you'd rather not heft the big plunger; and a cordless drill, which lets you drill holes and drive screws—anywhere.

► See *"Power Drive Your Screws"* on p. 81.

There are many additional tools and machines that can add to your shop's capacities. Some I own; some I'd like to own, but do happily without. The most useful ones are worth mentioning: a shaper, which is more powerful and accurate than a router table and lets you make really big moldings and work with wider, taller stock; a bench-top hollow-chisel mortiser, which lets you cut mortises affordably; a belt-disk sander, which is good for smoothing, but better for shaping and trimming parts to exact size; an oscillating spindle sander, which cuts aggressively and leaves a smooth surface, particularly in concave curves; a laminate trimmer, which is small and comfortable to hold, yet feels like a powerful mini shaper in your hand; a right-angle disk grinder fitted with a rotary blade, to hog out and dish wood in no time; a scrollsaw, for inlay or puzzle making

or when you need precise curved cuts and smooth-walled interior cuts; an air compressor plus small- and large-nail and staple guns, for driving fasteners with pin-point convenience; a vacuum pump and bag or a large veneer press (another space hog), for veneering without needing zillions of clamps; and for convenience's sake only, more routers, so you can keep dedicated bits in them for specific cuts or devote them to particular routing jigs.

Favorite Edge Tools

Edge tools, used for shaping, cutting, and smoothing wood, are probably more vital in my woodworking than all my power tools combined. That's because the degree of precision and surface finish available with these tools are unparalleled. A bonus is that they're quiet and relatively dustless. They *do* take skill to use. But an appealing indicator that you're beginning to master your edge tools is when you find yourself using finer and finer grits when it comes time to sand.

Some of my favorite edge tools, including a variety of handplanes, are shown on the facing page. I also favor wooden molding planes, from beading and rabbeting planes to hollows and rounds, when I want to work in peace and quiet or to supplement my power tools when they can't cut the profile I need. There are hundreds of molding planes available. Nowadays, only a few molding planes are produced commercially; instead, look for them at flea markets and through antique-tool dealers. Other important edge tools include handsaws, files, rasps, and chisels for all sorts of sawing and shaping tasks.

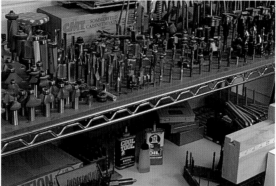

A plywood rack with holes drilled for various bit sizes helps organize your selection of router and drill bits.

Trusty edge tools. *Top:* bench planes, block plane, rabbet planes, spokeshaves, and scrapers. *Bottom:* bowsaws, backsaws, dovetail saws, flush saw, veneer saw, rasps, lathe chisels, bench chisels, and carving chisels.

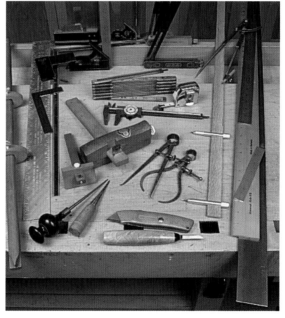

Essential layout tools (clockwise from lower left): pinch rod, small and large squares, bevel gauges, trammel points on stick and compass, measures, rulers, straightedge, inside and outside calipers, marking gauges, awls, knives, and dial calipers.

For drilling and routing, you'll need a selection of bits and accessories. Organizing your collection on a rack gives you quick access at a glance. Bits include ½-in.- and ¼-in.-shank router bits in as many profiles as you can afford for decorative edge work, grooving, rabbeting, mortising, and template work; regular twist bits, for drilling pilots and holes in wood *and* metal; brad-point twist bits, which cut very clean entrance and exit holes; Forstner bits, used primarily in the drill press for cutting large or small flat-bottomed holes; spade bits, less precise and less expensive alternatives to Forstner bits and convenient for use in a hand drill; and a variety of countersinks, counterbores, and plug cutters, for fitting screw shanks, screw heads, and wooden plugs.

Fundamental Layout Tools

There are some wonderful marking and measuring tools that will help you lay out joints, measure parts, and mark them accurately. Buy good ones; they'll work with the precision you need in this aspect of the craft. Some you can make yourself.

Marking and measuring gear should include a variety of tools from basic rulers and tapes to more specialized ones such as a pinch rod, which allows you to compare inside diagonals to ensure a square case. Depending on how serious you are about maintaining your own shop equipment, you may want some machinists' measuring tools such as dial indicators and calipers.

Also expect to use a compass and a large trammel for larger curves. And several sizes of straightedges always come in handy.

Sharpening Gear

As you start to acquire tools, your need for sharpening rises exponentially. Sharp tools are safer and more accurate than dull ones, but they don't stay that way unless you establish a sharpening regimen. My routine? When a tool is dull and won't cut properly, I sharpen it. I send out my carbide-tipped sawblades, router bits, jointer blades, and planer blades to sharpening professionals. But I regularly sharpen all my hand tools. Saws can be kept in tune with saw files. For plane irons, knives, and chisels, a grinding wheel will quickly dress nicked or damaged

edges, and a honing stone will sharpen and polish. In addition to acquiring these devices, setting up your sharpening area is just as important. A decent setup promotes your sharpening routine. In the hands of a skilled craftsman, sharpening is a quick and painless maneuver that lets you get back to work.

[TIP] **Keep a supply of extra plane irons for specific planes on hand. When the last of your irons get dull, sharpen them all at once. This way you can switch out dull blades for fresh ones during planing, instead of stopping your rhythm to sharpen.**

To dress edges properly, your grinder must be the right height, and it should have an adjustable yet solid tool rest. (There are many good grinder tool rests on the market.) A fairly high tool rest gives you more control over the tool and offers a better view of the cutting action. Keep the tool rest 40 in. to 46 in. from the floor, or the height your hands rise when you bend your forearms at a natural right angle to your body. This comfortable position lets you lock your elbows and pivot the tool from your shoulders,

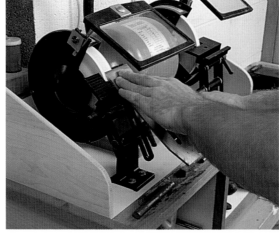

It's best to mount a bench grinder about chest high. This lets your arms extend comfortably and easily for more control.

This simple jig holds the chisel square for grinding.

which steadies the work and gives you great precision.

If you're new to grinding, it can be intimidating to try to grind an edge square. With practice, you'll be able to grind freehand quite easily and with great accuracy. But for beginners, the shopmade jig shown at right, which you push across a grooved tool rest, works great for holding narrow tools square to the stone.

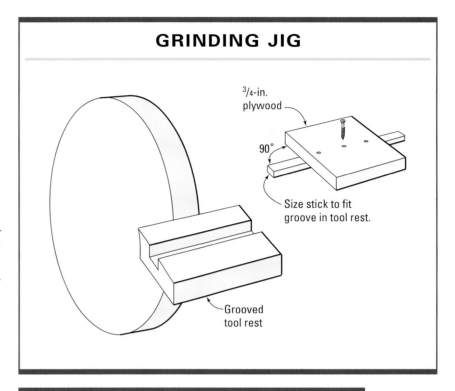

GRINDING JIG

³/₄-in. plywood

90°

Size stick to fit groove in tool rest.

Grooved tool rest

[TIP] **Overheating a tool during grinding will draw its temper and weaken the cutting edge. There are several tricks to keeping an edge cool. Always use a light touch and keep the tool moving across the wheel. Use a slow-speed grinder that runs between 1,700 rpm and 1,800 rpm to prevent burning; regularly rub the wheel with a dressing stone to remove glazed and impregnated debris.**

For honing and polishing, there are many types of sharpening systems that work very well, from ceramic and diamond plates and paste to natural India and Arkansas stones. Even sandpaper adhered to a flat surface works great. I've settled on synthetic waterstones for their speed and general cleanliness (although you might splash water when using them). To house my stones, which for the most part need to reside in water, and to sharpen with them, I use a homemade waterstone holder and work box.

Distinct from grinding, sharpening and honing take place on a lower surface, so you can use your upper body to control and place pressure over the tool. The correct height will allow you to move the tool edge with broad, even strokes across the stone. You can

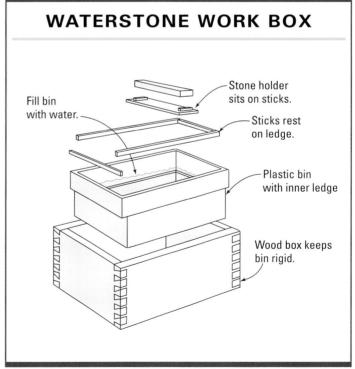

WATERSTONE WORK BOX

Fill bin with water.

Stone holder sits on sticks.

Sticks rest on ledge.

Plastic bin with inner ledge

Wood box keeps bin rigid.

This waterstone sharpening station provides a sturdy work platform as well as a place to keep the stones submerged when not in use.

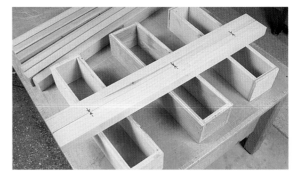

Clamping cauls should have slightly convex faces to help transfer pressure to the center of the board.

calculate the ideal stone height by letting your arms hang naturally at your sides, then measure from the tips of your fingers to the floor. It's about 30 in.

Clamps

Yes, the old saying is true: You can never have enough clamps. But it's worth investing in the most important ones. Pipe or bar clamps are the most essential for cabinet-making, in lengths from 2 ft. to 6 ft. or longer, for clamping edge-to-edge joints and case assembly. Quick clamps with 4-in.-deep jaws are my second favorites; they help position and hold work, clamp parts together, and are useful with jig and machine setups. If you can, collect a few deep-throat quick clamps for reaching into the center of wide work. Wooden handscrews, band clamps, spring clamps, and specialty clamps like miter clamps are best acquired as you need them. Don't skimp on quality; a good clamp should provide enough pressure without bowing or bending. And the clamp heads should grip securely and square to the work.

For reaching difficult-to-clamp areas, such as the middle of a wide panel, shop-made beams, or cauls, are just the ticket and

BOWED CLAMPING CAULS

Use paired cauls above and below the work to put pressure in the middle of wide stock.

Draw arrows to mark curved side.

Hardwood, 1³/₄ in. x 2¹/₂ in. x 40 in.

Lay out cure with flexible ruler or stick and bandsaw to line.

¹/₈ in.

Add ³/₄-in.-thick plywood platens to distribute clamp pressure.

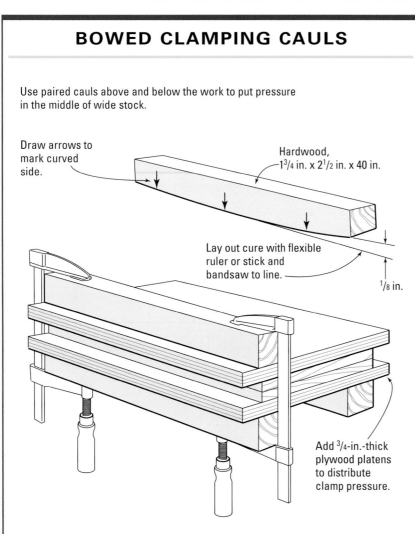

cost less than deep-throat clamps. Plus, they can be used along with plywood platens for pressing sheets of veneer. Because the beams are slightly curved along their length, clamping pressure is distributed evenly—even to the very center of wide work. I keep about 10 of these beams on hand for complicated glue-ups.

Storing all your clamps can pose a space problem. A cart with wheels is handy if you have the floor space, since you can move the clamps to where you need them. Don't overlook wall or ceiling space as real estate for your clamps. You can hang a multitude of clamps between joists as long as your ceiling height isn't out of reach. Another idea, which I picked up from my woodworking buddy Paul Anthony, is to make plywood hangers, as shown below. Attach the hangers to the wall; then hang your clamps within easy reach.

JOIST HOLDER FOR BAR AND PIPE CLAMPS

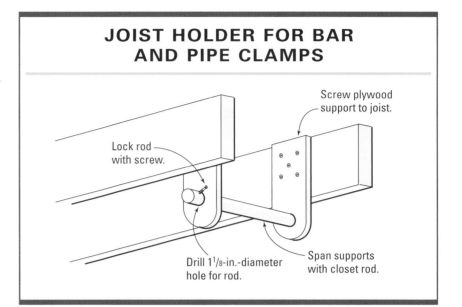

Screw plywood support to joist.

Lock rod with screw.

Drill 1$\frac{1}{8}$-in.-diameter hole for rod.

Span supports with closet rod.

An overhead rack can serve as convenient clamp storage.

WALL HANGER FOR BAR AND PIPE CLAMPS

Space according to particular clamp.

Screw or bolt backboard to wall.

12 in.

12 in.

$\frac{3}{4}$-in. lumbercore plywood

Glue and screw bracket to backboard.

A set of plywood wall brackets organizes your bar clamps, making them readily accessible.

Working Wood

A VITAL ASPECT OF MAKING quality furniture is having an intimate relationship with your material. What material to use, how and where to purchase it, and how it will behave from birth as rough stock to the ripe age of a 100-year-old piece of furniture are important pieces of information that will improve your woodworking, even before you pick up a chisel. And knowing your material will help you work wood safely, probably the most important skill in the craft. The following information should help you get started. For a more in-depth look at the technical aspects of wood and its properties, including plywoods and other man-made boards, read *Understanding Wood,* by R. Bruce Hoadley (The Taunton Press).

Working Wood Safely

The first and most important technique to learn and master in woodworking is to work safely. You can fix a woodworking mistake, but you can't take back a woodworking accident. Our shops are full of any number of sharp tools that can cause serious or permanent damage to your body. The good news is that safety won't cost you much. The biggest investment you'll make is in your mind. Or, more precisely, in your attitude. Although there is certainly plenty of safety gear that you should own, I believe that safe woodworking is primarily a mind-set you adopt every time you're in the shop. Be attentive to your energy level; if you're tired, don't fire up

a machine. And listen to your tools. Yes, with your ears. Any audible feedback—a change in pitch or tone—can warn you that danger is fast approaching and tell you to stop and re-evaluate what you're doing. If a procedure feels risky, find another way to do it. There is *always* another method that will work, and you should *always* feel safe and confident in the doing of it.

Safety gear is vital, too. Protect your ears with sound-deadening ear plugs or earmuffs, particularly when using high-decibel universal motors such as routers, miter saws, and benchtop planers. Keep your eyes safe from chips and dust whenever you're cutting material, swinging a hammer, or using compressed-air tools. Wear eye protection in the form of safety glasses, goggles, or shields.

Watch out that your lungs don't gather dust. Sweet-smelling shavings may highlight the romance of woodworking, but they often come cloaked as fine dust that floats languidly in the air for hours. These micron-size particles are known as some of the worst offenders when it comes to respiratory and other illnesses. Use a nuisance mask when possible and wear a powered air-purifying respirator when the dust is really bad. To overcome big chips and some dust, hook up major machines to dust vacuums or install a central dust-collection system. An air-filtration box, hung from the ceiling, is another way to capture really fine dust.

Like it or not, even the cleanest woodworking shop collects dust. And dry woodworking dust is a fire hazard. To keep things safe, clean and sweep your shop and regularly blow out electrical panels and outlets using compressed air. Always keep a charged fire extinguisher on hand, just in case.

During finishing, you'll want to protect your lungs, skin, and clothes from harsh chemicals. Latex gloves, similar to those used by the medical profession, are inexpensive and keep your hands clean. An organic cartridge-type respirator worn over your mouth and nose will prevent fumes and other noxious vapors from reaching your lungs. And a shop apron helps preserve your favorite T-shirt or pants.

Even more important than safety gear is reading about and understanding the finishes you use. Learn more by asking for a material safety data sheet (MSDS) from the manufacturer or supplier of the products you use. Remember that oil-based finishes generate heat as they dry and can burst into flames (spontaneous combustion)—so be sure to dispose of wet or damp rags in a sealed, metal container or spread them out on a bench outdoors until they're dry.

When it comes to moving wood past sharp steel and carbide, keep your fingers out of harm's way by using push sticks, push blocks, and featherboards. You can make them from scrap wood or buy them. Either way, use them whenever possible, instead of your hands.

[TIP] **Working safely on a woodworking machine involves total attentiveness to the task at hand. Advise your family, friends, and colleagues never to approach you from behind while you're working at a machine. A sudden interruption can break your concentration.**

Last, and certainly not least, are the safety guards and shields on your machines. They protect fingers and flesh, and they shouldn't be overlooked or taken for granted. Check to see that your guards are properly installed and use them. If possible, use a splitter, or riving knife, to reduce the likelihood of kickback on the table saw. If you find that a guard is inconvenient—table saws are the worst offenders—then look into replacement safety devices. There are plenty of good designs available from woodworking catalogs and stores.

Buying and Preparing Solid Wood

If you buy dimensioned wood at the lumberyard, save it for small projects—jewelry boxes and the like. Use rough lumber for furniture. Buying rough lumber lets you to take control of the dimensioning process, resulting in stock that's flatter, more stable, more consistent in color and texture, and prettier. All because you took the time to study your rough boards throughout the milling process.

For furniture making, it's vital that you work with dry wood. How dry? A good rule of thumb is 6 percent to 8 percent moisture content, which will keep the material in equilibrium with its intended surroundings indoors. You can buy kiln-dried wood, but don't overlook air-dried lumber. It's relatively easy to dry lumber yourself and save some money in the process, and there are many good articles and books on the subject.

The main thing to keep in mind, regardless of whether you use air-dried or kiln-dried lumber, is to make sure it's stored in an environment with a relative humidity of

Cut several inches from the end of a board to get an accurate reading of the moisture content from the interior.

Press both pins firmly into the end grain to take a moisture-content reading.

When laying out boards, it's a good idea to figure in about 4 in. on each end for planer snipe caused by the shift in pressure of the rollers as the board exits the machine.

and scientific supply catalogs, but a cheaper version works accurately if you keep it clean (hang it under a shelf to prevent dust buildup), mount it in an area with good air circulation, and check its calibration regularly. Monitor your hygrometer during the year to find out how much your shop's relative humidity level changes.

Once you become familiar with your shop's humidity level, use a moisture meter to check the actual moisture level in your lumber. For an accurate reading, cut the end of a board to read the stock's core and use the meter on the center of the end grain. The moisture meter shown at middle left has a digital readout, which lights up when a pair of steel pins are pressed into the wood. Use the meter to check your wood when you first bring it into the shop. Then check it regularly over the course of a couple of weeks. When your readings are consistent, the wood has equalized with the shop's environment and is ready for working.

[TIP] Buy or gather your lumber and store it in the shop well in advance of building a project. Stack and sticker the boards in a well-ventilated area and plan on waiting a few weeks for the wood to equalize with your shop's environment before working it.

With your stock at rest with your shop's atmosphere and at the correct moisture content, you'll want to lay out your boards and inspect them for defects before you begin the milling process. Look for stray hardware, such as staples or nails, and remove it with pliers. Mark around splits and unwanted knots. Then divide long boards into smaller lengths to make the milling process easier.

around 40 percent and that you store it in that location for a couple weeks before using it. Most woodshops have this ideal setting, which you can check by keeping an inexpensive hygrometer in your shop. You can buy expensive hygrometers from woodworking

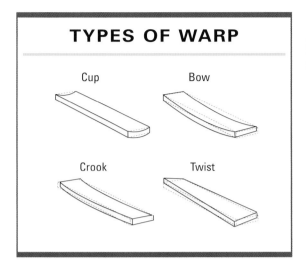

TYPES OF WARP

Cup

Bow

Crook

Twist

When face jointing a board, place the cupped side down and use rubber-coated push blocks so you can safely control the work.

Plan on losing about 4 in. on each end of a board owing to checking or from planer snipe. It's convenient to mark your cuts with regular chalkboard chalk. I like the "dustless" variety. White chalk shows up well on rough boards and, if you need to make a change, you can easily erase a mark by swiping the chalk with a damp sponge.

Now, if all went well, your lumber will be warped. Relax. This is a natural part of the drying process and *now* is the time to deal with it—not after you've built your furniture. There are essentially four types of warp, and you can easily train your eyes to spot each type in a board (see the drawing above). Knowing which kind of curve is in your board, and where, will help you determine the best course of action when it comes to removing it and milling your boards flat and square.

Face-jointing your lumber is essential if you want to make furniture that's flat and square. Many woodworkers commonly mistake the jointer as being solely an edge-straightening tool. Although it serves this purpose wonderfully, the best use of a jointer

is to flatten the face of a board before planing it to thickness. However, if you don't have access to a wide jointer, you can hand-plane one side flat instead.

► See *"Flattening a Board by Hand"* on p. 27.

Before jointing, sight along the board, looking for a cup or bow. Then place the cupped or bowed face down on the bed of the jointer. Set the knives for a light cut, about $\frac{1}{32}$ in., and be sure to use push blocks to control the work and to prevent your hands from contacting the knives.

With one face flat, you can thickness plane the stock to even thickness. Start with the jointed face down on the bed of the planer, orienting the stock so you plane with the grain to avoid tearout.

► See *"Working with the Grain"* on p. 28.

To minimize further warping caused by internal stresses in the wood, always take an even amount of wood from both sides of the

To avoid tearout on the thickness planer, always plane with the grain. Flip the board over after each pass to plane an equal amount from each side.

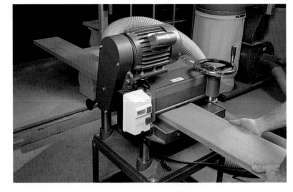

To ensure a square edge, press down and against the fence. Edge jointing cuts should be limited to about ¹⁄₁₆ in. maximum.

Align the grain where you want it, such as parallel to an edge, by drawing a straight line. A single bandsaw cut along the line establishes the new orientation.

TOP RAIL ℓ

To prevent long boards from wandering, sight along the rip fence rather than the sawblade as you push the board through.

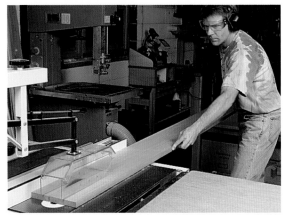

board. This means flipping the board over and end for end—to orient the grain direction—after every pass.

After planing, joint one edge of the stock. Pay attention to keeping the board snug to the fence, because this keeps the jointed edge square. For narrow edges, you can take off a little more than when face jointing. A depth of cut of about ¹⁄₁₆ in. is fine.

Once you've milled your lumber flat and to thickness, but before you cut out parts, it pays to get better acquainted with your wood. By studying your boards for grain pattern, color, and texture, you can learn to be a composer of wood grain in your work. Mark like-colored parts so they balance each other. For example, the two stiles on a door frame should come from similar areas of a board. And don't be ruled by straight edges; instead, follow nature's lines. Lay out your furniture parts, by studying the grain patterns, then draw straight lines in chalk, parallel with the pattern you want. Cut to your lines on the bandsaw; then clean up the sawn edges on the jointer and rip the opposite edges on the table saw. Now you have a board with the grain going where *you* want it.

When cutting out individual parts from a solid-wood board, it's best to rip pieces about ¼ in. over final width, placing a jointed edge against the rip fence. Use leverage when ripping long boards and focus your attention and pressure at the rip fence, not at the blade. Then go back to the jointer and re-joint an edge to remove any bowing caused by tensions released in the ripping process. (Look for cupping on the face, too. You may have to face joint the ripped stock and then thickness plane it once more.)

Then go back to the table saw to rip to final width, again referencing the jointed edge against the fence.

Finish up by crosscutting the boards to length on the table saw, using the miter gauge or a crosscutting jig.

➤ See *"Bottomless Crosscut Jig"* on p. 14.

Another alternative is to use the miter saw for cutting to length. A stop block lets you cut multiple parts to exactly the same length without having to measure and mark each board.

Flattening a Board by Hand

If you don't own a jointer, or your jointer is too narrow for your stock, you can still work wide planks into beautifully flat surfaces with some initial prep work from a handplane. Don't worry. This is not the sweat-drenching work our woodworking forebears carried out when they worked without power tools. Instead, it involves a sharp plane and your thickness planer.

At the bench, clamp the plank that you want to flatten cupped-side up, tapping wedges under the board at key points to prevent rocking. Use a long plane set for a fairly heavy cut and plane the high spots on the cupped face. Work the plane diagonally across the face. As you plane, use a straight-edge and a pair of winding sticks to check your progress, reading the face for cup and twist. Don't try to plane the entire surface; just make sure the perimeter, or outer edge, is flat.

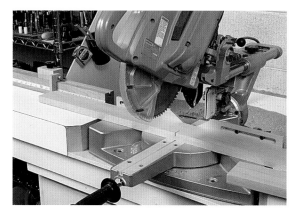

The flip-up stop block (to the left of the saw) allows you to easily cut multiple pieces to the same length.

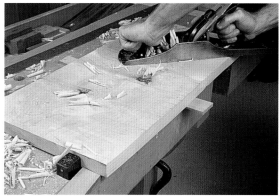

Wedges keep the workpiece from rocking as you plane the perimeter of a cupped board. Once the outside edges are flush, you can finish the job with a thickness planer.

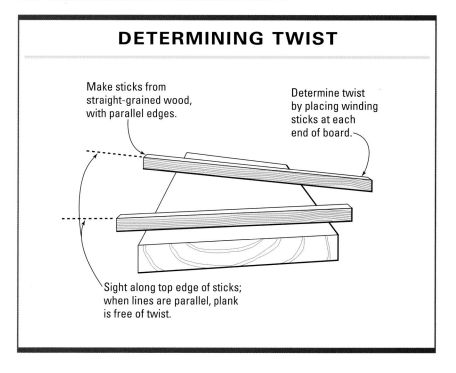

DETERMINING TWIST

Make sticks from straight-grained wood, with parallel edges.

Determine twist by placing winding sticks at each end of board.

Sight along top edge of sticks; when lines are parallel, plank is free of twist.

After handplaning, turn the planed side down on the bed of the thickness planer and flatten the top side.

Now flip the board over and send it through the thickness planer to flatten the opposite, unplaned face. A few passes is all it should take. When you've established a broad, flat surface on the second face, continue planing both faces evenly until you reach the desired thickness.

Working with the Grain

Working with solid wood demands that you pay attention to the direction of the wood's fibers, or grain. When you cut *with the grain,* such as when routing, planing, or even sanding, you'll produce smoother surfaces. Cutting *against the grain* pulls and lifts the wood fibers up, resulting in tearout, or a rough surface. Take the time to study the grain patterns in your boards to determine which direction to orient them for cutting. Most of the time, you can see the grain rising or falling by looking at the edge of a board. But certain woods can fool you. Sometimes you can pass your fingers along the long-grain surface in both directions and feel which direction is smoother. The technique is very much like stroking the fur of a cat. The final test is to cut the wood itself. If it tears, cut from the opposite direction.

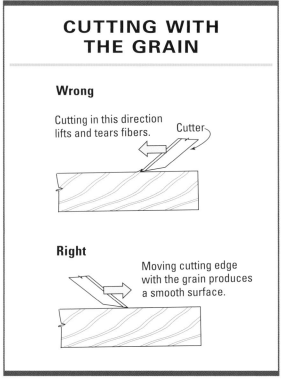

CUTTING WITH THE GRAIN

Wrong

Cutting in this direction lifts and tears fibers.

Cutter

Right

Moving cutting edge with the grain produces a smooth surface.

Smoothing with Edge Tools

Boards straight from the thickness planer or jointer (or the lumberyard) aren't smooth enough for furniture. Small millmarks—usually tiny ridges and hollows left by the rotation of a cutterhead's knives—will be glaringly apparent when you apply a finish. You can sand out these marks with a belt sander or a random-orbit sander, but it's dusty work and, worse, you risk leaving a surface that's far from flat. To remove marks and smooth any imperfections, a handplane is fast and efficient and leaves a flat, gleaming surface unsurpassed by any other tool.

If you're working with a flat surface, such as a long, wide board, clamp it to a flat surface such as your benchtop. If you try to plane on an out-of-flat surface, the plane will skip and skitter over small humps and valleys. Assuming your work has been accurately thickness planed, use a no. 4 or no. 5 plane for the initial smoothing. Make sure your plane iron is razor sharp and set the depth for a fine cut.

Body English is all-important when planing. To gain leverage, spread your feet apart, hold the plane directly in line with your wrist and shoulder, and use your legs to power the stroke. Plane in one smooth, decisive movement, letting your upper body pivot over the work as you push the plane. You should be able to plane a board about 5 ft. long without taking a step or moving your feet—and without huffing to catch your breath. Proper handplaning is a fluid, enjoyable action. For longer boards, take several passes by landing and taking off the plane from the surface, just like an airplane. This technique helps avoid stop and start marks.

From time to time, check your progress with a straightedge to ensure the surface is flat. If you detect a small hollow that the plane has skipped over, try skewing the plane to the direction of the cut to effectively reduce the length of the sole. If the wood is difficult and starts to tear, plane in the opposite direction. Sometimes it's quicker simply to reverse the plane and pull it rather than to reposition the board.

[TIP] **You can reduce friction and make handplaning easier by regularly oiling or waxing the sole of your plane. Light oil or paraffin (candle) wax works well, or rub some paste wax on the plane and buff it off with a clean cloth.**

For working difficult woods, when a handplane tears the grain—not uncommon

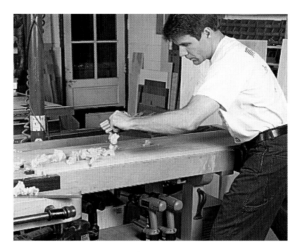

Lifting the plane off the work before ending a stroke prevents choppy plane marks.

The frequent use of a straightedge during planing helps ensure that surface is flat.

Skewing the plane while still pushing straight ahead helps reach slight hollows.

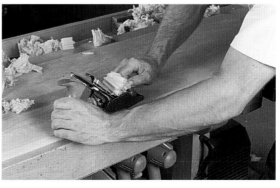

Pulling the plane is sometimes easier than changing places as you tackle difficult grain.

Use a sharp hand scraper, rather than a handplane, when working figured woods with difficult grain.

Sandpaper wrapped around a felt block provides a sensitive touch for hand-sanding, and uses sandpaper more effectively.

A granite block wrapped with sandpaper is great for getting into corners and for leaving a crisp edge with no fuzzy transitions.

Spray adhesive, sandpaper, and a scrap piece of MDF are used to make a sanding block with different grits on each side.

on wood with swirled or highly figured grain—use a hand scraper. Tilt the scraper at an angle to the surface until it begins to cut. A properly sharpened scraper makes shavings—not dust. Many books and articles describe how to sharpen a scraper, and it's worth reading about how to tune up this indispensable hand tool.

In most cases, you'll still have to sand to remove small ridges left by planing and to ensure that all your surfaces have an identical texture for an even finish. However, the surface left by a plane or scraper is so smooth that you can start sanding with a very fine grit, reducing sanding time—and dust—considerably.

Good Sanding Techniques

Proper sanding will yield flat, swirl-free surfaces ready for a fine finish. Careless sanding can result in scratches, or—much worse, in my opinion—rounded surfaces that reflect light unevenly and look downright shoddy. Not sanding at all can leave patterned machine marks or plane track marks and lead to hard edges or inconsistent-looking surfaces when the finish is applied. Take the time to look carefully at the surface and be sure to sand through each successive grit. Final sanding is always done by hand, *with* the grain of the wood.

Whenever you're sanding a surface by hand, wrap the paper around a block. A sanding block prevents rounding or dipping into surfaces, and makes the sanding process much more efficient. On broad surfaces, use a felt block for its sensitive feel to the hand and to the surface itself.

On edges, or arris, use a hard wooden block to gently round over the sharpness where the two planes meet. The denser the block, the better. Please don't sand an edge by hand. The results will be inconsistent. My favorite back-up block is a chunk of dead-flat granite, which is great for getting into corners for a nice, even look.

By far the most-used sanding block in my shop is a piece of MDF with a sheet of sandpaper glued to both sides. I make lots of blocks in a range of grits, spraying both sides of the MDF and the back of the paper with contact cement, and then sticking the paper to the block. You can use these blocks for leveling flat surfaces or for cutting or rounding over edges. And they're useful when sanding small parts, by clamping them to the bench and moving the work over the blocks, instead of the other way around. Think recycle, too. When the sandpaper loses its effectiveness, just heat the paper with a blow dryer or a heat gun and peel it off. Then apply a fresh sheet.

To keep your sandpaper organized, consider building a cabinet dedicated to storing full sleeves of sandpaper, cut paper, and all your other associated sanding gear. Size the shelves to fit sleeves, and then organize them by grit.

Keeping Parts Flat

Once you've flattened and milled your solid stock, and perhaps even sanded it, you still have to contend with the fact that wood left lying around the shop will warp if given a chance. (Letting the wood acclimate to your shop for several weeks before milling will help minimize this but won't stop it entirely.) In an ideal world, you would dimension the stock, cut all your joints, and assemble and glue all the parts together immediately. An

Sanding blocks clamped end to end with multiple paper grits are effective for sanding small parts.

Using a heat gun, you can peel the old sandpaper from a block; then apply a fresh sheet.

Building a cabinet with adjustable shelves lets you organize sandpaper by grit.

➤ CUTTING SANDPAPER WITH A JIG

I like to keep my sandpaper in sizes that fit my jigs and tools. To cut sandpaper into thirds, a convenient size for me, I use a home-made fenced jig. You can make the jig to suit your favorite size of sand-paper. Mine is 9½ in. by 10 in. To use the jig,

A piece of plastic laminate that's one-third the size of a sandpaper sheet helps the author tear off sections.

place several sheets against the two fences, position a piece of plastic laminate on top of the stack of paper, then lift and tear individual sheets to size.

When possible, dry-assemble case pieces while working on other components to keep the parts from warping.

Stacking and weighing precut parts prevents them from warping while you're away from the shop.

Small parts can be shrink wrapped to control wood movement.

assembled piece of furniture keeps itself flat and free from warping. However, most often we work piecemeal, and joints cut today may not see glue until weeks or months have passed. To keep parts flat and to accommodate a busy schedule, there are a couple methods to follow.

After milling the stock flat, sticker and stack it as soon as possible on a dead-flat surface. Make your stickers from shop scrap to a uniform width and thickness, typically ¾ in. by ¾ in., and stack the pile so that the stickers are in line above and below each other. After stacking, add another row of stickers on top of the stack and place weights on them. This simple routine will save you untold headaches later.

If you've cut the joints, but aren't ready for final assembly, it's a good idea to dry-

Panel Characteristics

Panel	Cost (A-2 grade)	Weight (¾ in. x 4 ft. x 8 ft.)	Flatness	Screw Holding	Rigidity
Softwood plywood	$ 20	68 lb.	Poor	Good	Good
Hardwood plywood	$ 45, birch $ 80, cherry	75 lb.	Fair	Good	Good
Solid-core plywood	$ 40, birch $ 60, cherry	80 lb.	Good	Fair	Fair
Lumbercore plywood	$100, birch $140, cherry	75 lb.	Fair	Excellent	Excellent
MDF	$ 25	100 lb.	Excellent	Fair	Fair
Particleboard	$ 20	100 lb.	Good	Poor	Fair

Information courtesy of Georgia Pacific Corporation, American Plywood Association, Hardwood Plywood and Veneer Association, and National Particleboard Association.

assemble the parts. This way, the joints themselves will hold the parts flat.

Another option that's particularly handy for smaller parts is to wrap them in plastic. I use industrial shrink wrap, which is strong and comes in wide lengths from shipping companies. Cover all surfaces—especially the end grain—and store the wrapped parts on a flat surface until you're ready to work them.

Plywood and Other Man-Made Boards

Using plywood, you can dimension all the panels for an entire kitchen in the time it would take to thickness enough solid stock for one piece of furniture. It's this ready-made width that's one of the most compelling reasons for choosing man-made boards. Another reason is the variety of panels or sheets to choose from, including the most common: hardwood plywood,

fiberboard, and particleboard. And the stability of man-made boards means you're free from the concerns of wood movement. The chart above shows some of the pros and cons of each panel type to help you decide which material has the characteristics you need for a particular job.

Plywood, available as veneer core, solid core, combination core, and lumbercore, can have softwood or hardwood face veneers. For furniture makers, hardwood plywood is the panel of choice. It is inexpensive; does a good job of holding hardware such as screws; and is relatively rigid, making it a good choice for shelving.

Newer hardwood plywood types, such as solid-core and combination core, offer inner plies of less-expensive particleboard or fiberboard and are generally flatter—an important consideration if you're building unsupported work such as floating door panels or

A, Hardwood veneer-core plywood with walnut face; B, Baltic birch plywood, C, softwood plywood with fir face; D, combination-core plywood with cherry face; E, MDO; F, lumbercore with birch face; G, MDF; H, hardboard (for example, Masonite); I, solid core of MDF with oak face; J, particleboard; K, MCP.

large tabletops. Lumbercore, as its name suggests, has a core of laminated solid wood, making it exceptionally stiff and rigid. One board, medium-density overlay (MDO), combines inner plies with a face of kraft paper impregnated with exterior glue, making it ideal for outdoor sign makers.

Keep in mind that the thin face veneers on hardwood plywood necessitates careful cutting, handling, and finishing to avoid breaking or chipping the face and exposing the inner plies. Typical hardwood plywood has random spaces or voids between the inner plies, which show up as holes along the edges of panels. The raw edges must be covered or banded to conceal the voids and the inner plies.

Three products—Baltic birch plywood, ApplePly, and Europly—are made from multiple layers of veneers and are void free. You can polish their edges for a finished

look. Also, their higher density and stability make them great for jig making.

[TIP] Use a *triple-chip* (TC) blade for clean, chip-free cuts in delicate faced panels such as hardwood plywood, melamine, and plastic laminate. A 60-tooth, negative-hook pattern reduces tearout on both the top and the bottom faces.

MDF is inexpensive and is the best choice for flat work because it's flat and stays that way. With its exceptionally smooth surface, MDF is a favorite for veneering or high-end paint work, and it's another great material for making jigs. The cons: It's heavy, making it difficult to handle in the shop; it won't hold fasteners well; it bends under heavy loads; the rough, porous edges of the panels need filling or edgebanding; and when exposed to moisture, it swells irreversibly.

Its "cousin" particleboard is made from chips—not the fine fibers used in MDF. The result is a coarser surface that's not suitable for thin or very fine veneers. It has most of the benefits of MDF—it's easy on your wallet and it's generally flat—and all of the cons. With its rough surface, particleboard is best as a substrate under thicker materials, such as plastic laminate. Melamine-coated particleboard (MCP) is, as its name implies, coated with a hard plastic, making it ideal for interior case pieces, since it provides a durable finished surface.

When buying particleboard, make sure to select the industrial, or high-density, grade; the builder's variety, called chipboard or flakeboard, is much too coarse and lacks the strength and rigidity of the denser grade.

Mixing solid wood and plywood can be an effective technique. Although the door frames, edging, and trim of this home library are made from solid mahogany, the panels are sapele plywood.

The desktop is made from sepele plywood with solid wood edging and leather.

Mixing Materials

There's no denying that the look and feel of solid wood has its advantages. But commercial hardwood veneered panels can be used in conjunction with solid wood to provide a rich feel to just about any project. For example, I made all the panel frames, door frames, edging, and trim in the home library shown in the photos above from solid mahogany. But the panels—including the desktop—are made from sapele plywood. The overall look is solid and luxurious.

Even when wood is the look you want, it's sometimes wise to mix it with other materials. A simple solution is to use prefinished panels for the insides of your utility cases and hardwood plywood for the outside. In the case shown at right, most of the inside—including the top, bottom, and dividers—is constructed from MCP. Melamine provides a hard-wearing surface, and you don't have

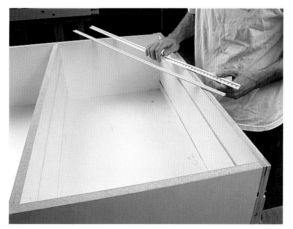

You can use melamine-coated particleboard inside a cabinet to create a durable surface.

On the outside of the same cabinet, maple plywood dresses up the public side.

The maple doors and visible exterior parts of this melamine cabinet create a natural wood look.

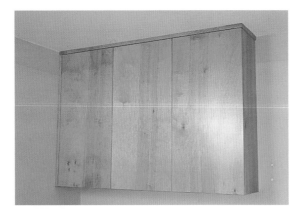

Working with a cutting list and graph paper, you can minimize waste by creating a cutting diagram for each sheet of plywood.

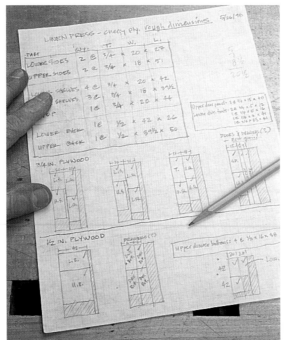

Use chalk to create the initial rough layout on a sheet of plywood.

to apply finish to the insides of the case, an often tedious task. The show sides of the case are maple plywood, and a coat of paint takes care of the interior. Once the wood doors are mounted on the outside of the completed cabinet, you see only maple in all its natural beauty (see the photo top left).

Laying Out and Cutting Plywood

While plywood affords you large, stable surfaces that need little or no prepping, the downside is handling such big sheets. That's why it's important to plan your cuts and to break up large sheets into more manageable bite-size chunks.

The first thing to do is to make a cutting list, including a sketch of each 4-ft. by 8-ft. sheet of plywood and how you plan to cut it into parts.

▶ See *"Using Cutting Lists"* opposite.

Laying out your cuts in this manner lets you create the most efficient cutting sequence. When you move from paper to panel, it helps to lay out the cuts on the actual plywood so you can more closely select grain patterns for individual parts. Using blackboard chalk lets you preview the cuts and makes it easy to change the layout; simply remove unwanted marks with a damp sponge.

Large sheets of plywood can be difficult to manage on the average table saw, even with side and outfeed support, so it's usually best to cut up the sheet into smaller parts first. The jig shown in the drawing opposite lets you cut sheets using a circular saw with very little setup. Simply clamp the jig to the

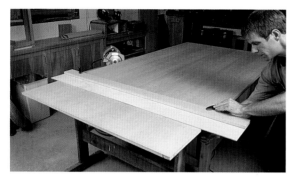

Simple jigs are often best. This circular-saw guide provides an easy way to cut up a sheet of plywood into manageable pieces.

This jig is easy to use because you place the edge directly onto the layout line; the saw is guided by the particleboard fence.

cutline and ride your saw on the base to make the cut. Once you have your sheets cut into smaller sizes, take them to the table saw to cut out the individual parts.

Using Cutting Lists

Making a cutting list is a good way to keep organized, and working from a list prevents mistakes during the building phase. For complex projects, make a list of each and every part and mark the dimensions of each piece on a single sheet of paper. Graph paper makes it simple to organize your thoughts. As you progress on the piece, check off each part as you cut it to dimension.

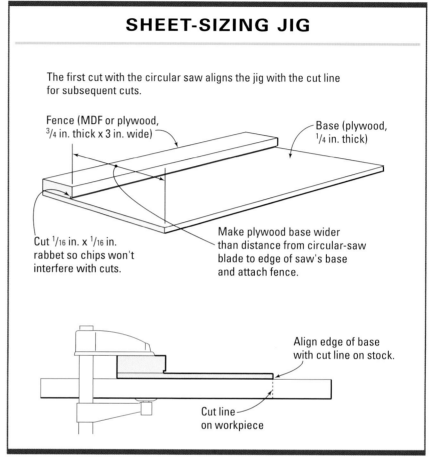

SHEET-SIZING JIG

The first cut with the circular saw aligns the jig with the cut line for subsequent cuts.

Fence (MDF or plywood, $3/4$ in. thick x 3 in. wide)

Base (plywood, $1/4$ in. thick)

Cut $1/16$ in. x $1/16$ in. rabbet so chips won't interfere with cuts.

Make plywood base wider than distance from circular-saw blade to edge of saw's base and attach fence.

Align edge of base with cut line on stock.

Cut line on workpiece

For projects with a lot of parts, a cutting list is an important tool for making sure everything gets cut to the proper size.

Making Your Mark

Like cutting lists, marking the work itself will keep you organized and reduce the time you spend looking for misplaced parts. For most work, an ordinary pencil works fine. On dark woods, consider using a white pencil, the kind sold in art-supply stores.

A marking knife is the most accurate method of transferring layout lines.

Mark the edges of your parts with triangle symbols so you can orient the faces and edges correctly during joint cutting and assembly.

An astounding variety of wood glues is available. Glues range from traditional hide glue to modern synthetics that bond instantly.

When you need a higher degree of accuracy, such as when marking out dovetails, the fine line left by a marking knife is best.

To keep track of parts in a project, you'll need some system of marking. I use a triangle and a straight line. You can make up your own marking scheme—the actual symbols aren't important. One of my favorite techniques is to designate front and top edges with two respective marks: a line to represent the front, and a triangle—or a series of triangles—to mark a top edge and inside edge. This simple system lets me keep track of the numerous parts in the right order.

Choosing and Using Glue

When it comes time for assembly, you'll grab your trusty glue bottle. But just as you wouldn't build cabinets strictly from one type of material or wood, you shouldn't rely on one glue for all your assemblies. Having said this, about 90 percent of my furniture goes together with ordinary woodworking white glue. Technically a polyvinyl acetate (PVA) glue, this glue comes in white and yellow varieties. White glue generally offers more open time (the time you have once you've spread the glue to get all the joints together), making it useful for complex assemblies. And like all the glues for woodworking, it's plenty strong for its intended purpose.

Other glues offer other compelling characteristics, such as the ability to take the work apart when you need to by nature of its reversibility, increased moisture resistance, or even waterproofness. The chart opposite helps you select the right glue for the job.

[TIP] Many glues have a shelf life of 1 year; some less. Look for a manufacture date on the glue you buy; if there isn't one, write the date you bought the glue on the bottle. Dating your glue lets you know how fresh it is.

Once you've chosen an adhesive, you need to learn the balance between using too much and using too little, because each approach has its respective drawback. Too little glue and you risk starving the joint line, especially when the pressure from clamps spreads the glue away from the joint. The result is a joint that's likely to fail. It's better to err on the side of too much glue, but not to the point that you have a gooey mess on your hands. Excess glue that's not removed will always haunt you later when it shows up as a bland smear under any finish. So how much is enough? A good rule of thumb is use enough glue so that you see an even bead squeeze out from the assembled joint.

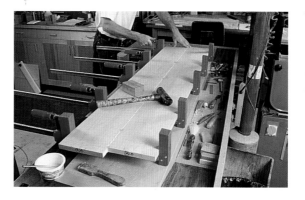

When applying glue, shoot for an even bead of squeeze-out after clamping.

Timely Glue Characteristics

Type	Open Time	Clamp Time	Comments
PVA (yellow and white)	3 min. to 5 min.	1 hr.	General woodworking; water cleanup
Cross-linking (type II water resistant)	3 min.	1 hr.	Good outdoors; water cleanup
Hot hide glue	Unlimited, with heat	Limited	Hammer veneer work; reversible
Cold (liquid) hide glue	30 min.	12 hr.	Reversible with heat and water
Polyurethane	20 min.	2 hr.	Moisture resistant; foams during cure
Plastic resin (resin powder/water powder)	20 min./20 min.	1 hr./12 hr.	Moisture resistant; veneer and bent laminations
Two-part epoxy (fast/slow)	1 min./1+ hr.	30 sec./24 hr.	Doesn't shrink; laminations; submersible
Cyanoacrylate glue (Super Glue)	5 sec.	5 sec.	Quick fix for small parts; filling cracks
Contact cement	30 min. to 3 hr.	Immediate bond	Plastic laminate work
Hot-melt glue	15 sec.	Temporary hold	Jig and template making

Designing Furniture

Average Furniture Sizes			
Furniture	**Height (in.)**	**Depth (in.)**	**Length/Width (in.)**
Tables			
Coffee	14–18	18–24	36–60
Card/game	29	30	30
End	30	15	24
Hall	30–40	15	24–40
Writing	30	24	36–40
Kitchen	30–32	30	42
Dining	29–32	42	60–84
Chairs			
Desk/task	16½	16–18	16–20
Dining	16–18	16–18	16–18
Couch/lounge	14–18	18–24	24–90
Cabinets			
Buffet	30	16–24	48–72
China/display	54–60	12–22	Any
Kitchen	32–36	12 or 24	Any
Other			
Chests	32–54	24	Any
Bookcases	32–82	14–18	Any
Desks	30	24–30	40–60

O WORK WOOD WITH CONFIDENCE and build furniture you'll be proud of, it's important to have a fundamental grasp of furniture design. Although designing good furniture is always a life-long challenge, the essence of it is dead simple.

When I make furniture or cabinets, I follow a fundamental principle of form following function. In plain English, this means the furniture has to be used by real people in a comfortable and satisfying manner, yet the piece should be pleasing to the eye. Using this theory, I'm careful to make sure a piece will *work* first, before considering its final shape or form. Think about how the piece will be used. For example, you wouldn't make the height of a desk incompatible with the chair used to sit in front of it. The chart at left lets you zero in on these important measurements.

Once you know the essential size of a piece, start with a sketch. *Please note:* You don't need formal training to sketch a project. The goal is to get down on paper the essential idea of the piece you want to make, so you can study it. Even crudely drawn, these sketches are full of energy and vitality. Later, refer back to your sketch to check your progress.

Now go build something. Of course, you'll use the right materials and sound joinery. And I guarantee, the *next* piece you make will be better. And the next from thereon.

To refine your design skills, there are things to think about as you build your furniture. Consider appearance, proportions, balance, line, shape, mass, color, and texture. These ingredients combine to create a pleasing piece of furniture. You'll figure all this out on your own.

There's always a risk involved with jumping in and designing as you go. Things may not work out. For a safer, more traditional route, you can develop a model and do some experimentation before building the real thing. For example, if you're designing a set of speakers, you might want to test the acoustical properties of various woods. Or a new door design might prompt you to experiment with various methods of hinging. To build these test models, use scrap wood and hold parts together with screws, hot-melt glue, or even tape.

Scale models are another test and can help you define a look before you commit. Dimension your parts carefully, using an architect's rule to determine accurate scale.

Scrap pieces of thin wood, plywood, MDF, cardboard—whatever you can get your hands on—make great materials for building these miniature portraits. Assemble with hot-melt or cyanoacrylate glue, and stand back to judge proportions and overall feel.

Sometimes, a scale model won't give you a feel for the actual piece. For the most

impact, build a full-size mock-up to visualize the real proportions of a piece. Make your mock-ups from common materials, such as 2x stock, rigid cardboard, and screws; then alter and change them until you like what you see.

Partly for their design value and partly for the building information they contain, I often make a set of working drawings, showing side and front views (elevations) and the top view. Your drawings can be full-size or scaled down and drawn with a ruler and a 30/60/90-degree drafting triangle, available from art-supply stores. Besides helping you visualize a piece, a working drawing can help you generate a cutting list should you need one.

► See *"Using Cutting Lists"* on p. 37.

Scale models can help you work out the proportions of a project. A scale ruler, or architect's rule (foreground), lets you transfer full-size dimensions to an appropriate scale size.

Understanding Wood Movement

All solid wood expands or contracts in response to changes in ambient moisture levels in the air. Because of wood's hygroscopic nature (the ability to absorb moisture from the air), nothing short of sealing the boards in a vacuum chamber can totally stop this movement—including the best glue or finish on the planet. Luckily, movement *with* the grain is negligible, so we don't have to be concerned about the length of the parts. But wood movement tangential to, or *across,* the grain can wreck havoc on your furniture if you don't take it into account. If you follow a few guidelines, your work won't buckle and bow and will be around for a long time.

As a rule of thumb, you can assume most kiln- and air-dried woods will change dimensions by as much as $\frac{1}{4}$ in. for every 12 in. of width, depending on the amount of seasonal swing in indoor humidity in your area. Certain species move very little; some change dimensions radically. For example, a 12-in.-wide plank of flatsawn black cherry will move a little more than $\frac{1}{8}$ in. when the wood changes from 6 percent to 12 percent moisture content (MC). The same width and cut of beech subjected to the same change in MC will move slightly more than $\frac{1}{4}$ in.

And the cut of wood affects its movement, too. Changing from plainsawn to quartersawn beech will reduce the movement to $\frac{1}{8}$ in. for that same 12-in.-wide board. Quartersawn wood is also more predictable than plainsawn, or flatsawn, wood, which moves unequally over its width because of its irregular grain, promoting warp. One of the lessons here is to use the more stable quartersawn wood for wide, unsupported panels, such as tabletops that aren't held to a rigid frame underneath. (For more in-depth information on specific wood species and their characteristics, see *Understanding Wood,* R. Bruce Hoadley, The Taunton Press.)

Allowing for wood movement is the key to building furniture that lasts. One of the best solutions, and perhaps most ancient, is making a frame-and-panel door. This savvy system relies on a narrow, grooved frame to house a wide panel. As the panel moves in response to changing moisture levels, it's free to change dimensions inside the grooves of the frame, swelling and shrinking without cracking or busting apart the frame.

Other strategies include aligning the grain of different parts of a case with each other. For example, if you orient the grain on the sides of a case vertically, the grain should run from side to side on the top and bottom. As the cabinet gains or loses moisture, the parts of the cabinet move in unison. Gluing or orienting parts cross-grain is a recipe for disaster, but there are exceptions. For example, gluing a mortise-and-tenon joint is fine. The joint remains tight because the cross-grain members are relatively narrow. And narrow stock (3 in. to 4 in. or less) moves very little. On wide stock, in which movement is considerable, one part swells and shrinks, pushing and pulling on its adjacent member relentlessly. Cracks or joint failure is the inevitable result. Even heavy buildups of finish can act like glue in the wrong place, promoting cracks.

Although a finish can't stop wood movement, don't overlook its protective powers. Any finish, including nondrying finishes such as natural oils, will to some extent minimize the amount of wood movement in a board. But be sure to apply the same number of coats to all sides of your work, particularly on free-floating panels. For example, while you may be more concerned about the beauty and luster on the top of a wooden desk, it's equally important to finish the underside. This way, the panel or top absorbs and releases moisture in an even manner. If you forget this rule of coating both sides, you'll end up with warped panels.

In addition to specific building techniques, it's important to understand the environment in which you work your wood and its relative humidity. For example, in most geographic areas, your wood will be drier indoors in the winter than in the summer. That's because the relative humidity is significantly lower at that time of year, due in part to the cold weather outside and in part to the central heat inside—both have a moisture-robbing effect. Knowing this, you'll wisely build parts a little less wide or a little less thick in the winter, because you expect them to swell during summertime humidity. The reverse is true for times when you're building during humid months: Build a little "fat" in the humid months to allow for shrinkage during drier times. You can check the exact swing in relative humidity over the seasons by monitoring your working environment with a hygrometer.

➤ See *"Buying and Preparing Solid Wood"* on p. 23.

Ultimately, I think the safest approach in coping with wood movement is to acquiesce to its inevitability. In other words, plan for the worst—and build accordingly. Assume

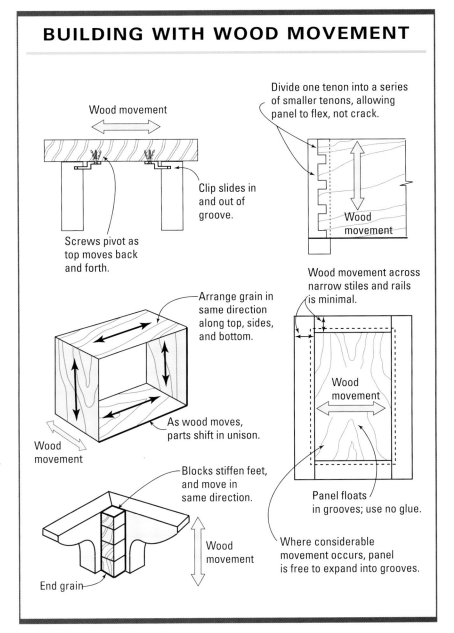

BUILDING WITH WOOD MOVEMENT

Wood movement

Screws pivot as top moves back and forth.

Clip slides in and out of groove.

Divide one tenon into a series of smaller tenons, allowing panel to flex, not crack.

Wood movement

Wood movement across narrow stiles and rails is minimal.

Arrange grain in same direction along top, sides, and bottom.

Wood movement

As wood moves, parts shift in unison.

Wood movement

Blocks stiffen feet, and move in same direction.

End grain

Wood movement

Panel floats in grooves; use no glue.

Where considerable movement occurs, panel is free to expand into grooves.

the piece will eventually come to live in the Southern Hemisphere, near water, somewhere in the tropics (where there are wild swings in humidity levels)—even though it probably won't. That way, you'll design and build for big swings in dimensional changes, and your furniture will to turn to dust long after you.

Basic Cases, page 46

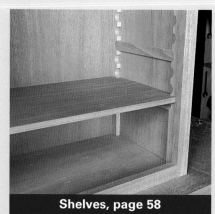
Shelves, page 58

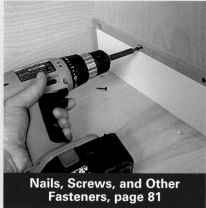
Nails, Screws, and Other Fasteners, page 81

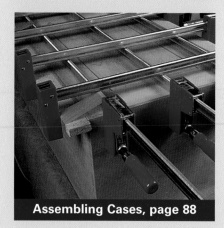
Assembling Cases, page 88

Cutting and Attaching Moldings, page 95

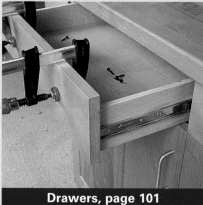
Drawers, page 101

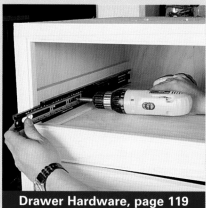
Drawer Hardware, page 119

PART TWO

Box and Case Construction

A S THE GROUNDWORK FOR ALL OF WOODWORKING, casework is much more than simply building a cabinet with six sides. Complex case designs can incorporate almost every joint you know and may include curves or involve great spans. But basic casework tackles some essential techniques, such as learning the art of producing flat and square surfaces—and keeping them that way. Creating a fair curve, when you shape a smooth line without hills or valleys, is also part of the craft. (For more on shaping, see *The Complete Illustrated Guide to Shaping Wood,* by Lonnie Bird, The Taunton Press.) And fitting parts. Yes—you'll be endlessly fitting parts in case construction. It's not for the weak of heart. But constructing all those little pieces into a recognizable whole as a box or a cabinet is good experience. Bit by bit, you'll learn to use your tools and materials more thoughtfully and, with luck, gain a higher level of control over them.

Basic Cases

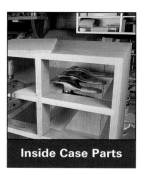

Inside Case Parts

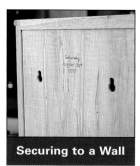

Securing to a Wall

CABINETS COME IN A NEVER-ENDING ARRAY OF STYLES and flavors to suit everyone's needs and tastes. But the basic box can be broken down into relatively few distinct styles, or types. Once you've decided on the flavor of your case, you still have many options for deciding how best to construct it.

Whether you're making a small jewelry box, a set of drawers, or a wall-to-wall entertainment center, basic case construction remains the same: You need to join two sides (at the very least) and add a top, a bottom, and a back. How you join the cabinet will in part depend on the material you're using—whether it's solid wood, man-made boards such as plywood, or a combination of the two. Yes, it's okay to put plywood into a solid-wood case; but there are certain rules to follow, or your new cabinet will come apart at the seams in no time because of solid wood's inevitable inclination to move.

➤ See *"Understanding Wood Movement"* on p. 42.

The drawings on pp. 48 and 49 show some of your options for joinery. For more details on making these joints, see *The Complete Illustrated Guide to Joinery,* by Gary Rogowski (The Taunton Press).

The next step in building a case is to lay out the interior, and its design greatly depends on the cabinet's intended use.

CABINET STYLES

Basic case styles leave plenty of room for personal aesthetics and use. For example, the same base style can serve as a filing cabinet or as a kitchen cabinet.

Wall-Hung

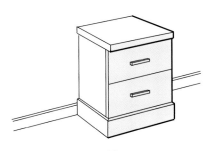

Freestanding

Can be tall, wide, or built in separate parts, such as an upper unit that rests on a lower case.

Built-In

Attached to wall, floor, or ceiling and scribed to fit.

Base

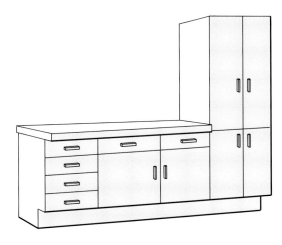

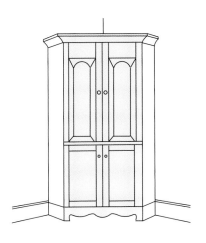

Display or Open Cabinet

32-mm System (Frameless)

Corner Cabinet

CASE JOINERY OPTIONS

You can use the same joinery on cabinets made from plywood or other man-made boards as you do for solid-wood cases, with the exception of the sliding dovetail, which doesn't have much strength when cut in plywood. When working with solid wood, orient the grain direction of the parts, as indicated by the arrows, to keep the assembly stable.

Butt Joints

Held with glue and nails or screws.

Knock-Down Joints

Metal connectors interlock with mating pieces.

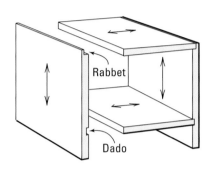

Bolt passes through side and engages nut in shelf.

Nut is inserted in blind hole under shelf.

Glued Dadoes and Rabbets

Rabbet

Dado

Biscuits

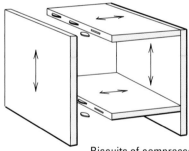

Biscuits of compressed wood glued into kerfs cut in mating pairs

Dowels

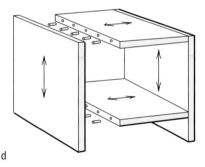

Dovetails

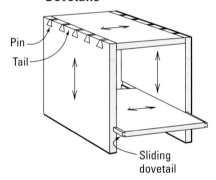

Pin

Tail

Sliding dovetail

Through dovetails join top corners; sliding dovetails secure bottom or shelf.

Mortises and Tenons

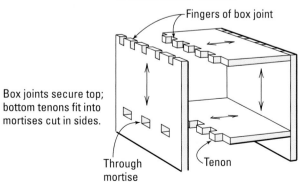

Fingers of box joint

Box joints secure top; bottom tenons fit into mortises cut in sides.

Through mortise

Tenon

Splines

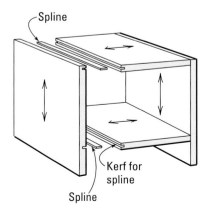

Spline

Spline

Kerf for spline

Spline

Dividers and partitions can section off a cabinet, maximizing the amount of usable space inside. If you're going to incorporate shelves, now is the time to think about the design, before you assemble the case.

➤ See *"Shelves"* on p. 58.

Cabinets that hold drawers or small trays will need runners and kickers that guide these parts in and out of the case. Of course, every cabinet has a back (or a bottom on a small box or drawer). And even though fitting the back to the case typically comes last in the assembly sequence, it's worth noting that most cabinets will need a rabbet or some form of structure to accept the back, and this should be designed or constructed before the case is assembled.

MIXING PLYWOOD AND SOLID WOOD

The key to mixing plywood and solid wood successfully in the same cabinet is to avoid gluing joints of 4 in. or more in width. If you must use plywood over a wide piece of solid wood, it's best to screw the parts together. The screws will allow the wood to move freely without binding. Or, instead of screws, make a plywood panel and house it in a solid-wood frame so there's no hardware on view. Plywood backs can be successfully glued into rabbets in the solid-wood sides, because there's practically no width to the rabbet.

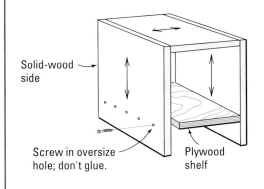

Solid-wood side

Screw in oversize hole; don't glue.

Plywood shelf

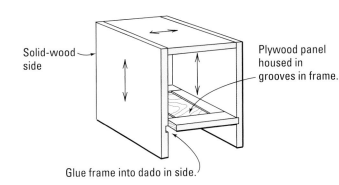

Solid-wood side

Plywood panel housed in grooves in frame.

Glue frame into dado in side.

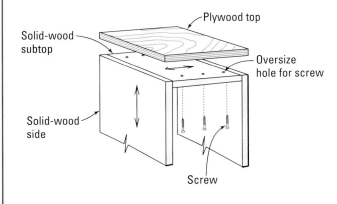

Plywood top

Solid-wood subtop

Oversize hole for screw

Solid-wood side

Screw

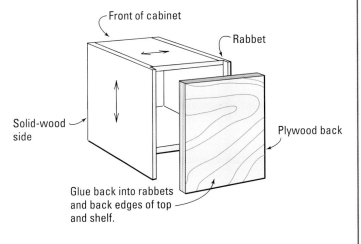

Front of cabinet

Rabbet

Solid-wood side

Plywood back

Glue back into rabbets and back edges of top and shelf.

INTERNAL ARCHITECTURE

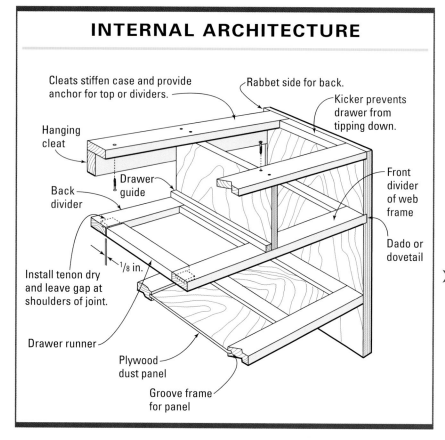

Cleats stiffen case and provide anchor for top or dividers.

Rabbet side for back.

Kicker prevents drawer from tipping down.

Hanging cleat

Drawer guide

Back divider

Front divider of web frame

Dado or dovetail

Install tenon dry and leave gap at shoulders of joint.

Back divider

¹/8 in.

Drawer runner

Plywood dust panel

Groove frame for panel

Finally, if the cabinet is to be hung on a wall, there are hanging systems to consider. Or perhaps you need to secure a base cabinet to the floor or wall. Weight is a big factor, since the cabinet will likely hold many times its own weight. Wooden cleats can do the trick in most cases and can be used to permanently fix a case to a vertical surface. But what happens if the cabinet is removed from its intended spot? Plan ahead and you can make a wall-hung case easily removable—without tools.

Before diving into the construction aspects of cabinets, decide on the basic style and function you require of the cabinet you're building. Often, a very basic design can be altered to suit a particular need, such as turning a simple base cabinet into multiples to outfit an entire kitchen.

Solid-Wood and Plywood Joinery

Once you've decided on a style, you'll need to investigate materials. Both solid wood and man-made boards (for example, plywood and particleboard) are used in casework. Each has its own distinct advantages and disadvantages when it comes to working it.

Your joinery approach will sometimes depend on the type of material you choose, but most likely it will hinge on the degree of complexity you want to invest in the work.

▶ See *"Working Wood"* on p. 22.

For example, there's nothing wrong with a glued-and-nailed butt joint. Done in a thoughtful and careful manner, a nailed joint can last generations, and it's a quick way of putting together a cabinet. Dovetailing a case on all four corners is the other side of the coin, requiring lots of careful planning and much toil at the bench. The point is that you can put as much time and energy as you wish into cutting simple—or not so simple—joints. It's often a matter of what fits best with your own personal sense of style, combined with the capabilities of your shop and skills.

The main thing to think about when determining case joints in solid wood is to take into account the direction in which the wood will move; then construct the piece to allow for that movement. The drawing on p. 48 shows the correct way to orient the grain in a variety of situations, particularly when gluing parts together. In hardwood veneered plywoods and other sheet goods with grain on the show surfaces, it doesn't matter what direction you orient the grain.

When combining the two materials (see the drawing on p. 49), you'll have to take wood movement into account once more.

Designing Inside a Cabinet

After settling on a style and choice of materials, you'll need to focus on what you want to do with the inside construction details. The internal architecture of a cabinet can serve many functions. Web frames joined to the sides of the case can stiffen it and provide a platform for drawers, and dividers help stiffen shelves and organize space efficiently. Cleats can replace wider panels and provide a means for attaching tops. Drawer guides help drawers glide smoothly in and out of a case, and drawer kickers are necessary to prevent drawer boxes from tipping downward as they're pulled out. And if you're building a wall-hung case, you'll need to think about a method for hanging the cabinet, which often involves strategically placed members hidden inside the case.

Partitions and Dividers

Web frames and dust panels provide the skeleton for the interior construction, to which you'll frequently add other dividers and partitions. Dividers not only break up the space in a cabinet but provide bearing surfaces for hardware and drawers or platforms for shelves. Position a vertical divider under a horizontal divider or shelf and you automatically stiffen the shelf to keep it from sagging. If you join the divider to the sides of the cabinet, you'll increase the overall strength of the case itself.

A vertical partition can help support a shelf or drawer and prevent sagging.

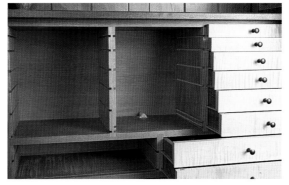

Combined with a vertical partition, a horizontal divider can provide solid support for drawers.

A series of thin vertical partitions create pigeonholes for storing small items.

DIVIDER CONNECTIONS

Dividers and partitions can become part of the overall structure of a cabinet, especially if the joints that secure them are strong. Butt joints and screws are a simple way of connecting a divider inside a case, and they fit the bill when you won't see the hardware. Wire supports provide an invisible joint and let you easily remove a divider.

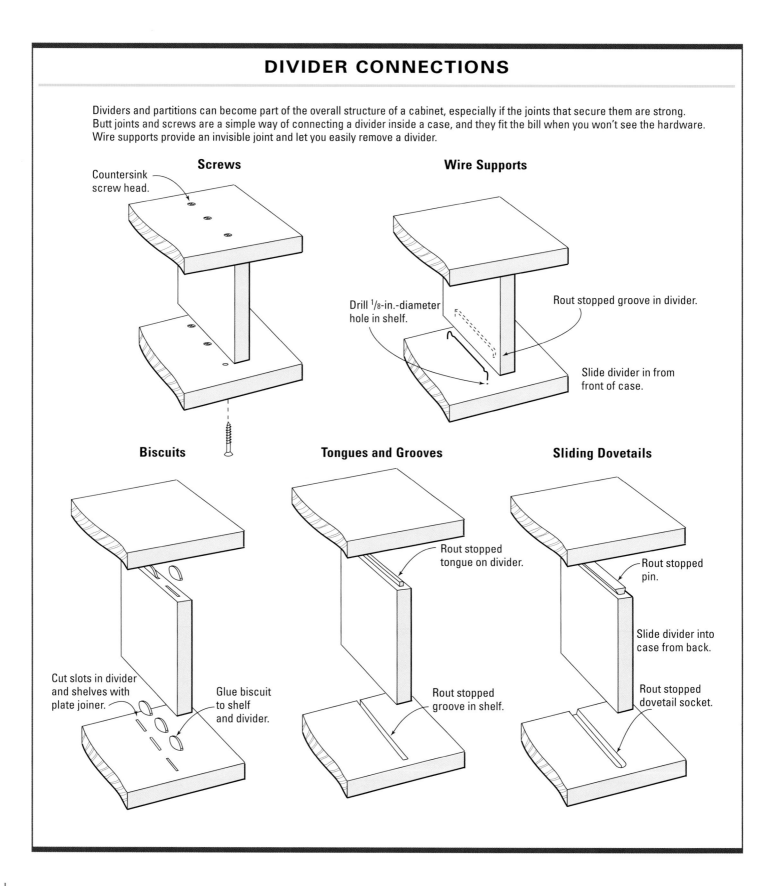

Screws

Countersink screw head.

Wire Supports

Drill 1/8-in.-diameter hole in shelf.

Rout stopped groove in divider.

Slide divider in from front of case.

Biscuits

Cut slots in divider and shelves with plate joiner.

Glue biscuit to shelf and divider.

Tongues and Grooves

Rout stopped tongue on divider.

Rout stopped groove in shelf.

Sliding Dovetails

Rout stopped pin.

Slide divider into case from back.

Rout stopped dovetail socket.

Web Frames

A web frame stiffens a case and creates a strong platform for housing drawers—all without adding excess weight to a cabinet—and its design allows for the movement of cases with solid-wood sides.

Start by sizing and cutting the frame parts to fit the interior dimensions of the cabinet. Prepare for the case joinery by first cutting mortise-and-tenon joints in the frame parts. Then cut the dovetail sockets and dadoes into the case sides. For accuracy, use one jig to cut both joints at the same time—but with two routers with different diameter baseplates (**A**). Shims placed on either side of the smaller router accommodate the difference in base diameter. Size the shims to suit your particular router. You can use this jig to cut both joints using only one router, but you'll have to either change bits (and bit depth) between cuts or reposition the jig for each cut.

Rout an $^{11}/_{16}$-in.-wide by $^{5}/_{16}$-in.-deep dovetail socket for the horizontal drawer divider using a $^{1}/_{2}$-in. bit. Using a bit that's smaller than the desired slot width puts a lot less strain on the bit and makes a cleaner cut in the wood. Place the shims on either side of the router and move the router in a clockwise direction, making contact with the shim on the left side and then with the shim on the right. Pencil lines mark the length of the socket, so it's a simple matter of stopping the cut when the bit reaches the mark (**B**).

Next, rout the dadoes for the drawer runners. Remove the shims and use the same jig and the second router, which has a larger baseplate. Use a $^{3}/_{4}$-in. plunge-cutting straight bit to cut a shallow $^{1}/_{8}$-in. dado between the dovetail slots (**C**).

(Text continues on p. 54.)

This dovetail dado-routing jig serves double-duty to rout $^{11}/_{16}$-in. dovetail sockets and $^{3}/_{4}$-in. dadoes in case sides. Using a $^{1}/_{2}$-in. dovetail bit in the first router, add shims on either side of the guide rails that provide $^{3}/_{16}$ in. of side-to-side play between the router and the rails. Rout the dovetails by moving the router from left to right as you push it away from you. To rout dadoes, remove the shims and install a $^{3}/_{4}$-in. plunge-cutting straight bit in a second router with a larger baseplate.

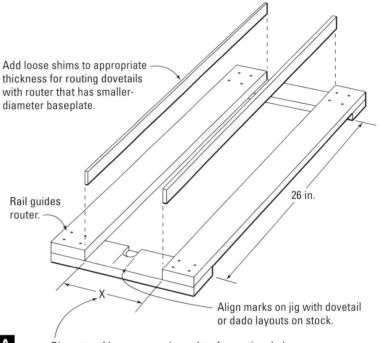

Add loose shims to appropriate thickness for routing dovetails with router that has smaller-diameter baseplate.

Rail guides router.

26 in.

X

Align marks on jig with dovetail or dado layouts on stock.

A Diameter of larger router baseplate for routing dadoes

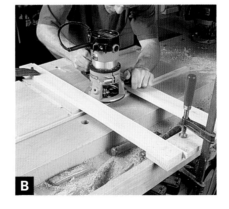

B

C

Working from the front of the cabinet, install the front dividers by gluing the dovetails into the sockets and clamping across the joints (**D**).

Next, turn the case over and install the drawer runner from the back by gluing it into the mortise in the front divider. Don't glue the runner into the dado. Instead, drive a screw through an oversize hole in the center of the runner and into the case side (**E**). On wider cases, use two or three screws through the runner. Adding screws may sound unconventional, but the technique stiffens the overall frame and—more important—helps keep the case sides flat over time.

Glue the back divider into the dovetail sockets at the back, but don't glue the rear tenons on the runners. Make sure to size the runners so you leave an ⅛-in. gap between the shoulder of the runner and the back divider (**F**). This arrangement allows for movement of the case sides. Waxing the rear tenons is also a good idea to promote easy movement of the runner. On the case shown here, where pairs of drawers run side by side, vertical dividers were dovetailed at the front of the case. Add wide runners behind the dividers using the same dry-tenon technique. Later, glue narrow guide strips onto the runner to guide the sides of the drawers.

➤ See *"Drawer Runners"* opposite.

Drawer Runners

If the cabinet contains drawers, some guide system is necessary. For the simplest cabinet, the side itself can guide the drawer. But guides are required, for example, when a face frame extends beyond the side of a cabinet or when a vertical divider divides two or more drawers side by side.

When your case doesn't involve horizontal front dividers and you want to maximize usable space, you can hang drawers directly above and below each other by attaching solid-wood strips to the sides of the case and then routing matching grooves in the drawer sides.

Rout a ¼-in.-deep stopped groove in the drawer side (**A**). Attach the strip to the case with screws. A piece of plywood registered against the case bottom keeps the strip parallel and helps align pairs of strips (**B**). Slide the drawer onto the strips and all you see is the grooves in the drawer sides (**C**). In the case of an extended face frame, just pack out the space with a plywood strip to accommodate the frame overhang; then screw the hardwood guide strip to the side of the case.

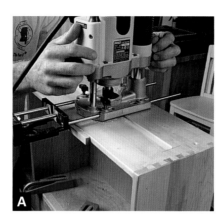

[**TIP**] **When a drawer has free space above the sides, install a kicker above the sides to prevent tipping. A couple screws or some spots of glue attach the kicker to the case.**

For divided drawers, rip and plane a strip equal to the thickness of the divider and mortise it into the front and back of the cabinet, or glue it directly to the web frame. To help align the guide strip square to the opening, use a pair of scrap boards cut to the exact width of the drawer openings. Clamp the boards in position with the guide strip between them. Then remove one board and glue and clamp the strip to the frame (**D**).

Dust Panels

There are two primary reasons for adding dust panels inside your cabinets: In bureaus, a panel helps prevent clothes from getting tangled in drawers above. It also helps seal the cabinet from airborne dust.

Before assembling the frame, groove the web members for the panel. It's quick to rout the slots with a slotting cutter on the router table (**A**).

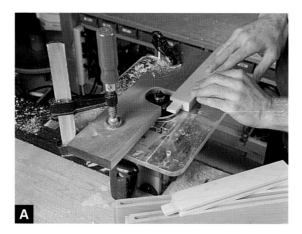

After installing the front divider and the runners, slide the panel into the grooves from the back. For extra rigidity, you can glue the panel into the front and side grooves, as long as you make it from plywood (**B**).

Add the rear divider by gluing only its dovetails into the sockets. Be careful not to glue the divider to the panel or the tenons on the runners to allow for movement of the case sides (**C**).

Hanging Cleats

An additional member fixed to the case is often needed when you're securing a cabinet to a wall, floor, or ceiling. For base cabinets, one horizontal strip of wood at the top of the cabinet in the back is usually sufficient to hold it securely to a wall. Or you can attach blocks underneath a cabinet's bottom that allow you to screw or bolt it to a floor.

For wall-hung cases, add a solid-wood strip inside the cabinet so it rests underneath the top (**A**) and add a similar strip underneath the case bottom (**B**). Drive screws or nails through both strips and through the case back to secure the cabinet. The strips support the top and bottom of the case, which is much stronger than simply screwing through the back. Be sure the fasteners you use enter the studs in the wall if you're attaching the cabinet to conventional wood-framed walls. Use masonry anchors for stone or concrete.

If you want your wall cabinet to be removable, you can hang it on a beveled strip secured level to the wall (**C**). Attach a matching beveled strip to the back of the case and add a block of the same thickness at the bottom of the case to keep the cabinet plumb to the wall. Then simply lower the case onto the wall strip (**D**).

For small cabinets, try routing a pair of keyhole slots in the case back with a keyhole bit in the router (**E**). If possible, position the holes so they correspond to the stud spacing in your walls; then drive a pair of screws into the studs and slip the cabinet over the screws.

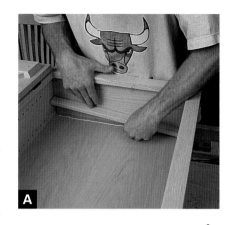

A

B

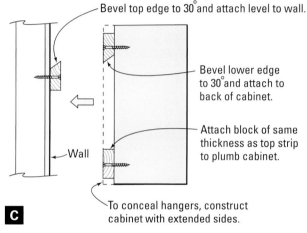

Bevel top edge to 30° and attach level to wall.

Bevel lower edge to 30° and attach to back of cabinet.

Attach block of same thickness as top strip to plumb cabinet.

Wall

To conceal hangers, construct cabinet with extended sides.

C

D

E

Shelves

Shelf Joinery

- ➤ Through-Dado Shelf (p. 64)
- ➤ Tapered Sliding Dovetail (p. 65)

Open Shelves

- ➤ Ledges for Open Shelves (p. 66)
- ➤ Wood Brackets for Open Shelves (p. 67)

Shelf Options

- ➤ Adjustable Shelves (p. 68)
- ➤ Wood Support and Edge Strip (p. 69)
- ➤ Pilasters and Clips (p. 70)
- ➤ Pins and Holes (p. 71)
- ➤ Wire Supports (p. 72)
- ➤ Torsion-Box Shelf (p. 73)

Dressing Up a Shelf

- ➤ Wood Lippings (p. 74)
- ➤ Flush-Trimmed Lippings (p. 75)
- ➤ Plugged Screws (p. 76)
- ➤ Biscuits (p. 77)
- ➤ Tongue and Groove (p. 78)
- ➤ Commercial Edgebanding (p. 79)
- ➤ PVA Glue and Veneer (p. 80)

THE LOWLY SHELF is one of the most important elements in casework. Where else will you find such useful horizontal storage space? Whether you're storing books, kitchen goods, office supplies, tools, or any of the myriad stuff we accumulate during the course of our lives, the shelf you build today will be pressed into service for many years to come.

Selecting the appropriate material for shelves is crucial. Solid wood can be decoratively shaped on its leading edge more easily than composite or man-made boards, such as plywood, to give your shelves a flair. Plywood, particleboard, and MDF have the distinct advantage of being available in large, flat panels, making the process of producing wide horizontal surfaces as easy as cutting panels to size on the table saw or with a circular saw. And the type of material you use can have a big effect on whether the shelves will bow or sag when they're loaded with favorite possessions. In general, solid wood is stiffer than plywood.

➤ See *"Designing Sag-Proof Shelves"* opposite.

When making the shelves, you have two options: fixed or adjustable. Adjustable shelving offers you the ability to move a shelf's position after the furniture has been built, increasing a cabinet's versatility. But this type of system often increases the complexity of your cabinet design. Fixed shelves are simpler to design and build, and they significantly increase the strength of a cabinet as well as stiffen each individual shelf. The most common method of making a fixed shelf is to dado it into the case sides. Dovetailing the shelf to the case is much stronger because of the increased glue surface and mechanical locking of the joint.

▶ See *"Shelf Joinery"* on p. 64.

You have many options with adjustable shelves, from shelf-support pins that fit into holes drilled in the case to more elaborate shopmade supports.

▶ See *"Adjustable Shelves"* on p. 68.

Designing Sag-Proof Shelves

Even a slightly bowed shelf in a cabinet or bookcase looks wrong. Good furniture should include shelves that are straight and solid looking. The trick is to figure out how to make your shelves strong enough to hold their intended load *before* you build them. There are several strategies you can employ from edging and ledges to dividers and torsion boxes. Other strategies include keeping the shelf span as short as possible and selecting the right material in the appropriate thickness. For the strongest shelves, thick hardwoods are your best bet. Also, a fixed

shelf is much stronger than an adjustable one because the joint itself helps stiffen the shelf.

▶ See *"Wood Lippings"* on p. 74.

Choosing Adjustable Shelf Supports

If you want adjustability and maximum versatility in your shelving, an adjustable shelf system is the way to go. You can choose from commercial hardware or make your own supports (see drawings on pp. 60 to 62).

Maximum Shelf Spans

The maximum length between supports for a moderate load (20 lb. per foot) on a 10-in.-wide shelf.

Material	Maximum Span (in.)
Particleboard, ¾ in.	24
MDF, ¾ in.	28
Hardwood plywood, ¾ in.	32
Softwood	
¾ in.	36
1 in.	48
1½ in.	63
Hardwood	
¾ in.	42
1 in.	48
1½ in.	66

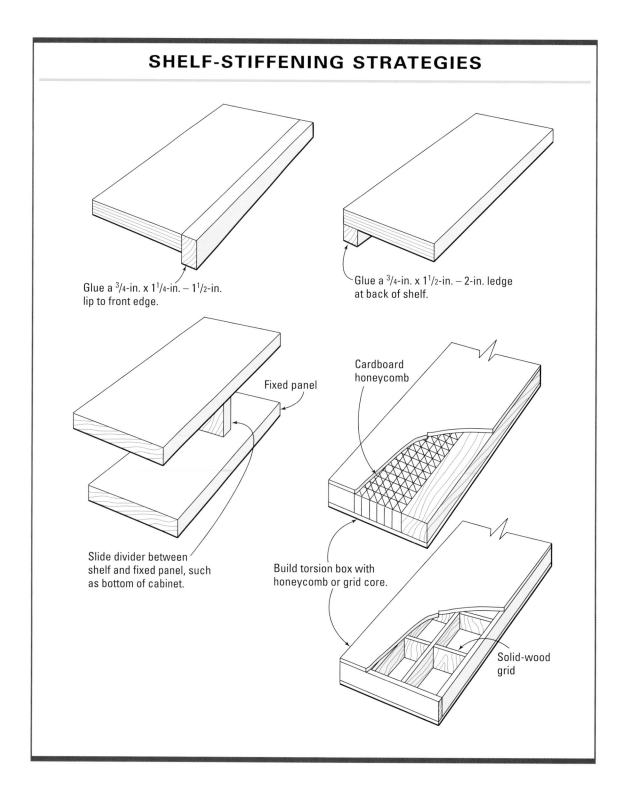

SHELF-STIFFENING STRATEGIES

Glue a $^3/_4$-in. x $1^1/_4$-in. – $1^1/_2$-in. lip to front edge.

Glue a $^3/_4$-in. x $1^1/_2$-in. – 2-in. ledge at back of shelf.

Fixed panel

Slide divider between shelf and fixed panel, such as bottom of cabinet.

Cardboard honeycomb

Build torsion box with honeycomb or grid core.

Solid-wood grid

TYPES OF ADJUSTABLE SHELF SUPPORTS

Commercial Hardware

Wall-mounted metal
standard and bracket

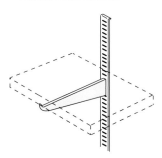

Metal or plastic pilasters
with shelf clips

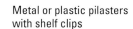

Clips and Pins

There are various metal and plastic
clips and pins that fit into pilasters
or into holes drilled in the case.

Pilaster clips

Pins

Metal sleeve

Wire support

Shelf pin

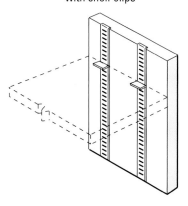

Stopped groove in shelf
accommodates wire support.

Shopmade Adjustable Shelving

Wood cleat

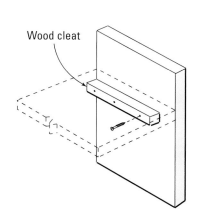

Wood cleat
with pins

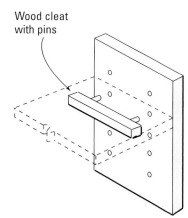

Wood support

Edge strip

Notch in shelf

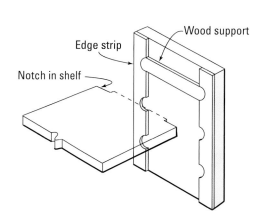

EDGE TREATMENTS

Routing, shaping, or molding a profile on the edge of a shelf can add a lot to the overall design of a piece of furniture. Here are some options.

Basic Shapes

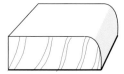

Roundover

Chamfer

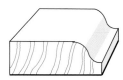

Cove

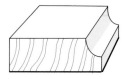

Ogee

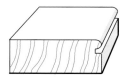

Bead

Variations

Roundover with fillet

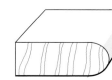

Bullnose

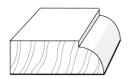

Thumbnail

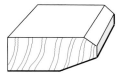

Chamfer top and bottom

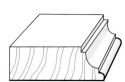

Chamfer top and bevel bottom

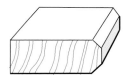

Cove and fillets

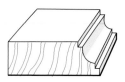

Cove and quarter-round

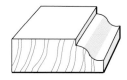

Roman ogee with fillet

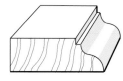

Reverse ogee with fillet

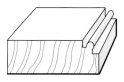

Corner bead

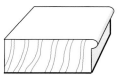

Cock bead

Wood Plugs That Disappear

Once you've selected the stock and the overall dimensions of your shelf, there are a number of strategies to increase its rigidity to prevent deflection under load. You can use screws or nails, for example, that support the shelf at several points. To hide the fastener on an exposed surface, you can use wood plugs.

For a super-tight fit in a counterbored hole, cut your plugs on the drill press using a tapered plug cutter. Be sure to select your material from the same stock that you're trying to fill, so the plugs will match the grain. It's best to set the fence so that the cutter is exposed on the edge of the stock as you drill. This trick keeps the cutter from overheating and dulling.

Apply tape to the drilled stock, rubbing it firmly over the ends of the plugs. Turn the stock on its side and bandsaw the plugs free from the blank. Eyeball along the bottom of the exposed plugs and cut to that line.

Before pulling off individual plugs, mark them to indicate the correct long-grain direction. This is important, because the bandsaw marks run at 90 degrees to the grain and will often fool you into installing the plug in the wrong direction. Install the plug *with the grain*, pare or sand it flush, and note how it practically disappears.

For a series of wood plugs, drill close to the edge so the cutter breaks through the side, reducing friction and heat.

Use a bandsaw to cut the plugs free, following the baseline of the plugs.

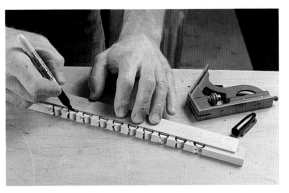

Mark the grain direction on all the plugs before separating them.

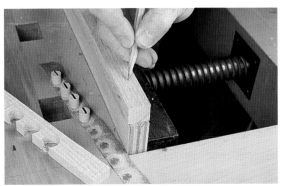

Plugs installed with the grain in the workpiece virtually disappear.

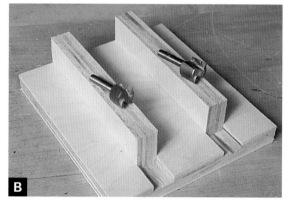

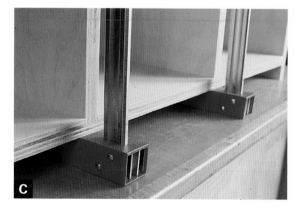

A Way to Make a Through-Dado Shelf

A strong shelf connection is to attach the shelf permanently to the case sides. This approach strengthens the case itself and helps stiffen the shelf and prevent it from sagging under a load.

The simplest method for making a fixed shelf is to cut through dadoes in the case sides to receive the shelf. Rout the dadoes with a straight bit guided by a straightedge. For a clean cut, plunge rout the dado in successively deeper passes to reduce tearout (**A**). Make your dadoes shallow—about ¼ in. deep in a ¾-in. panel—to keep the case sides strong and to leave enough material for nailing or screwing through the joint.

A tight-fitting joint is important for strength and good looks. Most plywood comes about ¹⁄₆₄ in. under nominal thickness, so you'll need to cut dadoes slightly undersize for a tight fit. The dado shown on the right in photo **B** was routed with a conventional straight bit, which resulted in a loose joint with a small gap. The bit on the left of the photo is specially sized for an exact fit with standard ¼-in. hardwood plywood, so the joint is strong and tight.

For a finished appearance, simply glue and clamp the joint (**C**). For case sides that won't be seen, add screws or nails through the side to ease assembly and to strengthen the joint.

Tapered Sliding Dovetail

The strongest connection is to dovetail the shelf to the case sides, tapering the joint along its length.

Cut the tapered dovetail sockets in the case first. Use a shopmade jig (**A, B**) to guide the router and a ½-in. dovetail bit. To reduce tearout, rout a notch into the back edge first, before routing the full width of the panel (**C**).

Next, tape ½₂-in.-thick shims to both sides of the shelf stock (**D**).

Using the same bit you used to cut the socket, rout the pin by making one pass on the router table on each side of the stock. Be sure to rout in scrap first to fine-tune the fit, moving the fence in or out from the bit, or adjusting the shim thickness, until the widest part of the tail almost—but not quite—fits into the wider end of the socket. Beams clamped to the stock remove any possible warp (**E**).

The dovetail pin should tighten as the joint is brought home. Having to tap the last ½ in. into the socket means a tight-fitting joint. Glue is optional, although with solid wood it's a good idea to glue about 2 in. at the front of the joint to keep the shelf flush with the case despite any wood movement (**F**).

This tapered-dovetail socket jig is sized to rout a $^5/_{16}$-in.-deep by $^5/_8$-in.-wide dovetail in a case side up to 14 in. wide, using a $^1/_2$-in. dovetail bit. The dovetail tapers $^1/_{16}$ in. over its length. For wider cases, use the same amount of taper and make the guide boards wider.

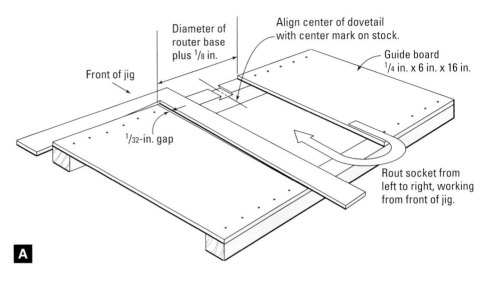

Diameter of router base plus $^1/_8$ in.

Align center of dovetail with center mark on stock.

Guide board $^1/_4$ in. x 6 in. x 16 in.

Front of jig

$^1/_{32}$-in. gap

Rout socket from left to right, working from front of jig.

A

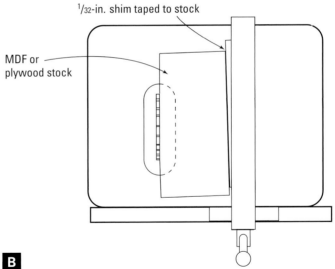

$^1/_{32}$-in. shim taped to stock

MDF or plywood stock

B

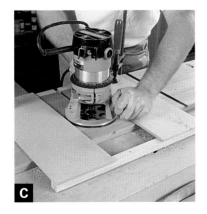

C

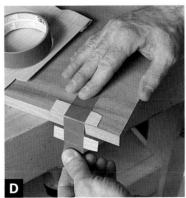

D

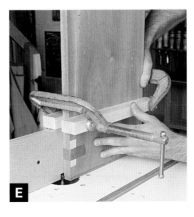

E

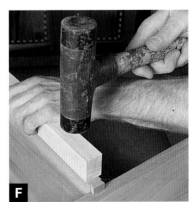

F

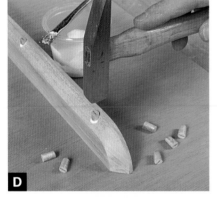

Ledges for Open Shelves

Display shelves often call for a ledge in the middle of a board, which can be screwed in place from behind.

To elevate your ledge from rectilinear boredom, first scroll the ends of the stock on the bandsaw (**A**) and then clean up the sawn surfaces with a drum sander or by hand.

For a more delicate feel, chamfer the underside of the stock on the router table. Use a piloted chamfer bit and begin the cut safely by rotating the stock against a starting pin. Don't rout the full chamfer in one pass; make successively deeper cuts by raising the cutter after each pass (**B**).

For a low-profile look, counterbore the stock with a ¼-in. Forstner bit and use trim-head screws to attach the shelf to the backboard (**C**). Once the shelves are secured, spread glue on a ¼-in. wooden plug and tap it into the counterbored hole. A mark on the plug indicates grain direction (**D**).

Once the glue has dried, pare and sand the plug flush with the edge of the shelf (**E**). Because the plug's grain runs parallel to the shelf's grain, the plug blends in seamlessly.

Custom-fitted ledges can make a distinguished statement. As shown here, I store my larger handplanes on shelves scrolled to the outline of each plane (**F**).

Wood Brackets for Open Shelves

Attached to the wall or placed in an open cabinet, wooden brackets can support a lot of weight and add a custom look.

If you're making one or two brackets, you can draw the desired shape on the stock and saw it out on the bandsaw. For multiple brackets, use a plywood template to trace the shape onto the stock (**A**).

Saw out the shape by cutting to the line on the bandsaw (**B**). Clean up the saw marks on the drum sander, sanding "downhill" to the grain for the smoothest surface (**C**). Pare the shoulders and flats with a sharp chisel.

When possible, screw through the back of the case or the backboard and into the brackets to conceal the connection (**D**). If necessary, you can also screw through the brackets themselves and into the backboard; then plug the screw holes for a finished appearance.

► See *"Wood Plugs That Disappear"* on p. 63.

You can simply let the finished shelf sit on the brackets or secure it from behind the backboard and below the brackets with screws or finish nails (**E**).

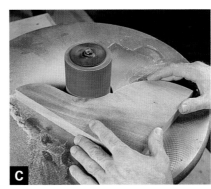

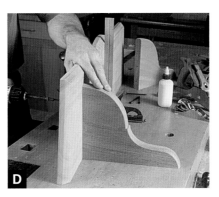

Adjustable Shelves

For maximum versatility in a cabinet or book-case, a shelf that simply rests on supports is the way to go. With this approach, you can easily reconfigure shelves on the fly. The type of support you choose is mostly an aesthetic decision, from simple pins that fit into holes drilled into the case, to more elaborate wooden hangers that add flair to your furniture.

▶ See *"Types of Adjustable Shelf Supports"* on p. 61.

Wood cleats used to support shelves are simple and effective. To improve their looks, keep the cleats as thin as possible (⅜ in. thick is about minimum) and install them with finish nails or small screws.

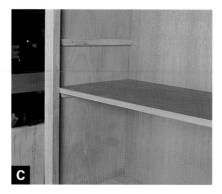

After ripping and crosscutting the stock to width and length, round over the front and bottom edge on the router table. Use a starting pin to begin the cut safely (**A**).

It's easier if you secure the cleats before fully assembling the case. Use a square to ensure each cleat runs dead square across the case (**B**).

The finished shelf rests on top of the cleats (**C**). To adjust the shelf, simply place it over another set of cleats.

Wood Support and Edge Strip

An elegant solution to adjustable shelving is to support each shelf on support cleats that nestle into half-holes drilled into wooden strips. The system is simpler to make than it looks, and a template-rounding jig helps you accurately make the round-ended supports (**A**).

Starting with a pair of 2-in.-wide boards, drill a series of 1-in.-diameter holes along the center of each board using a Forstner bit on the drill press (**B**).

Rip each board in half on the table saw to create two strips (**C**) and nail the strips into the corners of the case. A pneumatic brad gun makes for fast work (**D**).

After sizing the cleats to about ⅛ in. longer than the finished size, use a template-rounding jig and a pattern bit to reach the finished length, rounding the ends at the same time (**E**).

Install the supports between the edge strips at the desired height. The finished shelf sits on top of the supports (**F**). You'll have to notch the shelf to fit it around the edge strips.

> ⚠ **WARNING** Always remove rings and other jewelry when operating a drill press. Rings caught by a spinning drill chuck or bit can rip the flesh right off your finger.

Use this template-rounding jig on a router table to cut half-circles on the ends of wooden supports or anywhere you need a specific radius on the ends of stock. Rip the stock to finished width and about ⅛ in. over length; then bandsaw a curve on the ends slightly bigger than the desired radius. Using a top-bearing template or pattern bit, rout each support in four consecutive passes, each pass cutting one corner of the support.

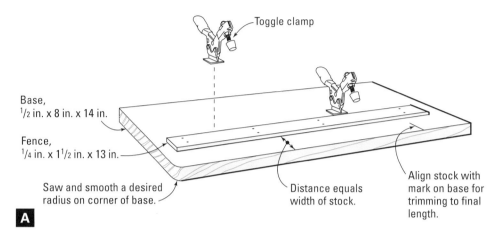

Toggle clamp

Base, ½ in. x 8 in. x 14 in.

Fence, ¼ in. x 1½ in. x 13 in.

Saw and smooth a desired radius on corner of base.

Distance equals width of stock.

Align stock with mark on base for trimming to final length.

A

B

C

D

E

F

Pilasters and Clips

Pilasters offer an easy way to incorporate adjustable shelves into cabinets, and they usually allow for incremental height changes of ½ in. or less—a real benefit for configuring shelves exactly where you want them. Some pilasters can be surface mounted, but recessed pilasters have a cleaner look.

Plow grooves in the stock for the pilaster using a dado blade or router, making sure to test the fit first in scrap (**A**).

Crosscut the pilaster strip to length using a crosscut-style carbide-tipped blade for aluminum, brass, or plastic (**B**). For steel, you'll need to use a hacksaw. It's important when using any style of pilaster that the slots or holes for the clips are equidistant from the ends of each pilaster, so measure carefully when cutting to length.

Tap the pilaster strip into the groove, using the assembled top and bottom of the cabinet to help register the strip (**C**).

With the cabinet fully assembled, you can hang the shelves. The plastic clips twist securely into this style of pilaster (**D**).

Pins and Holes

Drilling a series of holes in the case and using pins to support the shelves is another simple yet good-looking solution to adjustable shelving. But make a mistake in the hole layout and you'll end up with wobbly shelves. The key is to use a simple jig that lets you lay out dead-accurate holes in the case sides (**A**).

Clamp the jig to the case side with its edge flush with the edge of the panel. For this example, I used the biscuit joinery in the panel to help align the end of the jig. Use a center punch or an awl to mark the stock through the jig. Masking tape applied to the jig defines the row of holes you want to drill (**B**).

Drill the holes on the drill press using a fence clamped to the table and a brad-point bit. The fence is rabbeted so wayward chips don't interfere with alignment (**C**).

[**TIP**] **Shavings from a drill press (or a router table) have a nasty habit of lodging between the workpiece and the fence, most likely spoiling the work. A rabbet cut into the bottom of the fence provides a channel for the shavings and allows the workpiece to contact the fence.**

If you don't own a drill press, a good drilling option is to use a commercial drilling rig like the Veritas jig shown here. There's no marking out; just secure the jig to the stock and drill into the work through hardened steel bushings (**D**). Masking tape wrapped around the bit guides it to the correct depth.

A nice touch is to lightly chamfer the drilled holes with a handheld countersinking bit. Be sure to use the same number of rotations per hole for a consistent look (**E**). Brass pins provide a clean look (**F**).

This simple hole-layout jig allows for accurate layout of shelf-pin holes. To use it, align the bottom edge with the bottom of the case side or with the case's joinery, such as a dado or biscuits. Use an awl or a center punch to mark the hole locations by pushing the punch through the jig and into the workpiece.

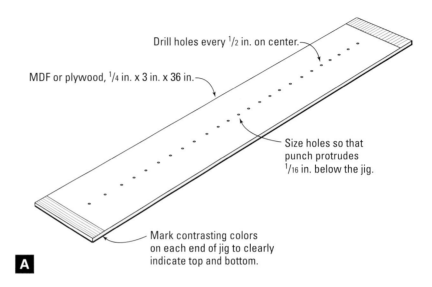

Drill holes every $1/2$ in. on center.

MDF or plywood, $1/4$ in. x 3 in. x 36 in.

Size holes so that punch protrudes $1/16$ in. below the jig.

Mark contrasting colors on each end of jig to clearly indicate top and bottom.

A

B

C

D

E

F

This wire support drilling jig lets you drill a pair of accurately spaced holes for a wire support. To use the jig, hold the fence firmly against the front edge of the stock and drill through the correct holes in the acrylic.

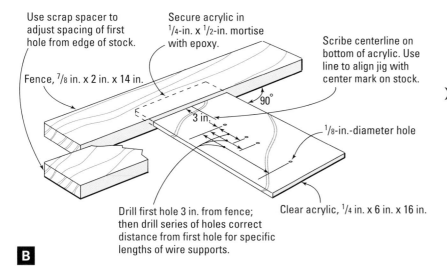

Use scrap spacer to adjust spacing of first hole from edge of stock.

Secure acrylic in 1/4-in. x 1/2-in. mortise with epoxy.

Scribe centerline on bottom of acrylic. Use line to align jig with center mark on stock.

Fence, 7/8 in. x 2 in. x 14 in.

90°

3 in.

1/8-in.-diameter hole

Drill first hole 3 in. from fence; then drill series of holes correct distance from first hole for specific lengths of wire supports.

Clear acrylic, 1/4 in. x 6 in. x 16 in.

Wire Supports

These imaginative little strips of wire—sometimes called invisible or "magic"wires—work great when you need to make removable dividers or partitions.

A pair of small bent wires engage slots cut into the ends of the shelf and small holes drilled into the case. To position the shelf, you simply slide it over the wires from the front of the case. There are two benefits to using wire supports: First, the holes you drill in the case are small (1/8 in. diameter), so they don't intrude glaringly into your design. Second, once the shelf is hung, you won't see any visible means of support.

> ▶ See *"Types of Adjustable Shelf Supports"* on p. 61.

Wire supports are available in roughly 6-in. and 9-in. lengths. If you need longer wires, for wider shelves, you can double up the wires to gain the necessary support. For narrow shelves, use shorter wires that you make yourself. Clamp a piece of stiff 1/8-in.-diameter wire—or an existing longer wire support—into a bending jig in a metal-working vise to form the bends (**A**).

Use a drilling jig to drill the 1/8-in. holes accurately in the case side for the wires (**B**). Tape placed on the drill bit lets you know when you've reached the correct depth (**C**).

Cut a groove in the ends of each shelf, stopping it about 1/2 in. from the front edge so you don't see the groove when the shelf is installed. Use an 1/8-in. slotting cutter on the router table and adjust the fence for the correct depth of cut. Pencil marks on the fence indicate where to start and stop the cut (**D**). The finished shelf slides into the case and over the wires (**E**).

Torsion-Box Shelf

For maximum stiffness, you can make a torsion box by sandwiching a panel of honeycomb material or a grid of wooden ribs between two thin plywood skins—similar to the construction of an airplane wing. The result is a shelf that's relatively lightweight but very rigid. Torsion boxes are also good for all sorts of furniture elements, including large conference tables and casework and anywhere you need a large surface that won't bend or deflect under weight.

Start by making the grid from ¼-in.- to ¾-in.-thick solid-wood ribs. Pine, poplar, or any lightweight wood works best. The wider the ribs, the stiffer the shelf. Make the spaces between the ribs about 4 in., depending on the thickness of the skin material that you're using—the bigger the spacing, the more chance that the skins will deflect. Use a staple gun to pin the parts together, making sure to staple both sides (**A**). You won't need glue here; the staples simply hold the grid together before you add the skins.

To make glue-up easy, spread a coat of glue on both sides of the grid with a roller (**B**).

Cut the skins from ¼-in. or ½-in. plywood or MDF, making them about ½ in. larger than the assembled gridwork. Glue the skins to both sides of the grid, using bowed cauls to distribute clamp pressure evenly (**C**).

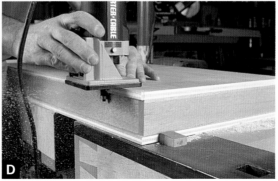

➤ See *"Bowed Clamping Cauls"* on p. 20.

Once the glue has dried, rout the skins flush to the core with a laminate bit (**D**). To dress up the shelf, you can veneer its surfaces or cover it with laminate or leather. Adding solid-wood lippings is an effective way to conceal the raw edges.

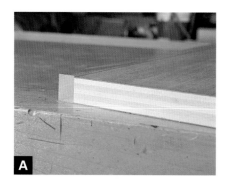

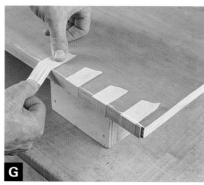

Wood Lippings

Covering up the edges of plywood shelves and other sheet goods with a band of solid wood or veneer is the best way to clean up the voids and variations that man-made boards exhibit. Lippings can be thick or thin, depending on the design of furniture, and there are a variety of methods for applying them. Once you've applied a solid-wood edge, you can then rout or saw into it to create a decorative effect—something you can't do with a raw plywood edge.

No matter what type of lipping you're adding to the edge of a shelf or case, it must be milled slightly thicker than the shelf material. This lets you accurately bring the lipping flush to the panel after it's applied. It's a good idea to mill the lipping stock about $\frac{1}{16}$ in. wider than the shelf is thick (**A**).

For a simple edge joint, apply glue with a roller to both the shelf and the lipping (**B**). Slip shims of veneer underneath the shelf to center the thicker lipping on the edge of the shelf (**C**).

Pipe clamps are very effective for pulling the lipping tight. A wide caul between the clamps and the lipping spreads the clamp pressure, allowing you to use fewer clamps (**D**).

For even more effective clamping pressure, glue two shelves at once, orienting the lippings so they face each other (**E**). The Jorgenson edge clamps shown in photo **F** allow for a quick and effective method for applying pressure, but you'll need plenty of clamps to close the joint.

On thin bandings—$\frac{1}{8}$ in. or less—you can get sufficient clamping power by using masking tape to pull the joint closed. Press the tape firmly to one side of the panel; then stretch it over the edge and onto the opposite side (**G**).

Flush-Trimmed Lippings

There are several methods for cleaning up a proud lipping once the glue has dried. If the lipping is thin, use a ball-bearing laminate bit to rout the lipping flush. A block clamped to the benchtop steadies the router (**A**).

My favorite method for flushing up a lip is to plane it by hand. It's very quick, quiet, and relatively dustless. The danger here is that if you plane too far, you'll plane through the thin veneer. Here's a foolproof method: Set the plane iron for a medium cut and plane close to—but not quite to—the surface of the veneer. Use your fingers to feel how far you have to go and skew the plane to help reduce tearout (**B**). Now adjust the iron for a very light cut and finish-plane the edging. You can see the difference in the plane adjustment by the gossamer-thin shavings (**C**). If you do cut into the veneer, you'll take only a very light shaving but not tear it.

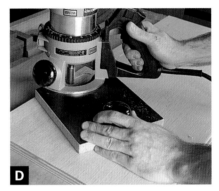

For really wide lippings and for gnarly, difficult-to-plane woods, you can rout the lipping by using a piece of melamine-coated particleboard screwed to a router. The board rides on the veneered surface while the cutter routs the lip flush. A four-flute end-mill bit leaves the cleanest cut for this operation, but any straight bottom-cutting bit will work (**D**).

Once you've trimmed the surface of the panel, you'll need to flush up the ends. If you plan ahead and cut your panel oversize in length and make the lipping slightly shorter than the panel, you can simply flush up the lipping at the ends of the panel with a couple of crosscuts on the table saw (**E**).

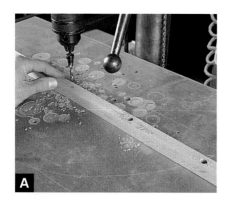

Plugged Screws

Screws are a great way to attach lippings, especially when you're on the job or can't easily get to the work with clamps. To conceal the screw holes, fill them with wooden plugs. And if you're careful with the way you make and install the plugs, the joint will virtually disappear.

Countersink and counterbore the screw hole in the lipping in one step with a counterbore/countersink bit on the drill press. In this example, I've spaced the screw holes about 5 in. apart; for wider lippings you can use fewer screws (**A**).

Drill pilot holes into the panel by drilling through the edging as you hold it in position. Then apply glue to the panel and lipping, and screw the lipping to the panel (**B**).

Spread glue on the plugs and tap them into the counterbored holes. Mark the plugs to help orient them with the grain direction of the lipping (**C**).

Remove most of the excess plug by tapping across it with a chisel and a mallet. Then carefully pare the plug flush to the lipping by hand (**D**). Finish up by planing the entire edging with a finely set handplane (**E**).

Biscuits

Biscuits aren't really necessary to strengthen most lippings, but for foolproof alignment, they can't be beat. Place a biscuit every 8 in. or so, and lippings will accurately line up with a shelf or case piece, taking the hassle out of shimming or carefully adjusting the lipping to the shelf as you clamp it. If you offset the biscuit slot in the lipping, you can offset the lipping to the shelf so that it stands slightly proud. This lets you flush up and smooth the lipping after gluing it to the panel.

No measuring is needed when cutting slots for biscuits. Just hold the lipping in position against the edge of the panel and draw a center mark across both pieces (**A**).

Cutting the slots in the panel is simple: Adjust the fence so the slot is centered on the edge of the panel and plunge into the edge at your center mark. Be sure to clamp small work (**B**).

Cutting narrow or short lengths of wood can be trickier and is often downright dangerous, because it's difficult to clamp the work effectively to keep your hands clear of the cutter. To make things safe, use the hold-down jig shown here for slotting small pieces (**C**). The jig is simple to make and adjusts to different sizes of small stock (**D**).

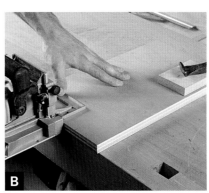

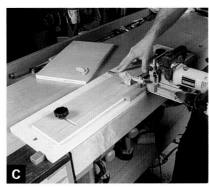

This hold-down jig lets you safely cut biscuit slots in short or narrow stock without having your hands near the cutting action.

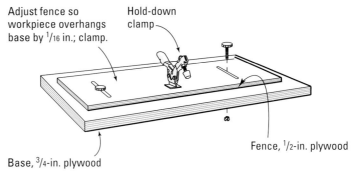

Adjust fence so workpiece overhangs base by $1/16$ in.; clamp.

Hold-down clamp

Fence, $1/2$-in. plywood

Base, $3/4$-in. plywood

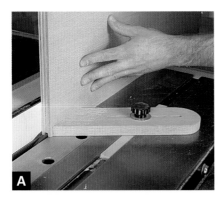

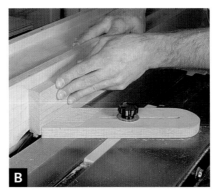

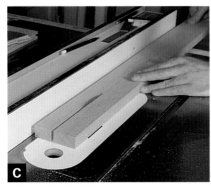

Tongue and Groove

Like biscuits, a tongue-and-groove lipping can facilitate a glue-up so that pieces go together exactly where you want them. And the additional glue surface of the tongue-and-groove joint means considerably more strength in the joint. This is an important consideration for times when you might need the extra strength, such as in wide lippings.

Plow a groove in the panel on the table saw using a dado blade. Make the width of the groove one-third the thickness of the panel. Use a featherboard to keep the stock tight to the fence (**A**).

[**TIP**] **Keep your hands clear of the blade when forming edge details by using oversize stock. Once the groove or detail is formed, rip the narrow section off the wider board.**

Install an auxiliary fence and use the same blade-height setting used to mill the tongue on the lipping. By cutting a rabbet on both sides of the stock, you automatically center the tongue (**B**).

Once you've milled the tongue, rip the stock to final width (**C**).

The glued lipping needs only flushing up on both faces and it's ready for service (**D**).

Commercial Edgebanding

Veneering the edge of a shelf is another option. Because the veneered edge is somewhat delicate and can't be shaped decoratively, this type of banding is usually reserved for more homely types of work, such as the interior shelves of a kitchen cabinet. The easiest method for veneering an edge is to use commercial edgebanding, which has a layer of hot-melt glue on one side. It comes in rolls in almost every species, and it's sized about $\frac{1}{16}$ in. wider than standard $\frac{3}{4}$-in. plywood. You can also buy plastic bandings in a variety of colors to match melamine and laminate surfaces.

You can use a commercial iron to apply the veneer, but a household iron will work just as well if you set the heat to medium. Keep the iron moving as you heat the glue and the veneer to prevent scorching. Use your other hand to guide the tape so it overhangs both sides of the panel evenly as you press it with the iron (**A**).

Immediately after heating the glue, rub the banding firmly with a hard block. Be sure to rub along the edges and ends to ensure a tight joint (**B**).

A wide chisel works best for trimming the ends of the banding, especially in coarse woods such as the oak shown here. Register the back of the chisel on the edge of the panel and move the chisel in a downward slicing action to get the cleanest cut (**C**).

You have a couple options for trimming the long-grain edges. An edge-cutting file is a safe bet for veneers that are prone to tearing. Hold the file vertically, tipping it a few degrees away from the face of the panel, and make the cut on the down stroke (**D**).

To cut both edges at once, use a commercial trimmer with knives on both sides. Be careful though; this tool can tear difficult woods if you cut against the grain (**E**).

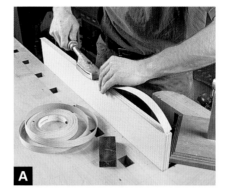

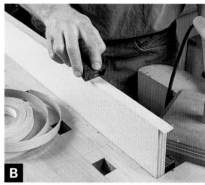

PVA Glue and Veneer

You can make your own veneer edgebanding and apply it without fancy glues or clamps. This technique relies on the thermoplastic qualities of white or yellow polyvinyl acetate (PVA) glues.

[**TIP**] **Use this method for attaching only small pieces of veneer, it's not reliable when you get into bigger jobs with wider veneered surfaces.**

Thin some white or yellow glue about 10 percent with water and brush an even coat on both the panel and the veneer. Don't use a roller here; it will leave small bubbles. Be sure to cover all the edges and corners, since these areas are naturally prone to lifting. To prevent the veneer from curling, wet the opposite side with a damp sponge before you apply the glue (**A**).

Sand the fully dried glue lightly with 80-grit paper to remove any nibs or dust (**B**). Then recoat both panel and veneer with the glue mixture.

Once the second coat has fully dried (the glue will appear clear and shiny), use an iron to reactivate the glue by heating it as you press the veneer firmly to the substrate (**C**). Trim the edges and you're done.

Nails, Screws, and Other Fasteners

Nails and Screws

➤ Nailing Joints (p. 84)
➤ Pneumatic Fasteners (p. 85)

Hardware Solutions

➤ Knockdown Hardware (p. 86)
➤ Bed-Rail Fasteners (p. 87)

FASTENERS ARE ESSENTIAL GEAR for the cabinetmaker. Screwing parts together saves time and is often the best method for clamping difficult-to-reach joints until the glue sets. Even the old-fashioned nail has its place in the shop, especially finish nails and brads for tacking together small projects and parts. And with the bevy of modern pneumatic nail guns and low-cost air compressors on the market, it's easy and economical for the small shop to power drive fasteners using compressed air.

For large cases that need to be assembled on site or for big woodwork such as beds, use knockdown (KD) hardware. This hardware comes in an endless variety and is used heavily by the furniture industry. If you've ever been faced with a piece too big to get out of your shop, knockdown hardware is the solution.

Power Drive Your Screws

Today's powerful battery drill drivers are perfect for driving screws. Although you can use the corded variety with the same results, a cordless drill/driver let's you get to the action quicker and without the headaches of tangled cords under foot. I equip my drill with a magnetic bit holder, which helps start the screw and allows a longer reach. This power-driving technique works best with Phillips-head or square-drive screws, but with practice you can drive traditional slot-head screws as well.

► CROSS DOWELS IN END GRAIN

Driving screws into end grain is risky at best. The threads mash the fibers; and instead of a strong connection, the fit is loose and is likely to fail if stress is placed on the joint. When you're faced with screwing into end grain, a nice trick is to introduce some long grain into the area that the screw will penetrate. The easiest way to do this is to drive a dowel across the joint.

DOWELS STRENGTHEN SCREW JOINTS

Glue dowels into the end-grain member to allow screws to get a grip.

Dowel

Screws pierce long-grain dowel for better holding power.

Proper driving technique is essential to avoid a common pitfall: bit spinning, in which you quickly strip the head of the screw. Two things to remember are keep the driver in line with the screw and maintain constant and very firm pressure (as much as you can apply) against the head of the screw as you drive it.

SCREW ANATOMY

To be successful in driving your screws, gauge the root diameter then drill a pilot hole to that size (or slightly under in softwoods). Next, determine the shank diameter and drill a shank hole to that size so the screw slips freely through the upper workpiece.

Screw heads come in different driving styles, so you need to match the driver tip to the screw. Slotted screws are prone to slipping, and the driver often jerks out of the slot. Phillips-head screws strip less, as long as you maintain pressure and stay in line with the head. Square-drive screws are king when it comes to not slipping, but they cost more than conventional heads. Combination drives work well with square drivers; in a pinch you can drive them with a Phillips-head screwdriver.

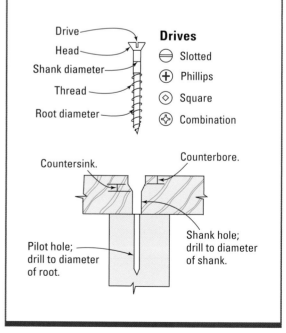

Drive

Head

Shank diameter

Thread

Root diameter

Drives

⊖ Slotted

⊕ Phillips

⊙ Square

✪ Combination

Countersink.

Counterbore.

Pilot hole; drill to diameter of root.

Shank hole; drill to diameter of shank.

Types of Screws

The vast array of screw types on the market can be bewildering to a woodworker. The good news is that there's a screw for practically every application and type of material. But for typical furniture work, you can pare down the options by selecting a few types that will work for most jobs. Once you've selected your screws, pick up a few drilling accessories for the drill as shown in the photo below right.

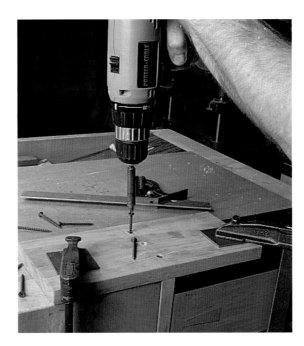

To prevent damage to the screw head, align the bit and the drill with the screw's shank and use firm pressure.

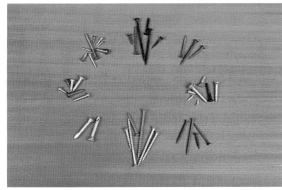

Screws for the woodshop (clockwise from top): production or particleboard screws, which grip well in plywood and particleboard; drywall screws; tapered wood screws, which come in the greatest variety of sizes and materials; trim-head screws with tiny, self-sinking heads; deck screws, which are coated with long-lasting epoxy; deep-thread or Confirmat screws, with exceptionally deep threads, making them the best choice for driving into materials without grain such as MDF or particleboard; pan-head sheet-metal screws for attaching hardware; solid-brass screws for the final touch on quality brass hardware.

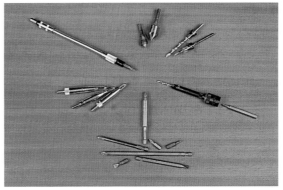

Equip your drill with some essential gear for sinking and driving screws (clockwise from top): countersinks to bevel the screw hole so the head of the screw seats firmly; countersink/counterbore drill bits to perform three operations at once (drill pilot hole, countersink for screw head, and counterbore for shank); quick-change drill/drivers to save time when changing drill bits and driver bits; magnetic bit holder and a selection of driver bits that slip into the holder; self-centering drill bits for hinges; flexible driver for tight spaces.

Nailing Joints

Sometimes a well-placed nail is all you need to firmly fasten a part in a cabinet or piece of furniture. Stay away from common nails, though. They're wonderful for carpentry, but too big for woodworkers. Box nails, however, are great for small work such as attaching a cabinet back. The shank is stiff and won't bend, yet the head is relatively small and won't jump out at you. Cut nails come in handy for period-furniture reproductions. Brads and finish nails are probably the most common nails used in furniture. Great for thin moldings and trim, a brad can be set below the surface in a hole so small you can barely see it. Finish nails can be puttied over to blend with your woodwork.

In contrast to pneumatic nailing, you generally need to pre-bore a pilot hole in solid wood for the nail you'll be hand driving, or the material is likely to split (**A**).

[**TIP**] **If you can't find the right size drill bit for a finish nail, you can snip off the head and use the snipped end to drill the pilot hole for the same size nail.**

Use a nail set of the appropriate diameter to drive the nail below the surface (**B**). This not only allows you to hide the head of the nail but helps seat the joint.

Finish up by puttying over the nail hole or by using a colored filler to match the finish (**C**).

Pneumatic Fasteners

Nothing beats the ease and convenience of pneumatic, or air-driven, fasteners. The powerful driving force of an air-driven nail lets you shoot together assemblies with speed and accuracy, since the parts don't have time to slip out of alignment. And you can leave your nail set behind: Nails or brads are set below the surface of the wood in the same stroke.

Although industry uses many types of pneumatics, the fundamental guns for a small shop are a brad gun or pin nailer, a small staple gun, a big staple gun, and a large finish nailer (**A**). You'll need an air compressor, but air demand is relatively small for these types of pneumatic drivers. A ¾-hp compressor with a tank will provide the 100 pounds per square inch (psi) necessary to drive a brad gun or finish nailer.

Brad guns and pin nailers accept 18- or 15-gauge brads in lengths from ½ in. to 2 in., and they're useful for attaching moldings and other small work. Brads generally won't split the wood. Preboring for the fastener is totally unnecessary; just point and shoot (**B**). The tiny holes the brads leave in the surface can be easily filled.

Finish nailers, which use thicker and stiffer nails, are great for finish-nailing case parts on a show surface. For unseen joints in relatively thick casework, such as all the ¾-in. interior dividers in a set of kitchen cabinets, use staples—and a large staple gun—which have more holding power than finish nails (**C**). For thin ¼-in. cabinet backs, use a smaller staple gun equipped with ⅝-in. or ¾-in. staples, which won't blow through the plywood.

> ⚠ **WARNING Air nailers can't tell the difference between wood and your fingers. Always make sure your hands are well clear before pulling the trigger.**

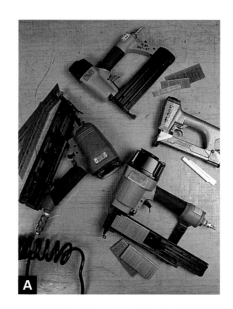

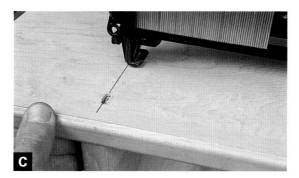

Bolt connectors can join vertical assemblies, such as two case sides, or can connect two panels face to face. Another variety allows you to make T connections, such as when a shelf joins a side. If you drill a stopped, or blind, hole for the nut in the underside of the shelf, you can conceal the cut from view.

Joining Face to Face

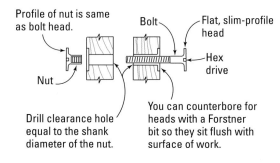

Profile of nut is same as bolt head.

Nut

Bolt

Flat, slim-profile head

Hex drive

Drill clearance hole equal to the shank diameter of the nut.

You can counterbore for heads with a Forstner bit so they sit flush with surface of work.

Joining a T

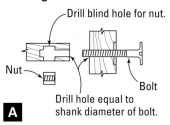

Drill blind hole for nut.

Nut

Bolt

Drill hole equal to shank diameter of bolt.

A

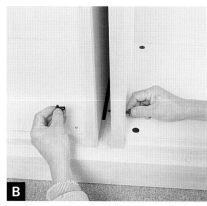

B

C

Knockdown Hardware

Sometimes the most appropriate fasteners are those that knock down or come apart, allowing you to transport furniture in pieces and assemble it outside of the woodshop. Knockdown (KD) hardware is especially useful for large or heavy pieces, such as beds and cabinets. (For more details on knockdown joinery, see *The Complete Illustrated Guide to Joinery,* by Gary Rogowski, The Taunton Press.)

My favorite type of KD hardware is the bolt connector (**A**). These connectors are easy to come by, easy to use, and very easy to *re-use,* an important consideration if the piece you're making is going to go through many cycles of being taken apart and put back together again.

Bolt connectors have two parts: A nut captured in a hole secures the bolt, which typically has a very thin profile that won't intrude aesthetically in the finished surface. Drill a hole through both pieces to be joined, checking that the hole is large enough for the diameter of the nut, which is usually the larger of the two parts (**B**).

Pull the parts together by tightening the nut onto the bolt. Most connectors accept a hex wrench, which allows you to get a good grip without heavy, protruding hardware (**C**).

Bed-Rail Fasteners

Gluing together any but the smallest bed frame in the shop is a big mistake; although you might get it out of the shop, the new owners will surely struggle to get it in the house. Knockdown bed-rail fasteners solve this potentially disastrous dilemma. There are two kinds of gear you can use—the bed bolt and the bed-rail fastener—and both work well.

The bed-rail fastener consists of two parts for each joint: a post plate with slots and a mating rail plate with fingers that fit into the slots. This fastener is a little fussier to install but allows for tool-less bed setup and knockdown. Rout and chisel a shallow mortise in the post for the post plate so it's flush with the surface (**A**). Before installing the plate, mark and drill clearance slots with a Forstner bit for the fingers of the mating rail plate (**B**).

Rout a mortise in the end of the rail for the rail plate and install it flush. The metal fingers of the rail plate wedge into the slots in the post plate (**C**). Installed correctly, the wedging effect increases as you place weight on the bed, helping stiffen the connection.

The bed bolt fastener is great because is easy to install without much fuss, and it's very strong (**D**).

A stub tenon on the rail supports the frame, but the bolt pulls the joint tight. Drill a hole through the post for the bed bolt; then drill a flat-bottomed hole on the inside surface of the bed rail with a Forstner bit. Now drill the same diameter hole through the stub tenon in the rail, ending in the flat-bottomed hole. Use a special wrench to turn the bolt and install a nut on the bolt so it bears against the wall of the flat-bottomed hole, tightening the joint.

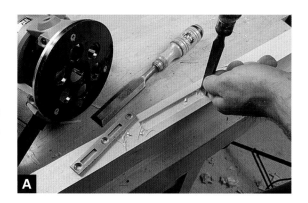

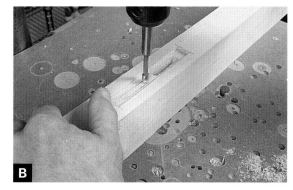

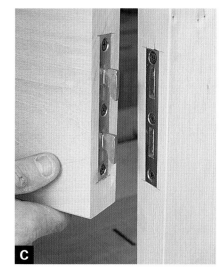

Assembling Cases

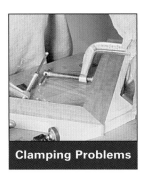

Clamping Problems

Whundredhen you're ready to assemble your furniture, you usually have only one shot to get it right. Once the glue is spread, there's no turning back. Glue up a cabinet out of square, and you'll pay dearly later in the construction process because your error will accumulate so that fitting subsequent parts becomes a nightmare. To get it right the first time, it's vital to have the right assembly tools on hand and to use the proper clamps and clamping technique. After all, who hasn't glued together what was a perfectly fitted miter, only to find the joint slipping out of alignment as you placed pressure on the joint? Learning and practicing the correct approach to assembly will save you untold hours of frustration.

The Dry Run

One of the best techniques I've come to learn about assembly (and learned it the hard way, meaning I had to make many mistakes first) is to always—and I mean *always*—do a dry run of any assembly. This means assembling all the parts without glue. Make sure you use all the necessary clamps you'll need and check to see that you can confidently close all the joints. In effect, you're practicing the entire assembly sequence.

And 9 times out of 10, you'll discover during a dry run that something is missing or you need more clamps in a specific area to bring an assembly together. Or perhaps you'll need to rethink the glue-up process and break the assembly sequence down into smaller, more manageable parts. It may take more time, but investing in a dry run is well worth avoiding the horror of applying glue, only to find that you can't quite put the parts together as planned.

Assembly Tools and Jigs

There are innumerable jigs and tricks used in assembly. All are aimed at making the process of putting together multiple parts easier, more accurate, and ultimately less frustrating. There's nothing worse than spreading glue only to find you don't have the right tools or setup ready to go. Here are some essential assembly aids that make glue-ups go a lot smoother.

Reading Square with a Pinch Rod

It's vital to square up a case or opening immediately after assembly—before the glue dries. One way to check for square is to read the diagonal measurements from outside corner to outside corner with a tape measure. When the two measurements are equal, the opening is square. But clamps often get in the way, it's practically impossible to get a reading on the back of the case, and reading the outside corners won't tell you whether the inside of a deep case is square. A more accurate method is to use a pinch rod.

A traditional pinch rod is simply two sticks, sharpened at one end, that you pinch, or hold together, in the center. The modified version shown at right adds clamping heads

that make things a little easier and more precise. Set the rod to the length of one of the diagonals; then check the opposite diagonal inside the case. Push the sticks into the case to read the entire depth. Keep adjusting the rod (and the case) until the rod fits equally between both diagonals.

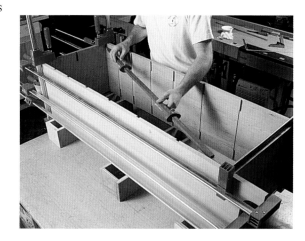

An adjustable pinch rod allows you to compare inside diagonals quickly and to any depth. If they match, the case must be square.

PINCH ROD

A pinch rod is the most accurate way to measure an opening for square. Any type of wood will suffice—even softwood—but make sure to use stock with straight grain.

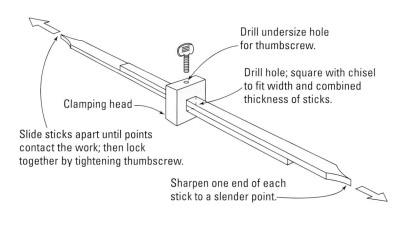

Drill undersize hole for thumbscrew.

Drill hole; square with chisel to fit width and combined thickness of sticks.

Clamping head

Slide sticks apart until points contact the work; then lock together by tightening thumbscrew.

Sharpen one end of each stick to a slender point.

A squared-up board cut to the width of the inside provides an easy way to square up a case.

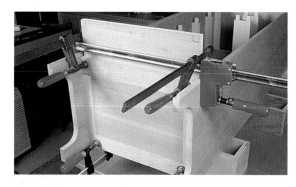

A box full of shim materials comes in handy during glue-up.

▶ DEAD-BLOW MALLET

Using a hammer to pound parts together is admittedly a part of woodworking. Your joints may be too tight, or the culprit may be the glue that has swelled parts at the critical moment of assembly. Either way, you should be ready with

Use a dead-blow mallet to help align parts during a glue-up.

some form of heavy-duty "persuader" to coax parts together when hand pressure or clamps alone fail. Better than a hammer is a dead-blow mallet. These weighted hammers pack a powerful punch without the jarring effect that metal produces. Backing up the surface with a block of hardwood can help distribute the force of the blow. The mallet shown here has different weights in each of the two heads, allowing gentle taps on one side and heavier, more powerful hits on the opposite.

Squaring a Case with a Board

As an aid to assembling a case square, cut a piece of plywood to the exact width of the case opening, making sure adjacent edges are square. Before you clamp the case joints, clamp the board inside the case, lining up one edge of the board with the case sides. Voila! No more twisted or out-of-square openings.

Shims and Blocks Align Parts

It's a good idea to keep on hand a variety of shims and blocks in varying thicknesses, from playing cards, squares of plastic laminate, and strips of leather to ¼-in.-, ½-in.-, and ¾-in.-thick blocks of wood. These spacers help align or position parts during glue-up, and they're great for protecting the surface of your work. Shown at middle left, small squares of MDF align the clamp heads over the center of the joint, while plastic shims prevent the pipes from dinging the surface.

Riser Blocks Raise the Work

Gluing up assemblies often means having to get underneath the work to attach clamps or other parts. The simplest answer is to raise the entire assembly on blocks of wood. But finding stock thick enough can be a pain. Just as strong, and easier to make, are sets of riser blocks made from ¾-in. plywood glued and nailed together. Blocks about 5 in. high by 2 ft. long are sufficient for almost all your glue-ups.

Clamping Cauls

Like blocks, cauls made from scrap material can prevent dings in your work. More important, cauls distribute more clamping pressure across a joint, allowing you to use far fewer clamps when gluing up. For broad gluing surfaces, use bowed clamping cauls.

➤ See *"Bowed Clamping Cauls"* on p. 20.

For narrow joints, scrap plywood or left-over sticks of wood work fine. The trick to getting the cauls to stay where you want them until you add the clamps is to tape them temporarily in place.

Dovetail Tapping Wedge

In many cases, you don't need to bother clamping dovetail joints, especially on small box constructions, such as a drawer. To assemble and fully seat the joints without damaging the pins, tap over the joint with a wedged-shaped block of dense wood. The shape of the block allows you to position it over the joint regardless of the size of the tail.

Simple plywood risers elevate the work for easy clamping.

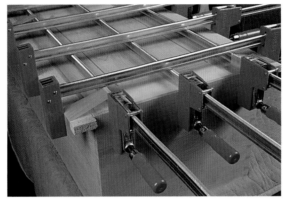

A piece of tape comes in handy as a third hand when positioning clamping cauls.

A wedge-shaped block helps seat dovetails in their sockets.

Assembling a Case

For most cabinets, there's a basic assembly sequence that will guarantee success—or at least a more comfortable heart rate. The trick is always to begin assembly from the insides out. In most instances, this means assembling any interior dividers or partitions to the top and bottom of the case. If the case is wide, clamp one side of the work while it sits face down on the bench (**A**). Then flip the assembly over and clamp the opposite side (**B**).

Tackle the outside of the case, often the sides or ends of a cabinet, after you've clamped all the interior assemblies. Depending on the type of clamps you use and the design of the cabinet, you might have to wait for the glue to dry on the interior parts before clamping the outside of the case. When possible, use long-reach clamps, because they can reach over existing clamps and let you clamp the entire case in one assembly session (**C**).

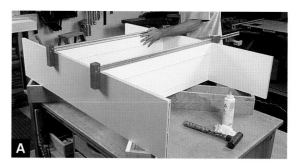

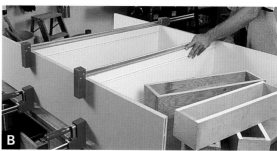

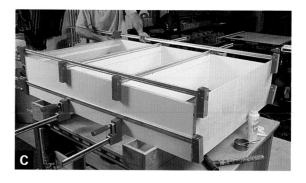

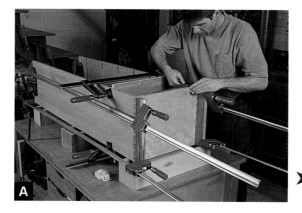

Clamping Corners

Corner joints constitute most of the casework in furniture—including small boxes and drawers—and it's necessary to find an effective way to clamp across what is typically a wide surface. Like edge work, the answer is to use cauls to help distribute clamping pressure.

▶ See *"Assembly Tools and Jigs"* on p. 89.

When joints protrude at the corners, such as in through dovetails or box joints, use notched cauls to bring the corner together (**A**). Make the notch cuts on the bandsaw or table saw. The blocks gain purchase and don't interfere with closing the joint, and they center over the joint to avoid bowing the sides.

Miter joints have a way of not closing at the most inappropriate times. To get good purchase on what is often a very slippery joint, there are several clamping strategies. The tried-and-true method is to clamp all four corners of a mitered frame at once with bar clamps. The deep throats of Bessey K-body clamps make it easy to get over and under the joint (**B**). Tighten each clamp a little at a time, like tightening the lug nuts on a car wheel. Make sure to check the frame for square before letting the glue dry.

The block-and-rod frame system shown here (from Lee Valley Tools) gives you very precise control when closing four miters at a time, and it doesn't require lots of clamping force (**C**). Like the bar clamp approach, tighten each corner a little at a time to align the miters.

One of the simplest ways to close the joint is to clamp shopmade blocks to the frame before assembly. Cut out the blocks on the bandsaw so that the clamping surfaces are parallel to each other when the frame is assembled (**D**).

A picture framer's vise is handy for closing one miter at a time (**E**). This is useful when you're nailing or screwing the joint, since you can assemble the frame one piece at a time.

Web clamps allow you to glue up all four corners at once, and they work well on both flat frames and boxes (**F**). You can use heavy-duty web clamps for large cases, but plan on having several on hand to close the joints.

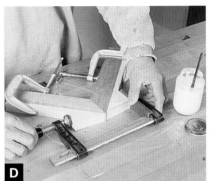

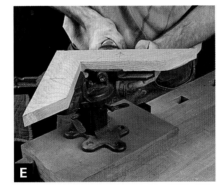

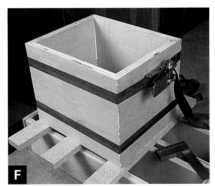

Clamping Difficult Parts

If your pipe clamps are too short, you can extend them with metal pipe joiners, available at plumbing-supply stores. Make sure at least one of your pipes is threaded on both ends so it can accept both the threaded joiner and the clamp head (**A**).

Another effective way to grip long work is to join two clamp heads together. Shims center the clamping pressure over the joints, and rubber pads slipped over the clamp heads prevent the work from being marred (**B**).

Get a grip on difficult pieces, such as a panel, by securing it with a wooden handscrew (**C**). A bar clamp holds the handscrew to the bench, leaving your hands free for more important tasks.

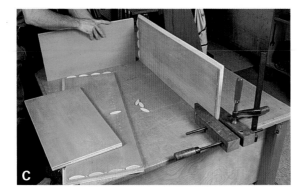

Cutting and Attaching Moldings

Working with Moldings

- ➤ Cutting Big Miters (p. 98)
- ➤ Shooting Miters (p. 98)
- ➤ Making Moldings "Grow" (p. 99)
- ➤ Sawing Delicate Miters (p. 99)
- ➤ Coping Large Moldings (p. 100)

MOLDINGS ACCENTUATE FURNITURE and often help tie two or more discordant surfaces together, such as when you join an upper case to a lower case in a two-part cabinet. By attaching waist molding between the two pieces, the case visually becomes one. Moldings also serve to anchor a piece visually (base moldings) and to finish off the top of a case (crown moldings).

Almost all your moldings will require some sort of miter cut to allow the molding to wrap around a corner or face. Although you can cut miters with a miter box and handsaw or on the table saw, I find it best to invest in a dedicated mitering tool such as a chopsaw or power miter saw. These saws can miter big or little stock and do so with great precision. However, for really small moldings or delicate profiles prone to splintering, you're better off sawing them by hand.

Gluing and nailing moldings to a piece of furniture is the easiest method of attaching them. If you set the nails below the surface and then putty over the holes, you can conceal the method of attachment. But with solid-wood surfaces, you have to take wood movement into account. There are several strategies you can employ. Also, sometimes it's inappropriate or even impossible to nail or effectively clamp a molding in place. In these cases, there are some clever techniques you can use to overcome the problem.

ATTACHING MOLDINGS TO SOLID WOOD

Glue molding to front of case.

Glue molding 3 in. at front; then nail at back with brads that flex to allow movement.

Case side

Screw rides in slot in case side, allowing movement.

Back part of molding slides along runner.

Rout dovetail slot in back of molding.

Screw dovetail runner to case side.

Glue holds the mitered molding at the front of the case. A single nail, set below the surface and puttied over, secures the back.

Attaching Moldings to Solid Wood

If you glue a length of molding cross-grain to the surface of a solid-wood panel, such as the side of a case, wood movement of the panel will eventually cause the molding to pop loose or, worse, split the case. Instead of gluing the molding along its full length, it's best to apply glue to only 3 in. of the molding at the front of the case side to keep it tight at the miter joint. At the back of the case, you have several options for attaching the molding. The easiest method is to use a small finish nail to secure the molding to the rear of the case side. If you set the nail head and putty over the hole, the connection becomes almost invisible. Other options include screwing through a slotted hole inside the case and routing a dovetailed slot in the back of the molding and joining the molding with a matching dovetailed key screwed to the case.

Clamping Difficult Moldings

There are times when it's impossible or inconvenient to nail or clamp moldings in place. One solution is to use masking tape as a temporary clamp to hold your molding in position until the glue sets. Stick the tape to one side; then firmly pull and stretch it over the molding and press it to the adjacent side.

When there's nothing for the masking tape to grab—such as on a flat panel—try some cyanoacrylate (CA) glue as a "clamp." First, spread a bead of regular white or yellow PVA glue on the back of the molding; then add drops of CA glue along the bead. Now press the molding into position. Presto! The water in the glue accelerates the cure of the CA glue, making it grab almost immediately. And the CA glue won't interfere with the bond of the PVA glue. Once the PVA glue has set, you have a permanent bond.

Immediately press the white glue and CA mixture to the work surface. In seconds, the molding is secure.

Wrap small moldings with masking tape until the glue sets.

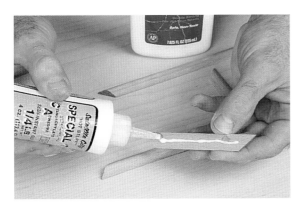

When applying moldings to flat work, spread a bead of white glue; then squeeze drops of CA along the glueline.

► SNEAKING UP ON A PERFECT FIT

When cutting miters on the miter saw, there are times you need to take off a shaving or two to get the miters to fit accurately. The difficulty comes in trying to judge just how much to take off. Here's a trick that doesn't require tedious measuring: Lower the blade so its teeth are below the table and push the sawn miter against the saw plate. Make sure no teeth contact the workpiece. Then lift the blade and, without moving the workpiece, make a cut. You'll take about $\frac{1}{64}$ in. off the miter, or the amount of tooth set on one side of the blade. It's a great technique for sneaking up on a perfect fit.

THE PERFECT FIT

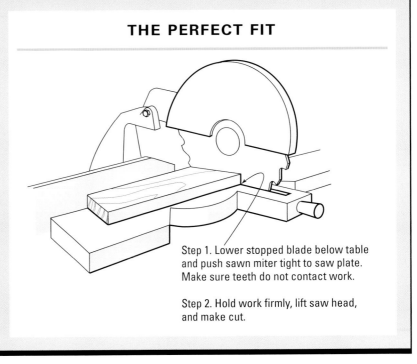

Step 1. Lower stopped blade below table and push sawn miter tight to saw plate. Make sure teeth do not contact work.

Step 2. Hold work firmly, lift saw head, and make cut.

A

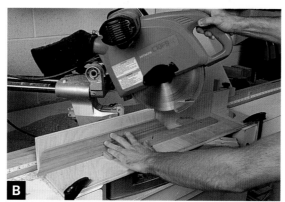

B

Cutting Big Miters

The power miter saw makes fast and accurate work of cutting moldings. But sometimes it's a challenge to cut miters in really large, wide stock, such as conventional crown molding. For these cuts, you have to place the molding upside down. To register and hold the molding securely, you can use an L-shaped jig clamped to the saw.

Make sure the two rear flats of the molding make full contact with the fence and base of the jig. Then add a strip of wood at the front of the jig to keep the molding from sliding forward as you make the cut. Use a scrap piece of molding to locate the strip. A pair of screws work great for holding the strip temporarily to the base, allowing you to reposition the strip for moldings of a different width (**A**).

Slide the molding into the jig, with its top edge facing down and against the strip. Then make the cut (**B**).

Shooting Miters

With large miters, it's important to have an exceptionally smooth cut to provide the best-possible gluing surface. If you use a sharp handplane, you'll produce a surface quality unmatched by any other tool. And a plane is a great tool for fine-tuning a miter that's a little off. To hold the stock and control the cut, use a jig to "shoot" the miter, as shown here (**A**). Position the molding in the jig slightly proud of the jig's mitered fence and clamp or hold the piece in place.

Any plane will work; but for more control and the best cut, use a large, low-angle plane to shave the molding. Keep the plane's sole firmly on the fence and shave the miter downhill, or with the grain (**B**). To avoid cutting into the jig, make sure to stop planing when the miter is flush with the fence.

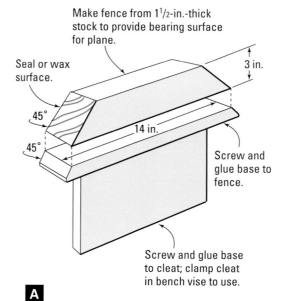

Make fence from 1½-in.-thick stock to provide bearing surface for plane.

Seal or wax surface.

45°

45°

14 in.

3 in.

Screw and glue base to fence.

Screw and glue base to cleat; clamp cleat in bench vise to use.

A

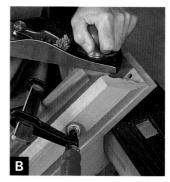

B

Making Moldings "Grow"

Who hasn't cut a molding too short, only to find that it's your last piece of stock? Don't despair. You can "grow" the molding, increasing its effective length, by taking a few shavings from its back side with a handplane (**A**). Remove material sparingly, tapering the cut, and check the fit until the miter meets its mate, as shown here (**B**). The tip of the opposite miter will protrude past the planed molding, but judicious carving or sanding at the joint will conceal the fact that the two miters don't line up precisely.

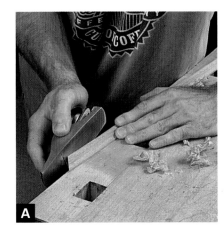

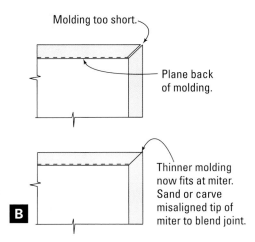

Molding too short.

Plane back of molding.

Thinner molding now fits at miter. Sand or carve misaligned tip of miter to blend joint.

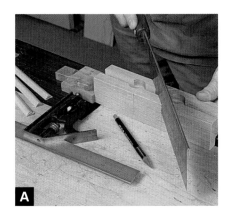

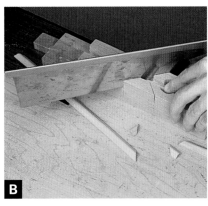

Sawing Delicate Miters

On small, delicate moldings that are likely to splinter when cut with a spinning sawblade, the safest approach is to use a handsaw to cut the miter. A shopmade jig helps you control the cut and guides the saw. To make the jig, first cut a deep groove along the center of a block of wood, equal to the width of the molding. Shallow holes drilled with a Forstner bit provide purchase for your fingers. Lay out the miter cuts on the block with a combination square; then saw down to the depth of the groove with a fine-toothed backsaw, following your layout lines (**A**).

Slip the molding into the block, lining up a mark on your molding with the miter cut, and use the same saw to cut through the stock (**B**).

Coping Large Moldings

When you're faced with joining large moldings at inside corners, such as when you're attaching crown molding around the walls of a room, the best approach is to run one piece full length, then cope the adjoining piece so that it fits precisely over the first piece. This way, if the moldings or the surfaces they're attached to should ever shift, you won't see a gap between the moldings. The coped cut is easier to make than you might think. Start by cutting an inside miter on the piece to be coped, using an L-shaped jig to support the stock (**A**).

► See *"Cutting Big Miters"* on p. 98.

For right-handers, it's easiest to cope the *left* piece (as it will be installed) to the right piece, so plan accordingly when laying out your cuts. Southpaws should start on the opposite side, coping the right piece.

At the bench, use a coping saw to saw straight across the square sections at the top, bottom, or middle of the molding. These sections must be butted, not coped. For the best fit, hold the saw at a slight angle to back-bevel the cut (**B**).

To saw the curves, follow the cut line of the miter cut. As before, angle the saw slightly to back-bevel the cut (**C**).

When the two pieces are held together (here shown upside down on the bench), the square sections butt together and the profiled area of the coped piece follows the curves of the opposite molding. Not a bad fit (**D**).

Drawers

Drawer Construction

Tray Construction

Drawer Interiors

D RAWERS ARE THE WORKHORSES of casework. They store, then offer up, a load of cargo that keeps you organized and makes your furniture a pleasure to use. As such, it's worth paying attention to the type of drawer you're making as to well as to its overall construction.

The technique of making a well-fitted drawer is very much like the carpenter's art of building a staircase. Both reflect the builder's skill and commitment. While a set of stairs must hold itself up in space and transport you from floor to floor, a drawer is more intimate. It often holds our personal belongings, and we sometimes stash our secrets inside to keep them from prying eyes. This intimacy suggests that our drawers should be well made and work flawlessly, with no binding or sticking. Often this means careful measurement and layout to get that elusive "perfect" fit. As a matter of habit, you should always keep planes and scrapers razor sharp; then use them to fine-tune the fit of a drawer.

Beyond the basic drawer are all sorts of specialty devices, from divided drawers and keyboard trays to leather-lined beauties and elusive "secret," or hidden, drawers.

Designing Drawers

Drawers can be one of the most beautiful parts of furniture to look at, with perfectly executed, hand-cut dovetails on the sides and custom-made handles that show craftsmanship. And when you operate them, they slide out wonderfully as if on a cushion of air. But some of the drawers I've seen made by woodworkers can be downright awful. Such drawers aren't appalling because of lack of skills but because of inattention to the drawers' proportions. Some general guidelines (see "Good Proportions" opposite) can help you build beautiful, functional drawers that look great.

Note the thickness of the sides of the drawer shown in the photo (opposite) in relation to the drawer front: It's no accident that the overall effect looks good. Keeping the sides about one-third (or less) the thick-

► HIDE UNSIGHTLY WIRES

With the appeal of today's electronic gear, you often end up with a mass of wires trailing under and over your beautiful woodwork. To organize and hide wires and plugs, you can install inexpensive grommets in the sides, tops, bottoms, backs, or shelves of your cases. Then run your wires through the grommets. Grommets come in a variety of colors to complement your woodwork.

To install a grommet, use the drill press to drill a 1⅞-in. hole through the workpiece. Clamp the work to the table and use a Forstner or a multispur bit to make the hole.

Tap the plastic ring of the grommet into the hole, then run your plugs and wires through the ring. A cap seals off most of the hole, allowing the wires to pass through. If you ever need to remove the wires completely, you can seal the hole with a small filler cap.

Use a Forstner bit to drill a hole equal to the ring diameter of the grommet.

Tap the barbed grommet into the hole. A plastic cap reduces the opening for smaller runs of wire.

ness of the front is the key. Also note that the dovetail pins on the sides are much smaller than the tails. This isn't necessary for the structure of the joint, but small pins always look more refined and elegant.

Material selection is also paramount in drawer making. Straight-grain wood is always the best to use, and when it won't ruin your budget, use quartersawn stock for its stability. Plywood is a wonderful material for drawers, but use it only for drawers that won't need subsequent fitting after assembly,

BASIC DRAWER ANATOMY

All drawers share a common theme: They must be joined at four corners and a bottom put in place to hold its contents. The type of joints you select is critical for a drawer to survive repeated cycles of opening and closing, and there are many options.

Bottom extends under back and is secured to back with screws or nails.

Back joins sides at corners and rests on top of bottom.

Front corner joint must withstand stress of repeated pulling forces.

Bottom, typically ¹⁄₄ in. to ¹⁄₂ in.

¹⁄₈ in. to ¹⁄₂ in.

Grooves in both sides holds bottom.

Groove in front holds bottom.

Drawer front

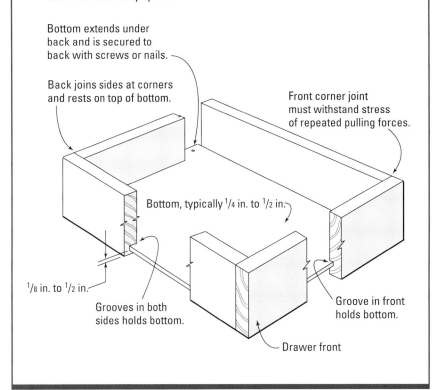

GOOD PROPORTIONS

Paying attention to the overall size of a drawer can pay off. Make a drawer too wide, and it will tend to rack in its opening, sticking when you try to pull it out or push it in. Too narrow, and you can't successfully store items. Make the sides thinner than the front; many woodworkers build sides too thick.

Sides thicker then ⁵⁄₈ in. are unnecessary. Small drawers can have sides as thin as ¹⁄₈ in.

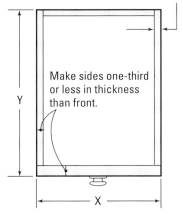

Make sides one-third or less in thickness than front.

Y

X

Aim for a width (X) that's less than the depth (Y) to avoid racking.

10-in. maximum drawer height

Keep drawer sides about one-third the thickness of the front for appealing proportions.

CORNER JOINTS

Butt

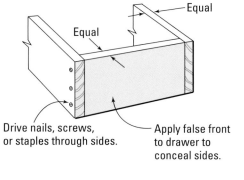

Equal

Equal

Drive nails, screws, or staples through sides.

Apply false front to drawer to conceal sides.

Rabbet

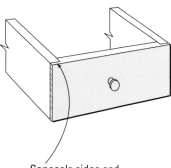

Conceals sides and provides more surface area for glue.

Rabbeted Tongue and Groove

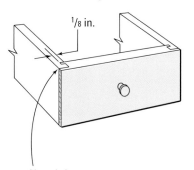

1/8 in.

No reinforcement necessary; lots of glue surface.

Through Dovetail

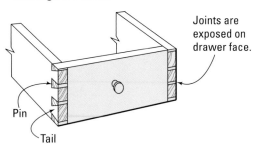

Joints are exposed on drawer face.

Pin

Tail

Sliding Dovetail

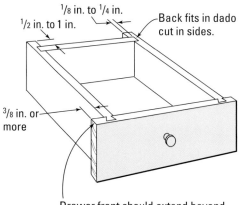

1/8 in. to 1/4 in.

1/2 in. to 1 in.

Back fits in dado cut in sides.

3/8 in. or more

Drawer front should extend beyond sides to maintain integrity of joint.

Half-Blind Dovetail

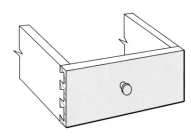

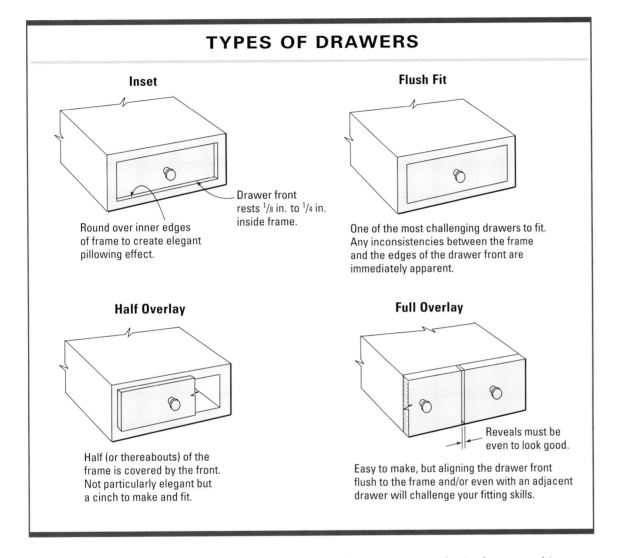

TYPES OF DRAWERS

Inset

Round over inner edges of frame to create elegant pillowing effect.

Drawer front rests $1/8$ in. to $1/4$ in. inside frame.

Flush Fit

One of the most challenging drawers to fit. Any inconsistencies between the frame and the edges of the drawer front are immediately apparent.

Half Overlay

Half (or thereabouts) of the frame is covered by the front. Not particularly elegant but a cinch to make and fit.

Full Overlay

Reveals must be even to look good.

Easy to make, but aligning the drawer front flush to the frame and/or even with an adjacent drawer will challenge your fitting skills.

such as a drawer hung with commercial drawer slides. Multi-ply plywood, such as Baltic birch, is preferable, since it's flat and solid throughout, so the edges of your drawers won't have voids in them.

Choose your joinery carefully when making a drawer. A drawer is asked to withstand a lot of abuse over time as it is pulled out from a case, so the corner joints must be sound and well made. (For more on drawer joints, see *The Complete Illustrated Guide to Joinery,* by Gary Rogowski, The Taunton Press.)

Once you master basic drawer making, there are four essential types of drawers you can make, as shown above. Outfitting the inside of a drawer offers many possibilities. One especially interesting approach is a French-fitted drawer designed to hold prized possessions. A fitted drawer looks beautiful and adds immensely to the organization of its contents. In the drawer shown in the photo on p. 106, I've fitted a set of prized wrenches. If I forget to replace a wrench, I can see in a heartbeat that it's missing from the drawer.

FRENCH-FITTED DRAWER

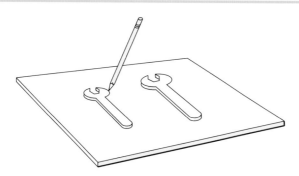

Step 1 Cut a ¹/₄-in. panel of sheet stock to fit inside the drawer. Position the items and trace around them.

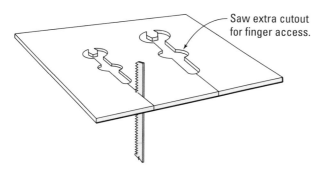

Saw extra cutout for finger access.

Step 2 Bandsaw to the outline, planning your cuts so you can enter and exit the panel in the same spot.

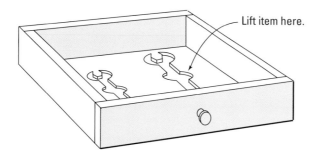

Lift item here.

Step 3 Glue the panel onto the drawer bottom. Cover with felt or flocking.

French fitting provides convenient and jiggle-free pockets for storage.

Making a French-fitted drawer is simplicity itself, as shown at left. After installing the panel that cradles the drawer's contents, you can line the drawer with traditional felt or use commercial spray flocking.

Hidden Drawers

Admit it: Woodworkers are a sneaky lot. We love to make things that nobody else can figure out, such as wooden puzzles or mechanical toys. It's a disease that's been around a long time, for if you study seventeenth- and eighteenth-century furniture, you'll find quite a number of cabinets that house "secrets." Most of these hidden drawers were designed to hold valuables from prying eyes and hands. Because it was long before the days of secure banks or consumer safes, these drawers were probably made more out of necessity than intrigue. But you can still wow your modern friends by creating a few of these fun, safe-keeping spots.

A wooden key hidden under the bottom drawer of Craig Bentzley's spice cabinet (above) allows you to drop down the back to reveal a hidden drawer (below).

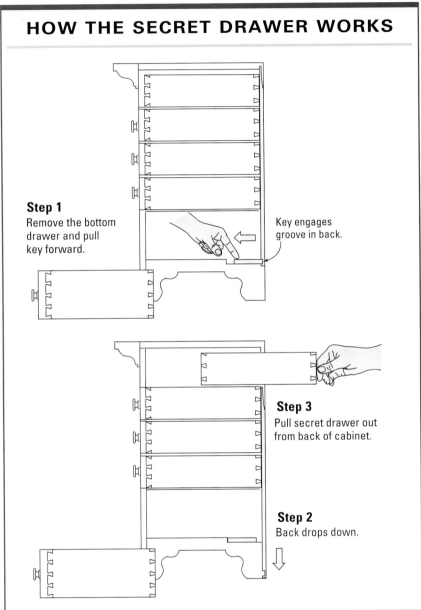

HOW THE SECRET DRAWER WORKS

Step 1
Remove the bottom drawer and pull key forward.

Key engages groove in back.

Step 3
Pull secret drawer out from back of cabinet.

Step 2
Back drops down.

Secret Drawer in the Back

The traditional spice cabinet by furniture maker Craig Bentzley of Pennsylvania offers a tantalizing puzzle at the rear of the cabinet (shown above). Start at the front by removing the lower drawer and reaching inside, where you pull forward a wooden key dovetailed into the case bottom. The back of the case drops down, revealing a small drawer at the top. Pretty underhanded, eh?

Hidden Boxes in an Apron

Push back both drawers in Joseph Seremeth's "My Brother's Table" (a sleek cherry coffee table shown on p. 108), to reveal what looks like a fixed center

The magic starts when you pull out a center drawer that looks like a fixed divider.

Put the drawer back in to start the next trick.

Push in a catch to engage a mechanism that attaches another drawer.

A second box now comes out with the drawer.

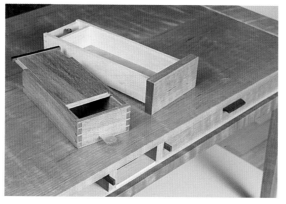

A sliding lid reveals the contents of the second secret drawer.

apron. Pull out the apron and you have a small drawer in your hands.

But wait, there's more. Put the little hidden drawer back into the table and reach inside one of the drawer openings to access a catch. With the catch engaged, pull out the hidden drawer; this time you also pull out a small box behind the drawer!

Dividers

Assorted sizes of drawers make for organized storage, but partitioning the interior of a drawer with dividers goes a step further.

DIVIDER OPTIONS

Vary height
of dividers.

Dividers press-fit together
with half-lap joints.

Glue slips to drawer
or to divider.

Grooved slips of wood hold dividers
and allow for changes in layout.

Cut ⅛-in.-deep
grooves in sides.

Cut shallow grooves in drawer sides before
assembly; dividers slide into them.

Insert narrow
divider in grooves
to retain block.

Coved block sits in drawer for holding
pens and pencils.

Dividers let you sort all your paraphernalia in a logical manner. The best examples are kitchen and office drawers, in which utensils and office supplies would quickly get lost or forgotten if left to fend for themselves in a big, undivided drawer.

Installing partitions can stiffen the drawer's overall construction if you add the dividers in such a way that they become a part of the drawer's joinery. However, because a drawer generally does fine by itself strength wise, I like to keep it simple when adding dividers, so I avoid unnecessary joints. You can divide the dividers or use other means to keep the dividers from shifting around inside the drawer. There are several options for both tasks.

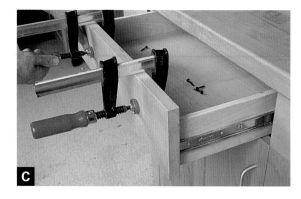

Full-Overlay Drawer

Found on Euro-style cabinets, a full-overlay drawer is one of the easiest drawers to make, but not necessarily the simplest to fit. The drawer front lays completely over the face frame of the cabinet, concealing the drawer opening.

Unlike other drawer types, the final fit of a full-overlay drawer often depends on its neighboring adjacent drawers. The idea is to have a ⅛-in. or less gap between all the drawers (and any overlay doors, too). The result is a seamless, contemporary look and feel. Achieving this small reveal between drawers is a challenge, but it's straightforward if you follow the right steps.

You can build the drawer as a complete unit, extending the front beyond the sides. I prefer a simpler method, that of building a drawer box and then attaching a false front to the box that overlays the face of the cabinet. Because the front overlays the box, you can use sturdy box joints or through dovetails for a long-lasting drawer, without seeing the joints from the front of the drawer.

Once you've constructed the drawer box, drill and countersink the back side of the front for screws (**A**).

Install the drawer box flush to the front of the case and use double-sided (carpet) tape to adhere the false front to the box (**B**).

Gently pull out the drawer and immediately clamp the front to the box (**C**). Then drive two screws from inside the drawer box and into the front.

Slide the drawer back into the case and check the fit (**D**). If the reveal is even, add more screws to secure the front permanently to the box. If the gap needs work, remove the drawer front and plane its edges or reposition the front by using screws in different holes. When the front fits correctly, add two more screws.

Flush-Fit Drawer

The Cadillac of drawers, a flush-fit drawer has the look and feel of fine craftsmanship. It's just as well—this type of drawer is more challenging to fit than any other. A flush-fit drawer involves many aspects of general drawer making, so it's a good exercise in mastering the art of a well-made and well-fitted drawer.

A fail-safe method for determining the correct height or width for the drawer parts is to measure directly from the opening. Hold a drawer front or side up to the finished opening and mark the exact height; then cut to your mark (**A**). This approach leaves you enough material so that you can plane the drawer down for the correct fit into the opening once you've assembled it.

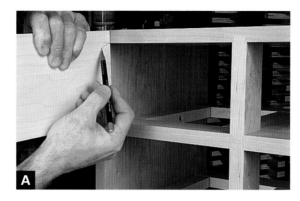

Usually, assembling a dovetailed drawer doesn't require the use of clamps. After tapping the joints together, and while the glue is still wet, check the drawer for square.

▶ See *"Dovetail Tapping Wedge"* on p. 91.

If the drawer is out of square, give the longer of the two diagonals a sound rap by tapping the rear of the drawer on a hard surface (**B**). When the drawer is square, set it aside on a flat surface until the glue dries.

After the glue has dried, use a smooth plane to level the top and bottom edges of the drawer. Periodically check that you're planing the drawer flat by checking it against a flat surface, such as your benchtop. To prevent tearing out the fibers, turn the plane around the corners as you work (**C**). Plane more off on taller drawers to allow for wood movement.

▶ See *"Understanding Wood Movement"* on p. 42.

(Text continues on p. 112.)

Next, set your plane for a very fine cut and shave the drawer sides down until the pins and tails are level. Clamp the drawer front in a bench vise and support the side on a wide board. Work in from each end to avoid breaking off any fibers (**D**). Check your progress with a straightedge and stop often to test-fit the drawer in the case opening. Keep shaving until the drawer slides in easily without any side-to-side play. Finish by sanding the sides lightly with 220-grit sandpaper wrapped around a felt block.

With the drawer stops in place, install the drawer into the case and mark the amount the front protrudes by scribing around the drawer (**E**).

▶ See *"Drawer Stops"* on p. 122.

Back at the bench, plane lightly across the face of the drawer to your marks (**F**). Now that you've fitted the drawer, add your favorite pull hardware.

Finally, rabbet a plywood drawer bottom and slide it into the grooves in the drawer (**G**).

[**TIP**] **On large drawers, glue the plywood for drawer bottoms into the grooves. It significantly increases the strength of the drawer and helps stiffen the corner joints.**

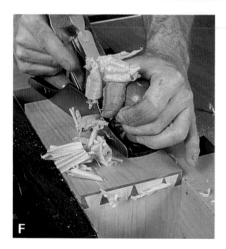

Finish up by driving screws or nails through the bottom and into the back of the drawer. If possible, use ⅜-in. or thicker plywood on anything but very small drawers. Thin ¼-in. plywood has a chintzy sound and feel.

Another option is to install a solid-wood bottom (*without glue!*) and let it extend past the back of the drawer to function as a drawer stop.

Half-Overlay Drawer

At the opposite end of the spectrum from flush-fit drawers are half-overlay drawers, often referred to as half inset. Because half-overlay drawers are so easy to fit into a drawer opening, this type of construction is perfect for utility drawers, kitchen drawers, and anytime you have multiple drawers and want to get the job done fast. A portion of the drawer front conceals the opening in the cabinet, so you can have as much as ⅜ in. of space between the opening and the back of the drawer front, allowing you to make a front with a "sloppy" fit. Half-overlay drawers are often used with metal ball-bearing slides, which further eases the installation.

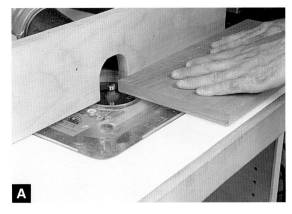

➤ See *"Commercial Slides"* on p. 124.

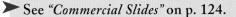

You can cut the drawer joints before or after you create the overlay in the drawer front. The order of construction isn't critical. To make the half overlay, start by rounding over the edges of the drawer front on the router table using a ¼-in. roundover bit (**A**).

Next, set up the table saw with an auxiliary fence and a dado blade and cut a ⅜-in.-deep by ⅜-in.-wide rabbet on all four sides of the front (**B**).

A typical bank of half-overlay drawers shows gently rounded edges (**C**). You can space adjacent drawers relatively far apart by incorporating the drawers into a face frame made from wide stiles and rails. This saves you from having to fit the drawer fronts to exacting reveals.

Bow-Front Drawer

Making a curved or bow-front drawer is identical to building a conventional drawer, except you curve the drawer front. The tricks are to cut all the drawer joints and to groove the parts for the drawer bottom while the stock is still square, allowing extra thickness in the front stock for your desired curvature. Once you've cut the joints, lay out the curve from a pattern or use a thin, flexible stick or batten that's bent to the desired arc (**A**).

Saw to the waste side of your layout line on the bandsaw (**B**). Clean up the saw marks with a small plane or use a flat-bottom spokeshave. Skewing the shave to the work helps reduce chatter and makes a smoother cut (**C**). As you shave, feel with your fingers to check that the curve is fair. Sand the curve; then assemble the bow-front drawer as you would any other drawer.

Pull-Out Drawer

Great for easy access inside a cabinet, a pull-out drawer can be made as you would any standard drawer. The difference is that it stows inside the cabinet, typically behind a door. Pull-outs work best with full-extension metal slides. To conceal the slides, construct the drawer front so it extends past the sides, as you would a full-overlay drawer.

Use an alignment spacer to install the metal slides on the drawer side (**A**). With a shim supporting the hardware at the correct height and parallel to the case bottom, screw the slide into the cabinet. A plywood spacer glued to the case side prevents the slide hardware from hitting the doors when the drawer is pulled out (**B**).

Install the drawer by sliding it onto the hardware in the case (**C**).

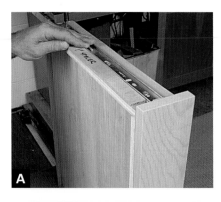

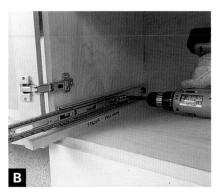

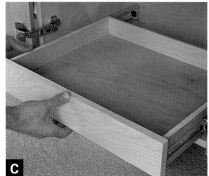

Keyboard Tray

A custom keyboard tray will enhance any home-made desk. The tray shown here is 10 in. wide by 26 in. long, big enough for a standard keyboard and mouse pad.

Make the tray from ¾-in. hardwood plywood and edge it with solid wood. Use a ½-in. lipping at the front so you can round the corners of the tray (**A**). Trim the lippings flush with the plywood and round the front corners on a spindle sander or with a few chisel cuts. Then round over the lippings with an ⅛-in. roundover bit on the router table (**B**).

Sculpt a wooden wrist support by using a selection of router bits, chisels, and sandpaper. With the stock face-side down, use a large thumbnail bit on the router table to cut the front and ends (**C**); a small roundover bit eases the back edge. Round the corners as you did on the tray.

Screw the wrist support to the tray from underneath (**D**). The support is shorter than the full length of the tray, which leaves about 6 in. for the mouse pad.

A

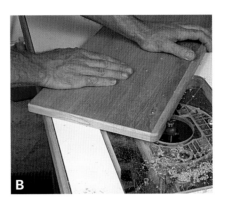
B

C

D

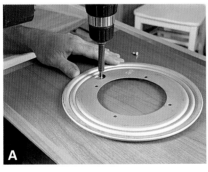
A

B

C

Lazy Susan

A lazy Susan is basically a turntable. It's great inside a cabinet where you want to store a lot of small items (spice jars are ideal); it can also support a TV.

A large hole lets you screw through the swiveling plate and into a shelf (**A**). To cover the hardware, add a shelf above the turntable. You'll have to drill an access hole through the shelf for screws to secure it to the turntable. If you don't want a hole to show, simply stick the shelf to the platform with double-sided carpet tape (**B**). Once installed, you can swivel the shelf a full 360 degrees (**C**).

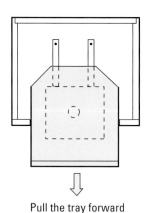

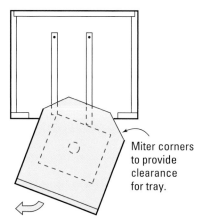

Pull the tray forward
and out from the cabinet.

A

Miter corners
to provide
clearance
for tray.

Rotate the tray to change
the viewing angle.

B

C

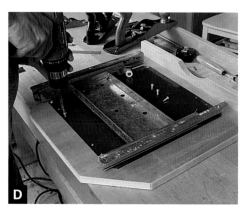

D

E

TV Swivel

It's always a hassle to get to the back of a big TV to access the wiring, especially if the TV is housed in a cabinet. Not so if you mount the set on a swivel. A swivel lets you pull out the TV to get at the back and lets you adjust the viewing angle of the picture tube to cover practically any seating arrangement in the room (**A**).

Buy the hardware first; then build a tray to fit over the swivel. A simple plywood panel edged in solid wood will support a large TV (check the manufacturer's load rating on your swivel first). Size the tray to accommodate your set and the cabinet or shelf where it will go. Before adding the wide front lipping, miter the back corners of the tray so the tray won't bind in the cabinet when the swivel is rotated (**B**).

Make the front strip wide enough to conceal the hardware that will reside under it, less about ³/₁₆ in. of clearance. Cut out a curved notch in the strip for a hand pull. Then glue the strip to the front edge with the tray upside down. A wide caul gives the outer clamps purchase (**C**). Trim the front lip flush once the glue dries.

Screw the swivel's metal platform to the underside of the tray (**D**). Then install the assembly into the cabinet with screws or, better yet, bolts; now you're ready to swivel (**E**).

Felt-Lined Drawer

There's nothing like a felt-lined drawer. It makes a classy drawer classier. Master craftsman Frank Klausz starts with a small dovetailed drawer. Begin by measuring the interior of the drawer; then cut pieces of cardboard or mat board slightly undersize. Cut each felt piece about 1 in. larger all around than the board; then cut away the corners of the felt at roughly 45 degrees, so the felt just touches the board at the corners (**A**).

Lay the board over the felt and spray a light coat of contact cement along the edges of the board and on the exposed felt (**B**). Then fold the felt over onto the board and smooth it down with your hand (**C**).

Run a couple beads of regular woodworking glue over the backside of each liner; then clamp the liner into the drawer (**D**).

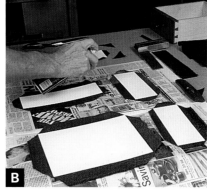

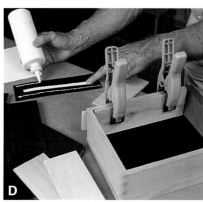

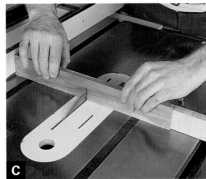

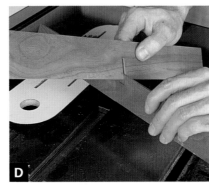

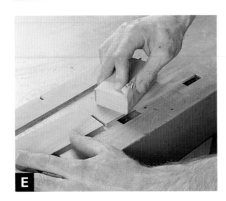

Divided Drawer

One of the simplest ways of dividing a drawer or other box-type opening is to join the dividers themselves with half-lap joints cut on the table saw. If you cut the dividers a hair short of their intended resting spot and add strips of felt to each end, you can press-fit the dividers in place. Start by finish-planing the divider material (**A**). Then cut the stock ⅟₃₂ in. smaller than the drawer or case opening. Lay out the joints with a square, making the notches equal to the thickness of the planed stock (**B**).

Saw the first notch on the table saw by making a couple of passes using the miter gauge (**C**). Check the fit. The joint should *almost* fit but be too tight to put together fully (**D**). Repeat the procedure to cut the notch in the second piece.

Sand the dividers for the final fit with 220-grit paper wrapped around a felt block (**E**). Self-stick felt applied to the ends of each finished divider holds them in tension against the drawer or case opening (**F**).

Drawer Hardware

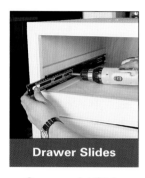

Drawer Slides

➤ Commercial Slides
(p. 124)

➤ Under-Mount Slides
(p. 125)

Computer Hardware

➤ Keyboard and
Mouse Hardware
(p. 126)

Drawer Pulls

➤ Installing Pulls
(p. 127)

➤ Shopmade Pulls
(p. 128)

➤ Protruding-Strip Pull
(p. 129)

➤ Curved Pull (p. 129)

A
FTER BUILDING YOUR DRAWERS, the next step is to install them into the case. If you've already built web frames into your cabinet, you're done.

➤ See *"Web Frames"* on p. 53.

But for many drawer-making operations, you will want to consider other types of drawer-guiding hardware as well as some clever jigs that can help you accurately lay out parts to fit them into the case. Today's commercial metal slides are beautifully made, with silky smooth action and respectably quiet operation. But many woodworkers like to make their own drawer-guide systems.

Another consideration when installing drawers is how they are going to stop once they're all the way in the case. Also, you should decide whether you want to limit how far the drawers can be pulled out of the case, so you can avoid accidents.

Finally, there are knobs, pulls, and other great pieces of gear that will allow you to grasp the drawer and actually get inside it. Here you have a choice between commercially available knobs and the shopmade variety.

WEDGING A KNOB

Turn tenon on knob slightly longer than thickness of drawer front.

Drill $1/8$-in. hole th-rough tenon.

Saw $1/16$-in. kerf up to hole on bandsaw.

Drawer front

Glue knob into hole front. Glue and drive wedge into kerf; saw protruding tenon and wedge flush.

Full-extension slides provide access to the back of a drawer.

Commercial Drawer Slides

Commercial drawer slides may not belong in fine furniture with hand-cut joinery, but they certainly have their place in case construction. Used appropriately, commercial slides let you hang a drawer quicker than a sneeze; and today's designs are quiet, smooth, and easily hidden.

Remember that most metal slides require 1 in. of clearance between the case opening and the sides of the drawer, or $1/2$ in. for each side. Good slides have a "slop" tolerance of about $1/16$ in., meaning that if you build your drawer a little too wide or too narrow, the slides will still work fine. Be sure to buy your slides first, and follow the manufacturer's specifications before building your drawers. And think about the load that the drawer will carry. Choose a slide rated at or preferably above that load. Use a full-extension slide when appropriate, such as for file drawers or wherever you need to get to the back of the drawer.

Shopmade Guides

Shopmade drawer hardware has a look and action that commercial slides can't compete with. Wood runners have a special feel and are well worth the extra effort. The good news is that you have several options for using wood runners, and they suit several applications.

The drawing opposite shows some options for using wooden runners that ride in grooves. One popular method is to rout grooves in the sides of the drawers and hang the drawers on wooden runners installed in the case. Or, if you want to make a design statement, attach the runners to the drawer

GROOVES AND RUNNERS

Runners on Case

Rout stopped groove in drawer side.

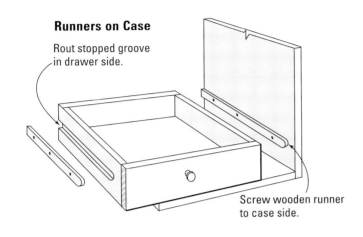

Screw wooden runner to case side.

Runners attached to the case side allow you to conceal the means by which the drawer travels.

Runners on Drawer

Rout stopped groove in case.

Screw runner to drawer side.

Runners attached to the drawer become a visible design element at the front of the cabinet.

Twin Guide Strips

Rout twin grooves in sides before assembly.

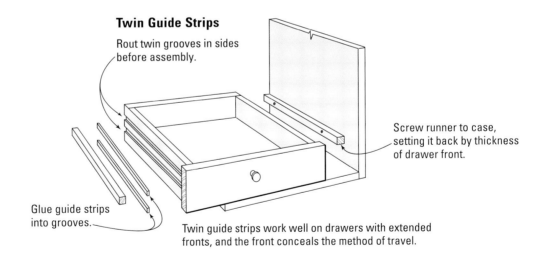

Screw runner to case, setting it back by thickness of drawer front.

Glue guide strips into grooves.

Twin guide strips work well on drawers with extended fronts, and the front conceals the method of travel.

instead and rout grooves in the case. The ends of the runners show up as little rectangles at the front of the cabinet.

A third method involves pairs of guide strips and works well with drawers with fronts that extend beyond the sides. Rout twin grooves in the sides before assembling the drawer; then glue wood guide strips into the grooves so they extend beyond the sides but not quite as far as the extended front.

Pairs of hardwood guide strips work well for drawers with fronts that extend past the sides.

You can extend a drawer bottom to act as a stop. A slot for a screw provides room for expansion on a solid-wood drawer bottom.

Rip some runner stock and plane it to fit between the guides; then temporarily screw it to the sides of the cabinet. Hang the drawer and make any necessary adjustments to the fit by removing the runners and hand-planing them. When the drawer operates smoothly, glue and screw the runners permanently to the case.

Drawer Stops

Besides the overall fit and action of a drawer, there are two other key movements to question when building drawers: What stops the drawer on the way in? Do you want to stop the drawer on its way out?

On cases with solid-wood sides, you can use a solid-wood drawer bottom as a drawer stop. Let the bottom extend about ⅜ in. beyond the back of the drawer so it contacts the case back. As the sides of the case expand and contract, so does the drawer bottom, keeping the drawer front flush to the front of the case.

Orient the grain of the bottom from side to side, *never* front to back. If the grain were to run front to back, any expansion would force the sides apart, binding the drawer and weakening the joints. And don't glue the bottom into the grooves in the drawer. One handy method is to use a screw and a washer through a slotted hole—cut on the table saw—to hold the bottom in place. As the bottom swells, it moves toward the back of the drawer.

If you allow for some extra wood when making a solid-wood bottom, it's easy to get a perfect flush fit at the front of the drawer by shaving some material off the back edge.

The same technique works for cabinets with plywood sides, except that you must use a plywood bottom in the drawer instead of solid wood.

A wooden strip glued to the front rail of a case makes a convenient drawer stop and allows for more accurate tolerances when it comes to solid-wood cases. To cushion the drawer, you can glue leather to the front of the strip if you like. It makes a nice touch and softens the action. Drawers stopped at the front are more likely to stay aligned with the front of a solid-wood case when the case swells and shrinks over the seasons. This technique works only when the drawer front and sides extend below the drawer bottom, usually by about ¼ in.

Clamp the stop strip to a scribed line equal to the thickness of the drawer front. The stop material must be thin enough to clear the drawer bottom—³⁄₁₆ in. is usually sufficient—and short enough to allow clearance for the sides of the drawer. Once the stop is secured, fit the drawer flush to the case by shaving the front with a handplane.

▶ See *"Flush-Fit Drawer"* on p. 111.

Use a marking gauge to mark the setback for the door stop strips. Set the gauge by the thickness of a drawer front.

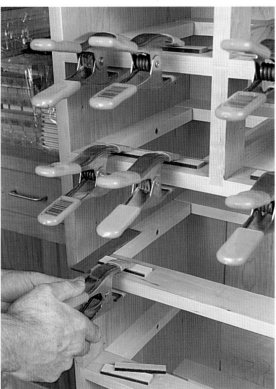

Spring clamps hold the stops on the gauged lines while the glue sets.

Commercial Slides

Side-mounted slides remain popular with many cabinetmakers and kitchen designers. Affordable and easy to install, they come in left and right pairs for each drawer, and each slide consists of two parts: a runner, which is screwed to the drawer side, and a housing for that runner, which attaches to the inside of the case.

When installing the runners on the drawer, use a jig to align the runner accurately. At this point, install only two or three screws in the elongated holes—enough to hold the runner in place (**A**). How high on the side should you position the runner? You should aim for aligning the runner with the height of your drawer pull or handle. For example, if you plan to mount the handle centered on the drawer front, then center the runner on the side. This gives you the best action and feel.

Use a plywood spacer in the case opening to align the slide housing in the cabinet. The shim ensures that the slides on both sides of the case are level with each other and that they're square and parallel to the case (**B**). After hanging and fitting the drawer to the correct depth of the cabinet, add the remaining screws (**C**).

Under-Mount Slides

When the thought of looking at metal hardware on the side of your carefully crafted drawer gives you the heebie-jeebies, use an under-mount side.

Mount the case and drawer slides as one member into the case. Then drill a hole in the bottom edge of each drawer side, near the front of the drawer (**A**). Slip the drawer into the case and lower the drawer so the holes you've drilled engage pins at the front of the slides (**B**). When you pull out the drawer, you won't see any hardware at all (**C**).

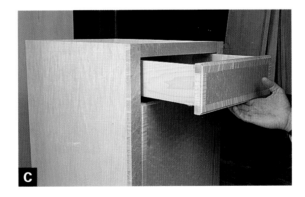

Keyboard and Mouse Hardware

The mail-order woodworking catalogs are full of home-office and computer gear, and one of the more useful devices you can find is hardware for holding a keyboard and mouse tray. Good hardware lets you pull out the tray as you would a drawer and then swivel the tray from left to right to suit your typing or mouse-clicking style.

The keyboard hardware consists of a plate and a tray-holding mechanism that slides along the plate. Installation is simple. Just screw the plate to the underside of your desk surface (**A**). Mount the sliding mechanism onto the plate (**B**); then attach a commercial or shopmade tray. To make an invisible connection, attach the tray to the mechanism by driving screws from underneath .

► See *"Keyboard Tray"* on p. 115.

Once you've installed the tray and support mechanism, you can fine-tune the position of your keyboard for optimum performance. Extend the tray beyond the desk by simply pulling it out, or tuck it out of view by pushing it underneath. To rotate the tray, just grasp it and swivel it into position. You can adjust the height of the tray below or flush with the desk surface by loosening a knob. Finally, set the desired angle or tilt of your keyboard by pulling a lever located underneath the front of the tray (**C**).

Installing Pulls

U Pulls U-shaped pulls typically install with screws through the back of the drawer front. Finding the center of the screw holes is the key to mounting them successfully. To make the job easy, create a template with the centerlines of the screw holes carefully drilled through it; then use the template to mark the holes' locations in the drawer front (**A**).

If possible, drill for the screws before you assemble the drawer. Use the drill press so your holes are precisely square to the face of the drawer front (**B**).

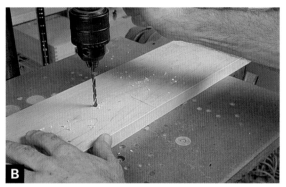

Bail Pulls Bail-type pulls are elegant pieces of gear. Unfortunately, on pulls for which you install a pair of loose posts to connect the bail, you'll often encounter one drawback: The pins on the bail can be slightly out of square and not parallel with each other. After you drill the holes for the posts and install the pull, the bail binds, because the pins won't rotate freely in the posts.

To avoid the problem of out-of-square pins, always check all of the pulls for a project before drilling the post holes. Make a jig from scrap wood with the desired hole spacing drilled into the jig. Then check each pull by installing the posts and bail in the jig. If a reluctant bail won't rotate easily, spread it open or squeeze it closed a little with your hands to square up the pins. If the bails still bind, try re-drilling a new set of holes in the jig and check again (**C**).

When all the bails swing freely in the jig, draw center marks on the jig and corresponding center and height marks on the drawer fronts. Position the jig on each drawer front with the marks aligned and mark through the jig to locate the holes on the work (**D**).

Shopmade Pulls

Making your own pulls or handles is a very satis-fying aspect of furniture making and is tons of fun. There's no limit to the designs you can incorporate into your work, and it personalizes your furniture in a way that commercial hardware can't. The pulls shown here are just a sampling of what you can make if you let your imagination roam free. And all these designs will work great as door pulls, too.

▶ See "*Doors*" on p. 130.

Here's a chance to use those prized leftover scraps of wood you've been saving since the last millennium. This pull is as simple as it gets, and that's probably why I like it so much. Use a live-edged piece of wood—burled or highly figured woods are my favorites—to make each pull unique. Sculpt the shape of the pull on the band-saw however you wish; just be sure to keep the mounting face flat. Try beveling the ends for a dramatic effect (**A**).

Drill and countersink the inside of the drawer front for screws and drill pilot holes in the back of the pull. Spread some glue on the pull and secure it to the drawer with screws driven through the back of the drawer front (**B**).

Protruding-Strip Pull

To make a very simple but very effective pull, apply a strip to the top edge of the drawer front. If you select your stock carefully for color and grain, you can fool the eye into thinking that the pull was carved into the front, instead of being simply glued in place. The best method is to shape the strip before gluing it to the drawer.

Cove the underside on the router table using a coving bit. Make the cut in successively deeper passes (**A**). Then round over the top and bottom of the leading edge (**B**).

Glue and clamp the strip to the drawer front (**C**). When the glue has dried, clean up any small misalignments with a goose-neck scraper and planes.

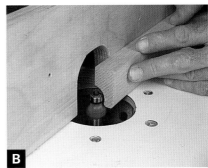

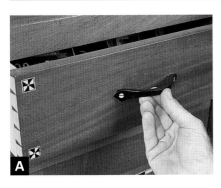

Curved Pull

Made from any dense, close-grained hardwood such as maple, rosewood, or ebony, a curved pull has a sophisticated look (**A**). The faux screws shown here add to the charm, although their main function is to conceal the screws that secure the pull to the drawer.

Lay out the pull profile on the stock using two plywood templates, one for the side of the pull (**B**) and one for the top (**C**). Cut out the shape on the bandsaw.

Use a drum or spindle sander to help fair the curves and remove the saw marks; then counterbore, countersink, and drill a shank hole at a slight angle through the pull for screws (**D**). Plug the hole with a dowel made from a contrasting wood; but before you glue in the dowel, saw a kerf in one end with a handsaw. Install the dowel and tap a wedge into the kerf made from contrasting wood to mimic the slotted head of a screw.

Building Doors, page 132

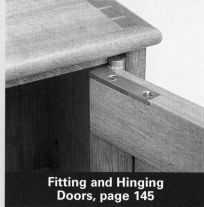

Fitting and Hinging Doors, page 145

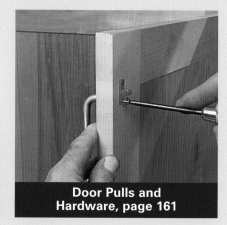

Door Pulls and Hardware, page 161

PART THREE

Doors

CABINET DOORS ARE THE GATEKEEPERS of furniture making, dressing up the entrance to our furniture in a variety of patterns, textures, colors, and styles. A well-made door will invite us to explore the contents within. On a practical level, doors keep out dust and dirt, and they dissuade prying eyes from the insides of our cabinets. Plus they're expedient at hiding the clutter of our lives. They provide the opportunity for us as woodworkers to conceal the good and the bad and to provide access to both by designing and building good-looking and trouble-free doors.

Your design choices when making doors are plentiful, thanks to the ready supply of natural woods and man-made goods like veneered hardwood plywood. The style of door you decide to make can also be affected by small details, such as introducing a curve for flair or adding moldings for depth and contrast. Of course, you can always keep it simple and construct a simple flat panel. The choice is up to you.

Building Doors

Doors with Panels

➤ Flat Panel (p. 136)

➤ Raised Frame and Panel (p. 137)

➤ Arch-Top Frame and Panel (p. 139)

Solid Doors

➤ Board and Batten (p. 141)

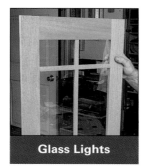

Glass Lights

➤ Dividing Up a Door (p. 143)

THE FIRST DECISION YOU'RE FACED WITH when making a door is to decide on its style. Choices abound here and include the use of solid wood, veneers, and moldings. The next step is to ensure that the door you build will stay together through years of use. There are few items in furniture making that get more abuse than the typical cabinet door, so the joinery you select has to stand the test of time. Joints must also be strong enough to keep the frame of the door from racking under its own weight. Proper glue-up techniques can save you the hassle of dealing with out-of-flat surfaces and cocked joints, which lead to doors that won't fit well or hinge poorly.

When it comes to door types, there are plenty of structures to pick from. Used extensively in Euro-style kitchen cabinets, an austere, flat panel is the easiest type of door to make and can be surprisingly elegant when used side by side in neat, orderly rows. Probably the most oft-used construction is the frame and panel. This design dates back thousands of years and was conceived as a solution to the problem of excessive wood movement seen with wide, solid-wood panels. Other more complicated doors include frames with arching tops and glass doors with divisions made of wood strips.

Designing Doors

The design possibilities for doors are limitless. But some basic ingredients are available for expanding your door palette. If the look and feel of solid wood is what you're after, then you need to think about wood movement and its associated structural concerns. Frame-and-panel construction takes this movement into account, as does a board-and-batten door. Using man-made sheet goods like plywood and medium-density fiberboard (MDF) lets you expand your design parameters to include veneers, leather, and other materials on the surface of your doors. And moldings are an endless source for adding bands of light and shadow to the surface of a door, making it more three-dimensional.

Joinery Options

Doors—especially cabinet doors—take a lot of abuse during their lives. Who hasn't slammed a door or accidentally swung a door open so fast it pulled on the hinges? To counteract this mistreatment, you need solid joints to keep doors together.

In frame-and-panel construction, the corner joints hold the frame together. The mortise-and-tenon joint is time tested to hold up well, especially if the tenons are 1 in. or longer. Other options include paired biscuits and paired dowels. Mitered frames can be splined to strengthen weak end-grain surfaces. And introducing plywood or any type of stable, man-made board inside the frame allows you to glue the panel to the frame, greatly increasing the overall strength of the door.

Gluing Up Flat and Square

There's no describing the frustration of building a beautiful door and fitting it with expensive hinges only to have it hang twisted in the cabinet once it's installed. The good news is the door, and not the cabinet or those really

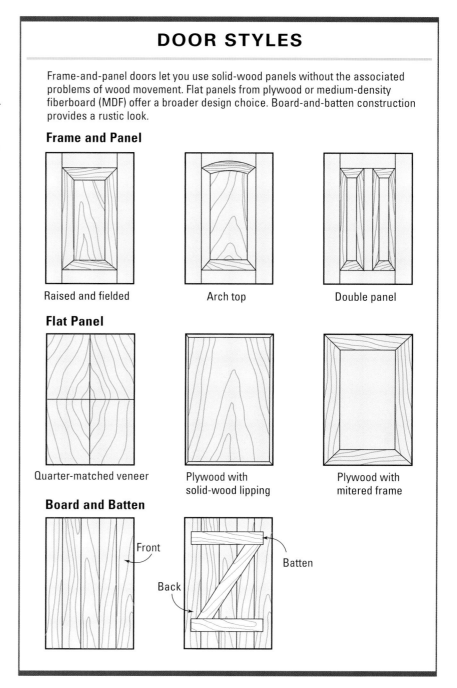

DOOR STYLES

Frame-and-panel doors let you use solid-wood panels without the associated problems of wood movement. Flat panels from plywood or medium-density fiberboard (MDF) offer a broader design choice. Board-and-batten construction provides a rustic look.

Frame and Panel

Raised and fielded   Arch top   Double panel

Flat Panel

Quarter-matched veneer   Plywood with solid-wood lipping   Plywood with mitered frame

Board and Batten

Front   Batten   Back

fine hinges, is the most likely culprit. The problem usually shows up during the clamp-up stage of construction, when you unwittingly introduce twist into the frame. For a flat and square glue-up, think in terms of two planes: the face, or broad surface of the door,

DOOR JOINTS

Mortise and Tenon

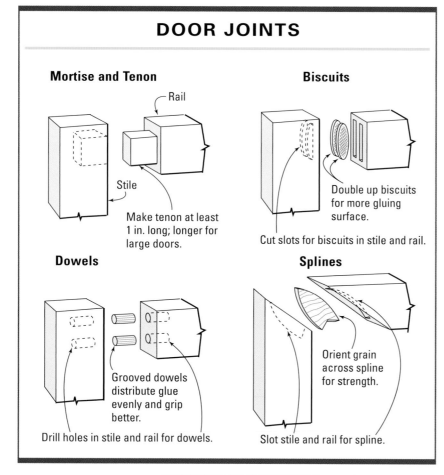

Rail

Stile

Make tenon at least 1 in. long; longer for large doors.

Dowels

Grooved dowels distribute glue evenly and grip better.

Drill holes in stile and rail for dowels.

Biscuits

Double up biscuits for more gluing surface.

Cut slots for biscuits in stile and rail.

Splines

Orient grain across spline for strength.

Slot stile and rail for spline.

and the door's edge. Always clamp your work on a dead-flat surface, or any twist in the table will transfer itself to the face of the door. Then position your clamps over critical points on the door's edges and face.

As you look at the edge of the door, check to see that the center of the clamp's screw is

CLAMP ALIGNMENT

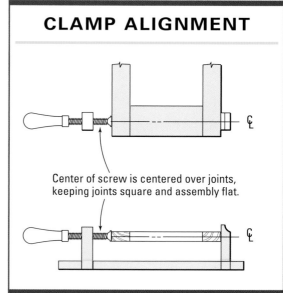

Center of screw is centered over joints, keeping joints square and assembly flat.

PANEL PROFILES

Raising, fielding, and molding create different effects with light and shadow.

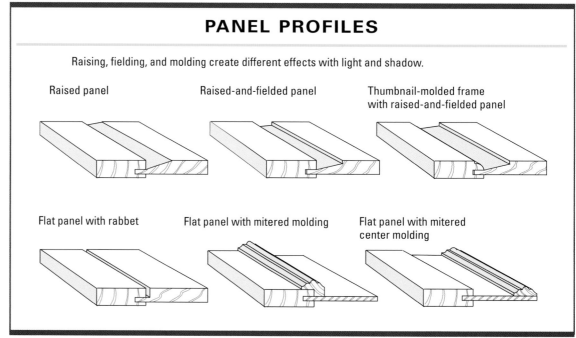

Raised panel

Raised-and-fielded panel

Thumbnail-molded frame with raised-and-fielded panel

Flat panel with rabbet

Flat panel with mitered molding

Flat panel with mitered center molding

► REINFORCING A COPE-AND-STICK JOINT

One of the most hotly debated joinery issues is whether or not to reinforce a cope-and-stick joint. An obvious fact is that the increased gluing surface and stub tenon of a cope-and-stick frame is simply no match for the strength of a long tenon. On cabinet doors that see a lot of daily use, the joint can fail, even when pinned from behind with brads. One method of reinforcing the joint is to glue dowels into the stiles and rails. The strongest solution is this: First rout a separate mortise into the edge of the stile and into the end of the rail; then glue "loose," or floating, tenons into both mortises. Make sure the tenon is housed at least 1 in. into each part.

Properly fitted and made from a hardwood, a loose tenon can be stronger than a conventional mortise-and-tenon joint—and in many cases easier to construct for the small-shop woodworker. (For more on joinery, see *The Complete Illustrated Guide to Joinery,* by Gary Rogowski, The Taunton Press.)

**COPE-AND-STICK
WITH LOOSE TENON**

Rail is coped to fit sticking with stub tenon.

Tenon

Mortise for tenon in stile and rail.

Sticking

---

centered over the thickness of the frame member. This is easy if you position scrap sticks of the correct thickness over the clamps. Centering the work in this manner prevents twisting the stiles and keeps the door flat. Look down on the surface of the door to make sure the clamps are centered over the width of the rails, ensuring that the joints come together square.

Don't turn the clamps with the strength of a gorilla; undue pressure can buckle the frame and compress the wood. When the clamps come off, the wood springs back and the joints open. Be sensitive to the pressure you apply. If a reluctant joint needs encouragement, by all means crank those clamps. But back them off a little once the joint line is tight. Then check the assembly for flat with a straightedge.

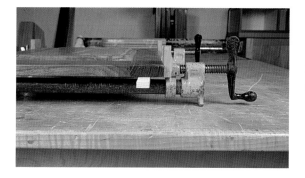

Raising a door on some scrap and in line with the clamp's screw prevents the style from cocking.

The clamping pressure should be centered on the width of the rails to keep the frame square.

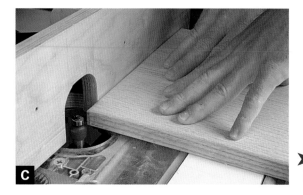

Flat Panel

The most basic of all doors is a simple flat panel. Although you can make a panel from solid wood, there's a high probability that the door will warp if it's of any considerable width or length. A better choice is a man-made material, such as MDF, because of its inherent stability. But MDF needs a surface covering of veneer or paint to conceal its bland appearance. Veneered hardwood plywood is another choice, but like MDF, you'll need to conceal the raw edges. For edging on doors, I prefer thin solid-wood banding over veneer edgebanding. If you make your banding from the same species as the plywood veneer, with similar color and grain patterns, it will blend inconspicuously with the panel. Make the banding about ⅛ in. thick, which provides enough material for easing over the sharp edges without exposing the plywood core.

Dimension the panel to account for the combined thickness of the edging; then glue and clamp the two edges that will become the vertical surfaces on the door. Make sure to cut the banding slightly thicker and longer than the panel (**A**). Once the glue has dried, rout the excess with a laminate bit or trim it flush with a handplane.

➤ See *"Flush-Trimmed Lippings"* on p. 75.

Add the two horizontal bandings, making a butt joint at the corners (**B**).

You can ease over the edges of the banding with a plane or rout a small ⅛-in. roundover (**C**). Once the door is installed, the corner joints will be invisible from the top of the door.

Raised Frame and Panel

For solid-wood doors of any size, frame-and-panel construction solves the problem of warping and natural wood movement. The frame, made from stiles and rails that are on the narrow side, is relatively stable and thus not prone to warp. Inside the frame is a wide panel captured in grooves cut in the frame. The panel "floats" inside the frame so it can move freely as it expands and contracts, without stressing the framework around it (**A**).

Cut the frame joints, then groove the stiles and rails for the panel. Dimension your panel to the exact size of the inside perimeter of the frame plus the full depth of its grooves.

➤ See *"Dust Panels"* on p. 56.

You can raise panels on the router table using a panel-raising bit or use a panel raiser on the shaper. (For more on raised panels, see *The Complete Illustrated Guide to Shaping Wood,* by Lonnie Bird, The Taunton Press.) Making a full-depth cut in one pass will overload the cutter and the machine, plus it can be dangerous. Instead, make the cut in two or three passes. A subfence temporarily clamped to the shaper fence lets you make a shallow cut on the first pass (**B**). To make the final, full-depth cut, remove the subfence (**C**).

> ⚠ **WARNING** Always unplug the machine when making bit changes on a router or shaper.

(Text continues on p. 138.)

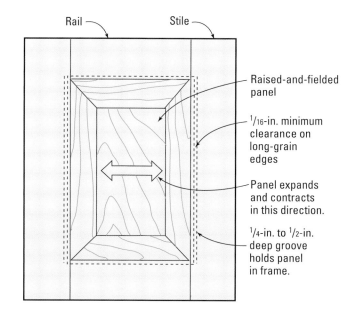

Rail — Stile —

Raised-and-fielded panel

$^{1}/_{16}$-in. minimum clearance on long-grain edges

Panel expands and contracts in this direction.

$^{1}/_{4}$-in. to $^{1}/_{2}$-in. deep groove holds panel in frame.

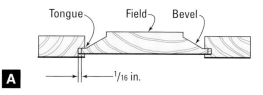

Tongue — Field — Bevel —

$^{1}/_{16}$ in.

A

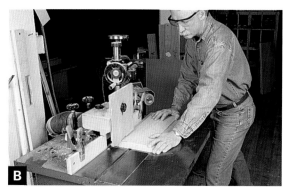

B

C

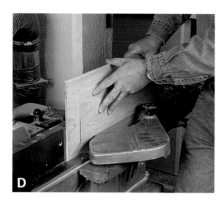

Before assembling the door, there are three important steps to take. First, joint $\frac{1}{16}$ in. to $\frac{1}{8}$ in. off each long-grain edge of the panel. This allows room for the panel to expand in the groove of the frame (**D**). (For more on calculating expansion and contraction of solid-wood panels, see *Understanding Wood,* by R. Bruce Hoadley, The Taunton Press.)

Next, if the finished door will be colored, prefinish the same long-grain edges of the panel with the stain you'll use to color the door (**E**). That way, when the panel shrinks during the dry season, it won't expose the lighter colored lip of the panel.

Last, to keep the panel from rattling in the frame, pin the panels from the back in the center or use spacers between the panel and the grooves. One method is to use little rubber balls (sold as Space Balls through many woodworking mail-order catalogs) that fit into $\frac{1}{4}$-in.-wide grooves and compress when the panel expands (**F**).

Align your clamps carefully over the joints and glue up the frame and panel. Make sure no glue migrates from the joints to the edges of the panel, or the panel will bind in the frame and eventually crack. Furniture maker Edward Schoen's glue-up table has notches that automatically center pipe clamps for easy assembly (**G**).

A variation on the frame-and-panel style is a flat panel fitted in a frame. You can significantly increase the overall strength of the door if you make the panel from veneered plywood or MDF—or any stable sheet stock—and glue it into the grooves of the frame. To dress up the perimeter of the panel, you can miter decorative molding inside the frame and glue and nail it to the panel (**H**).

Arch-Top Frame and Panel

Introducing a simple arch at the top of a door is easier than you might think, as long as you follow the construction sequence step by step. The first step is to make a full-size drawing of the door, including the curve of the top rail. One warning: Don't aim for a small radius on the rail, because the shoulders will have weak short grain and can snap off if the angle is too severe. A curve with a radius of 10 in. or larger is ideal. (For more complex curves, see *The Complete Illustrated Guide to Shaping Wood,* by Lonnie Bird, The Taunton Press.)

Choose your door stock carefully. Whenever possible, use straight-grained material for the stiles. For the curved rail to look its best, select a board with curving grain and cut the rail stock to follow the curve. Cut the frame joints first while the stock is still square; then transfer the curve of the rail on your drawing onto the rail stock by setting a large compass to the correct radius (**A**).

Bandsaw the curve in the rail, staying to the waste side of your layout line (**B**). Then clean up the sawn surface with a spokeshave or a spindle sander (**C**). For the smoothest surface, sand downhill to the grain.

Groove the frame members on the router table with a ¼-in. ball-bearing slotting cutter. Use the fence for the straight pieces; then remove the fence and ride the curved rail against the bearing. Use a starting pin and a guard (not shown) to make the cut safely (**D**).

(Text continues on p. 140.)

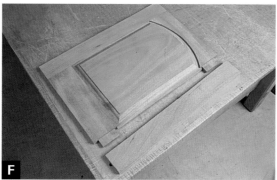

Use the same layout method to mark the curve at the top of the panel, increasing the radius for the panel by the depth of the groove you cut in the rail. Now bandsaw the curve and smooth the surface as before; then raise the panel on the router table using a bearing-guided panel-raising bit and a starting pin (**E**). Make several passes, raising the height of the bit in increments until the panel fits the grooves in the frame. The panel should slide easily into the stiles and rails without rattling (**F**).

[**TIP**] **Sanding in the right direction can result in much smoother surfaces. Like planing wood, the key is to sand so that the fibers of the wood are pointing away from you. Whenever possible, follow the "downhill" sanding technique, flipping over the workpiece when necessary.**

Board and Batten

A board-and-batten door has a rugged, rustic appeal. If you pay attention to the details, it can be quite elegant, too. This type of door is made from boards laid edge to edge and held together by splines and by stout battens at the back. Start by milling individual boards to length. Your boards can be random in width or you can make them all the same for a more symmetrical effect. You can chamfer the edges of the boards where they meet, rout beads, or simply leave the edges square.

Use a slotting cutter in the router table to mill ¼-in.-wide by ⅜-in.-deep grooves in the edges of the boards (**A**), Be careful not to cut grooves in the outer edges of the two outside boards.

Rip some spline material to fit the combined depth of the two grooves. To prevent the splines from falling out of the door, spot glue one spline into each board, except for a single outer board (**B**).

Fit all the splines and boards together, dry-clamp them, and check the panel for square. Don't glue the boards together or they'll split or curl as they move against the battens. Then attach the battens onto the backside of the panel with screws through countersunk holes (**C**). I like to use trim-head screws for their low profile. You can add plugs to cover the screws if you wish, but I think the little holes make a nice detail.

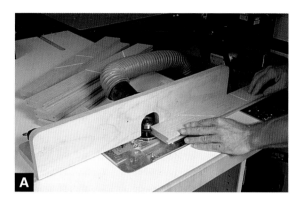

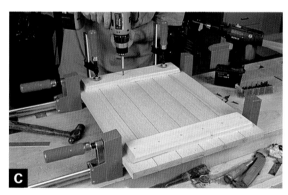

> ⚠ **WARNING** Cut against the rotation of the router bit when slotting. Failure to do so can cause the router to grab the workpiece and pull your hands in.

(Text continues on p. 142.)

Add a diagonal brace between the battens. The brace stiffens the construction and prevents the door from racking. Getting the brace to fit tightly between the battens can be tricky. The best approach is to clamp the brace stock across the battens and knife two lines at each end of the brace where it meets the inside edge of the batten (**D**). Then square your marks onto the face of the brace and cut a miter on each end.

Attach the brace in the same manner as the battens by screwing it into the back of the door (**E**). The front of the finished door (**F**) does not reveal the bracing and screws.

Dividing Up a Door

Here's a simple approach to making divided or glass-light doors based on a little router jig (**A**). Construct and assemble a door as you would a standard frame; then level the joints if necessary with a plane and trim the door to fit its intended cabinet.

Once you've trimmed the door, rout a ⅜-in.-wide rabbet into the inner edge on the back side of the frame. The actual rabbet depth isn't critical. I usually make the rabbet about half as deep as the frame's thickness. This leaves plenty of room for the glass and a wood strip or some caulk to hold the glass in the frame. Make sure to lay a sacrificial sheet under the door or raise the door on blocks to avoid routing into your benchtop. An oversize baseplate on the router serves as a stable platform for riding the frame, making it easier to cut the rabbet to a uniform depth (**B**).

Square the rounded corners of the rabbet with a chisel. For accuracy, extend the straight edges of the rabbet onto the frame with a ruler; then chisel to your marks. Work slowly up to your marks by taking thin slices, using a mallet to chop the end-grain shoulders and paring the long-grain shoulders by hand (**C**).

After finishing the rabbet, measure the thickness of the remaining ledge below the rabbet and mill the muntin strips to the same thickness by ⅝ in. wide. Cut each strip to the correct length by holding it in position over the rabbets and marking where the ends meet the frame. Then use a dado blade to rabbet the ends of the muntins by half the muntins' thickness and to mill dadoes where adjacent muntins overlap. Remember to flip one of the muntins over when cutting the

(Text continues on p. 144.)

With this glass-light jig, you can rout ³/₈-in.-long by ⁵/₈-in.-wide pockets in a rabbeted frame for ⁵/₈-in.-wide glass muntins. Sandpaper under the jig lets you hold it in position without clamps.

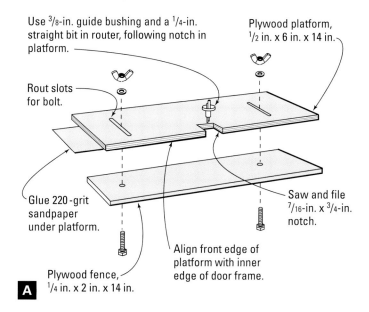

Use ³/₈-in. guide bushing and a ¹/₄-in. straight bit in router, following notch in platform.

Rout slots for bolt.

Plywood platform, ¹/₂ in. x 6 in. x 14 in.

Glue 220-grit sandpaper under platform.

Saw and file ⁷/₁₆-in. x ³/₄-in. notch.

Align front edge of platform with inner edge of door frame.

Plywood fence, ¹/₄ in. x 2 in. x 14 in.

A

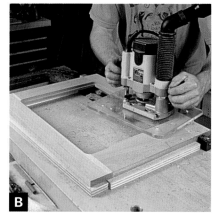

B

C

intersecting dadoes so the rabbeted ends in both muntins will face the same direction (**D**). Make test cuts in scrap until the two muntins fit together with their surfaces flush.

Fit the muntins together and lay them into the rabbeted frame; mark where they rest on the rabbets. Then cut ⅝-in.-wide pockets in the rabbets for the muntins using the router jig, aligning the jig to your marks. If necessary, you can square up the rounded corners of the pockets with a chisel or simply round the ends of the tongues on the muntins. Remember, the joint won't be seen once the glass retainer strips are in place (**E**).

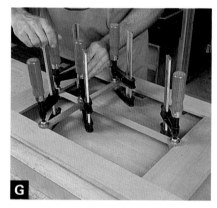

Spread glue on the tongues of the muntins and in the pockets in the frame; press the assembly into the pockets (**F**). A few clamps will pull the joints together and keep everything tight until the glue sets (**G**).

Have a glass shop cut the glass ⅛ in. smaller than the rabbeted opening, and lay the glass in the rabbets. You can use caulk to hold the glass in the frame or miter wood strips to fit into the rabbet. Tack the strips temporarily into the frame to check the fit (**H**). Then apply a finish to the door before permanently installing the glass. From the front, you won't see any of the overlapping joinery (**I**).

Fitting and Hinging Doors

Installing Basic Hinges

Specialty Hinges

Shopmade Hinges

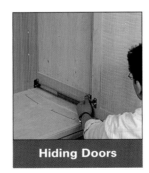

Hiding Doors

Once you've built a door, the next steps are to fit it to the case and then install the hinges and hang it. Achieving the perfect fit of door to case is a telltale mark of craftsmanship. Your aim is to have even reveals, or gaps, all around the door, whether the door is inset into the case or lying over the case frame. Once you've fit the door to the opening, fitting and applying hinges to the door are the keys to completing the job successfully. Properly hung, a door should open with effortless ease and swing quietly on its hinges.

As a general rule, it's best to construct your door a little oversize and then trim it after assembly to fit the case. This gives you more control over the final reveal, because you can saw, plane, or sand the edges to the exact size needed. You can trim edges on the table saw using a cut-off sled to keep the door square.

➤ See *"Bottomless Crosscut Jig"* on p. 14.

The jointer is another useful tool for trimming a door to size. For the final fit and finish, a handplane is by far the most accurate tool to use. Once you master the technique of planing an edge flat and square, you'll find that a handplane can remove shavings as thin as 0.001 in., a degree of accuracy no other machine or hand tool can match. You'll have to sand the surface at some point, but be careful. Use fine sandpaper and a felt block, or you're likely to round over the surface and quickly bring an edge out of square.

Once the door fits the case opening, you're ready for hinges. You have many hinge types to choose from, and your choice will depend on the type of door you're making, not the least of which includes making your own hinges from wood or other materials.

Choosing Hinges

Everything about the final fit and feel of your doors relies on its hinges. From the look and feel of the hinges on the outside, to the positive action of the door as it swings around them. It's not enough to simply make or buy good hinges. You'll need to learn the characteristics of each type so you can choose the right hinge for your project and then install it properly. Some hinges can be used interchangeably for flush, half-inset, and overlay doors; others cannot. Make sure to select the correct hinge before committing to its installation.

As a friend of mine wisely notes, it's worth picking your battles. You can choose a hinge that needs precise mortising into both the case and the door or you can get the same results with a hinge that simply screws to the surface of both parts. Knowing the outcome will help you to determine the best course of action. What you see on the outside of the cabinet once the door is hinged

can affect your decision, too. At one end of the spectrum is the surface-mounted hinge, which puts both leaves and knuckle on display for all to see. Or perhaps you want to downplay your hinges and install an inconspicuous knife hinge, which reveals a low-profile knuckle, or use a barrel hinge so you don't see any hardware at all.

Regardless of the hinge you use, it pays to treat the process of installing hinges with the same approach used for cutting joints: Tune up your tools and hone them razor sharp. And take the time to lay out parts accurately. This attention to detail will pay off in a well-hung door that will provide years of service.

Three Types of Doors to Fit

Before you can hinge a door, it must be accurately fitted to the case. Of the three door types—flush fit, full overlay, and half overlay—the flush-fit door is by far the most demanding to install. Overlay and half-overlay doors are fitted just as you would a drawer of the same type.

► See *"Full-Overlay Drawer"* on p. 110 and *"Half-Overlay Drawer"* on p. 113.

But a flush-fit door requires that the edges of the door meet the perimeter of the frame or case sides in an even gap, or reveal. And the surface of the door must be flush with the surface of the case. I use a simple shopmade jig to ease the process and to make the art of fitting more accurate.

Start by building the door to the exact size of the case opening. If you dimension the door correctly, it shouldn't fit into the

TYPES OF HINGES

Butt

Use for inset and overlay.

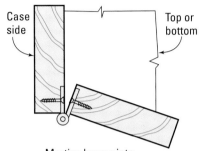

Case side

Top or bottom

Mortise leaves into case and door.

Continuous

Use for inset and overlay.

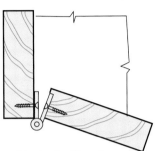

Mortise leaf into door.

Surface Mount

Use for inset and overlay.

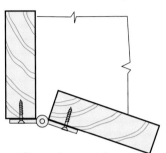

Secure leaves to face of door and case.

Knife

Use for inset and overlay.

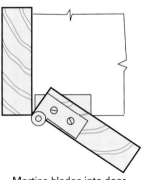

Mortise blades into door and case top and bottom.

Barrel

Use for bifold, inset, and overlay.

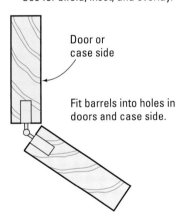

Door or case side

Fit barrels into holes in doors and case side.

Cup

Use for inset, half overlay, and overlay.

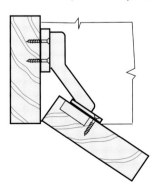

Fit cup into hole in door; mount baseplate inside case.

Pocket

Use for inset and half overlay.

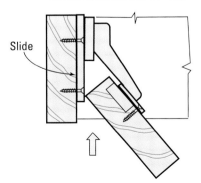

Slide

Fit cup into door; mount baseplate and slide inside case.

Prevent a jointer from tearing the end grain of a door stile by following the door with a back-up block.

For a uniform opening, support the doors in position and use a compass to scribe the desired gap onto the door.

Carefully plane the doors to the scribed marks, using a back-up block to prevent tearout on the end grain of the stile.

opening. To get the initial fit, joint all four edges of the door to remove about $\frac{1}{32}$ in. on all edges. Use a back-up block to guide narrow edges and to prevent tearout on the stiles.

With the case facing up on the bench, place the door into the case on shopmade hangers. Check the gap around the door; if it's not uniform, use a compass to scribe around the door by referencing against the case opening. If the hangers get in the way during scribing, use a straightedge at the bench to join your scribed marks.

Finish the fit by planing the edges of the door with a bench plane, shaving to your marks. A block clamped to the stile prevents tearout.

Commercial Hinges

With the door ready to receive hinges, you can venture into the vast world of commercial hinges. Using store-bought hinges has

DOOR HANGER

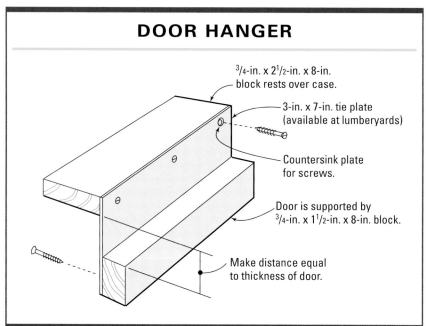

$\frac{3}{4}$-in. x $2\frac{1}{2}$-in. x 8-in. block rests over case.

3-in. x 7-in. tie plate (available at lumberyards)

Countersink plate for screws.

Door is supported by $\frac{3}{4}$-in. x $1\frac{1}{2}$-in. x 8-in. block.

Make distance equal to thickness of door.

▶ DETERMINING HINGE SETBACK

The rule of thumb for accurately locating butt hinges is to measure from the center point of the hinge barrel to the outside edge of one leaf; then subtract about $\frac{1}{16}$ in. and lay out the width of the mortise to this measurement. Laying out a hinge in this manner ensures that the door won't bind on the face of the cabinet when it's opened, yet keeps the barrel unobtrusive when the door is closed.

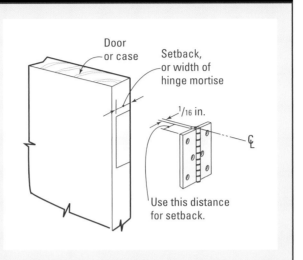

Door or case

Setback, or width of hinge mortise

$\frac{1}{16}$ in.

C̶L̶

Use this distance for setback.

many advantages over making your own. You'll save time (but be prepared to spend money) and you can select the right hardware from a wide assortment to complement the particular style of furniture you're making, including historical pieces. Lucky for us, there's a commercial hinge for practically every type of door we'll ever make.

Once you settled on a particular hinge, it pays to buy the best you can afford. Quality hinges have some distinct characteristics. Look for thick leaves—$\frac{1}{8}$ in. or so

is generous—that are flat and without twist, and accurately placed and crisply drilled and countersunk screw holes. Knuckle joints should be accurately machined and the joints tight, yet able to rotate freely. A good hinge should swing open smoothly without any play. Solid brass is preferable over plated varieties, and "bright brass" should be polished to a mirror shine. If you buy good hardware, it will be a pleasure to install and will truly complement the fine doors you build.

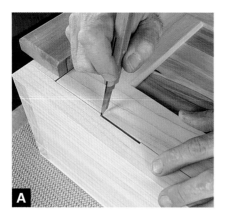

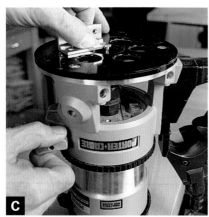

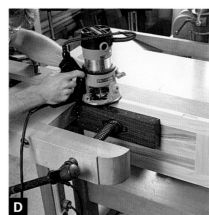

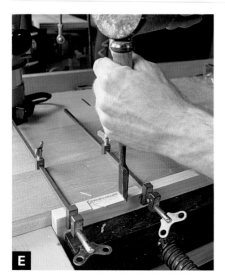

Butt Hinges

With a butt hinge, you'll need to mortise the leaves into both the door and the case. Whenever possible, lay out and cut the mortises in the case side before assembling the cabinet. Then fit the door and use a marking knife to transfer the mortise location to the door (**A**).

▶ See *"Three Types of Doors to Fit"* on p. 146.

Here's the process for accurately laying out and cutting the mortises for the leaves: First, determine the correct depth of the hinge into the door and the case. Next, lay out the length of each hinge by squaring lines across the work with a pencil and a square. Then use a marking gauge to mark the long-grain shoulder (**B**).

Install a ¼-in. straight bit in the router and adjust the bit height to the thickness of the hinge leaf. The simplest way to do this is to lay the leaf directly on the baseplate of the router (**C**). Make a test cut in scrap to check the depth before routing the real thing.

Rout freehand inside your layout lines, staying about ¹⁄₁₆ in. from the marks (**D**). Then clean up the shoulders by hand with a sharp chisel. Back up the delicate long-grain shoulder by clamping a block behind the door stile (**E**).

Install the hinges by placing each hinge into its respective mortise and using a self-centering drill bit to drill accurate pilot holes for screws. At this point, drill only one hole for each leaf (**F**). Hang the door on a single screw through each leaf and check the fit. If you need to make adjustments, back off the first set of screws, shift the door into position, and drill and install the second set of screws. Once the fit is perfect, install all the screws.

Surface-Mounted Hinges

One of the easiest hinges to install is the surface-mounted hinge. There are many varieties, including hinges for inset or half-overlay doors and hinges that close by themselves via springs concealed in the barrels. Usually, a surface-mounted hinge is used when a decorative effect is desired, such as the butterfly hinge shown here (**A**).

Fit and position the door into the case; then lay the hinges into position, making sure the centerline of the hinge barrels are centered between the door and the case. Drill pilot holes for screws with a self-centering drill bit. To facilitate driving the screws, wax the threads with a little paraffin or beeswax (**B**). Then install the screws and you're done.

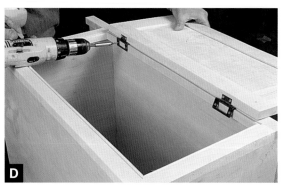

No-Mortise Hinges

A type of butt hinge, the no-mortise hinge is great for hanging doors quickly and without fuss, and it works with frame or frameless cabinets. The best part is that there's no mortise to cut in either the door or the case, which makes the job of hinging much easier.

To locate the holes for the screws, turn the hinge over and snug up the barrel against the face of the door stile; then drill pilot holes through the leaf and into the stile (**A**). Now turn the hinge over and install it right-side up on the door.

With the door fitted and positioned temporarily in the case opening, mark the location of the hinge onto the front of the case. Use the center sections of the hinge barrel to eyeball the marks (**B**).

Remove the door and use a spare hinge to drill pilot holes in the cabinet. You can accurately position the hinge without measuring by holding the barrel tight to the frame and aligning the center barrel sections to your marks on the case (**C**). Then replace the door with the hinge leaves open and drive the screws to attach the door to the cabinet (**D**).

Knife Hinges

Knife hinges are one of the most elegant and inconspicuous types of hinges; and installed correctly, their action is delightfully smooth (**A**). The best hinges have separate blades. You mortise the pin blade into the case; the pinless blade is mortised into the door. There are two types of knife hinges: straight hinges for overlay doors and offset hinges for inset doors (**B**). Make sure you buy right-hand offset hinges for doors hinged on the right side of the case and left-hand offset hinges for the opposite side.

Cut the hinge mortises in the case before assembly and fit the door to the case before cutting the door mortises. Correct layout of the mortises is crucial for a good fit. Mark the outlines of each hinge with a sharp pencil or knife; then rout freehand to the exact thickness of the blade, staying within the marked lines. Use a ¼-in. straight bit and clamp a scrap block level with the door to prevent the router from tipping (**C**).

Pare the case mortises to the exact size of the hinge, but leave the door mortises a hair short for now (**D**).

Install the pin blades into the case, press the door blades onto the pin blades, and slide the door between the blades. Install a single screw in each door blade and check the fit of the door. Make adjustments by lengthening one or both door mortises with a chisel. When the door hangs evenly, drive in the final screws (**E**).

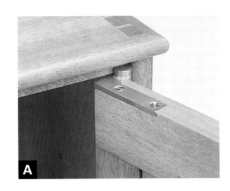

A

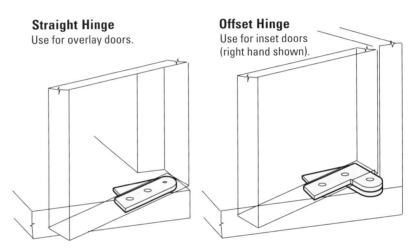

Straight Hinge
Use for overlay doors.

Offset Hinge
Use for inset doors
(right hand shown).

Hinge Layout

Lay out the pin leaf on the cabinet's top and bottom, flush to the sides of the case. For clearance, lay out the pinless blade on the door so it overhangs the door's edge by ¹/₃₂ in.

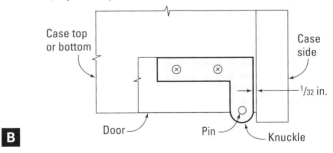

Case top
or bottom

Case
side

¹/₃₂ in.

Door

Pin

Knuckle

B

C

D

E

Overlay

Half Overlay

Inset

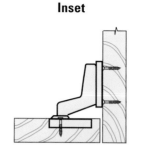

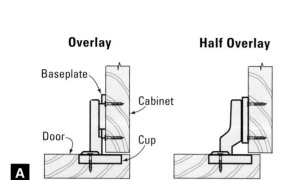

Baseplate

Cabinet

Door

Cup

A

B

C

D

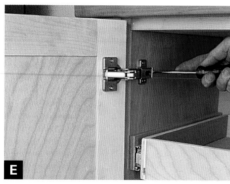

E

Euro-Style Hinges

Cup hinges, also called Euro hinges, are part of the gear used in the 32mm cabinetry system in Europe. They're appropriate for doors that get everyday use, like kitchen cabinets. Each hinge consists of a cup, which is mortised and screwed into the back of the door, and a base-plate, which screws into the case side. Once the door is hung, you can adjust the door up and down, in and out, and side to side.

There are three styles of cup hinges: overlay, half overlay, and inset. All the hinges are available in different degrees of opening (**A**).

Installation is easy. Mark a centerline on the door stile for the height of each hinge. Refer to the manufacturer's directions for the correct setback, or distance from the edge of the door to the center of the hinge mortise, and set up a fence on the drill press to establish that distance. Use a 35mm hinge-boring bit to drill the holes for the cup (a 1⅜-in. Forstner bit works in a pinch). Set the depth stop on your drill press accordingly to drill the correct depth (**B**).

Install the hinges into the door by drilling pilot holes for the screws. For accuracy, use a square to align the hinge to the edge of the door; then drill the holes (**C**).

Measure the height and center-to-center distances of the installed hinges on the door and transfer these measurements to the case to locate the baseplates. Install the baseplates on the cabinet with screws (**D**). Then slide the hinges over the baseplates and secure the door (**E**).

[**TIP**] **When you have a number of doors to install, it helps to transfer the correct layout dimensions to a piece of ¼-in. plywood and use that to mark the hinge locations. That way, all the hinge locations are uniform and layout is quick.**

Barrel Hinges

Barrel hinges are great when you want an invisible hinge connection. They mortise into the inner edges of both the door and the case, so they disappear when the door is closed. These hinges are especially useful for hinging bifold doors, because their 180-degree opening allows for the full swing of both doors, giving you better access inside a cabinet.

To install barrel hinges on bifold doors, clamp the doors face to face with the ends of the doors aligned and mark across the doors with a square to locate the hinges. Then drill a ⁹⁄₁₆-in.-diameter hole for each barrel of the hinge. Masking tape acts as a flag to gauge the correct depth (**A**). Because of the expanding nature of the barrel, it's fine if each hole is a little oversize. You'll take up any slack when you install the hinge.

Install a pair of hinges in one door by pushing the barrels into the door holes; then turn the small screw in each barrel to expand the hinge and tighten it against the walls of the hole (**B**). For heavy doors, you can drive a screw through the machined recess on the side of the barrel to further wedge the hinge. Then join both doors by installing and tightening the barrels in the adjoining door (**C**).

Once you've installed the hinges, hang the doors by hinging one door in the conventional manner.

Continuous Hinges

A continuous hinge, or piano hinge, is one of the strongest pieces of gear you can use to connect a door to a frame, making it well suited for heavy doors. For relatively small piano hinges, you can surface mount the leaves directly to the door edge and the case frame. But bigger hinges—those with ⅝-in.-wide leaves or larger—require setting into the door to avoid ending up with an unsightly gap between the case and the door.

Instead of cutting a mortise, you cut a rabbet in the door. To determine the correct rabbet depth, position the hinge in the closed position with the leaves parallel to each other and measure the thickness of one leaf plus the barrel. Then cut the rabbet to that depth (**A**). You can mill the rabbet on the table saw or with a router and straight bit.

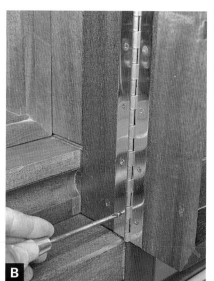

Drill pilot holes for the screws and mount the hinge on the door frame by securing one leaf in the rabbet. Hang the door by surface mounting the opposite leaf onto the case (**B**).

Knuckle Hinges

The surface-mounted knuckle hinge is a nice touch on small cabinet doors or box lids and allows the door or panel to open slightly past 90 degrees. To keep the hinge strong, choose a hard, dense wood, such as rosewood, hard maple, or wenge, as shown here. The hinge uses a brass rod for the pin.

To make a pair of hinges, lay out the knuckles on two pieces so that the grain runs parallel with the tongues. Then cut the tongues and notches in the stock with a dado blade on the table saw. For the hinges to work correctly, it's important that you set the height of the blade equal to the thickness of the stock. For safety, attach a tall auxiliary fence to the miter gauge to guide the workpiece. Cut the notches first; then cut the tongues so they fit tightly into the notches (**A**). After cutting the knuckles, rip the stock to width.

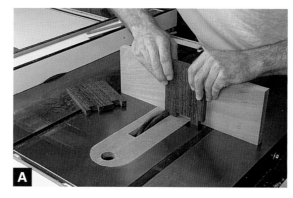

Now fit each hinge together and drill a hole through the exact center of the knuckle for an ⅛-in.-diameter brass rod. Clamp the stock securely so it won't wander as you drill (**B**).

To provide clearance for the leaves to pivot, round over the tongues on both sides with a block plane and rasp (**C**). Smooth the curves with some careful sanding.

Assemble the hinge by tapping the rod through the joint (**D**). Then crosscut the leaves to the finish length and drill holes for mounting screws. Install the wooden hinge as you would an ordinary surface-mounted hinge.

▶ See *"Surface-Mounted Hinges"* on p. 151.

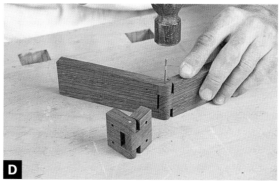

A

B

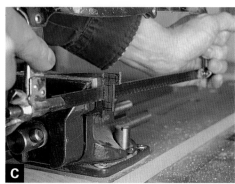
C

D

E

F

Brass Knife Hinges

Cabinetmaker Yeung Chan likes to make his own brass knife hinges, like the offset hinge shown here in his Ming's Cabinet (**A**). The process is satisfying, and it's straightforward without requiring any specialized metal-working tools.

To make an offset hinge, start with a template for accuracy. Using stiff paper or card stock, lay out the contours of the hinge and mark centerlines for the screw holes. A draftsman's circle template is handy for generating the rounded ends of the blades (**B**).

Use the paper template to transfer the outline of the hinge onto ⅛-in.-thick brass stock. Then cut as close as possible to your layout lines with a hacksaw. Don't try to cut the rounded ends at this point (**C**).

Drill for and install an ⅛-in.-diameter brass pin through both blades. The pin can be longer than necessary for now. The fit should be tight, yet allow the blades to pivot around the pin. With the pin and blades together, drill and countersink the screw holes on the drill press (**D**).

Keeping the blades together, use a mill file to shape the rounded ends and refine the edges (**E**).

Slip a brass washer between the blades and saw and file the pin flush to the surface of the hinge. Then take apart the hinge, sand the surfaces up to 320-grit to smooth and polish the brass, and your hinge is ready for installation (**F**).

> ⚠ **WARNING Freshly cut brass edges are very sharp. Handle carefully and dull the edges with a file as soon as possible.**

Wood Knife Hinges

This straight knife hinge (**A**), made from walnut by woodworker and designer Ellis Walentine, works on overlay doors when there are frame members above and below, as shown in his CD cabinet (**B**).

There are four uncomplicated parts to each hinge: a wood hinge blade, into which you glue an ⅛-in.-diameter brass post and a washer, and a screw, which secures the blade to the case (**C**).

To install a pair of hinges, rout mortises in the top and bottom of the case to accommodate the blades. The blades should fit flush in the mortises. Then drill ⅛-in.-diameter holes in the top and bottom of the door for the posts. Slip the posts with their blades into the holes and slide the blades into the mortises in the case (**D**). Position the door where you want it, making any adjustments by sliding the blades left or right. When the door hangs evenly, open it gently and drive screws through the blades and into the case to secure the door.

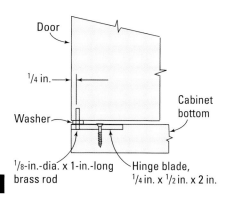

Door

¼ in.

Washer

Cabinet bottom

⅛-in.-dia. x 1-in.-long brass rod

Hinge blade, ¼ in. x ½ in. x 2 in.

A

B

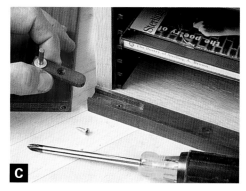

C

D

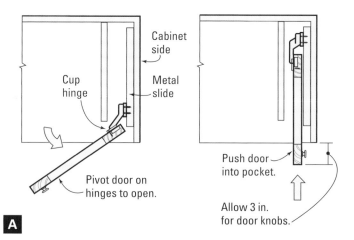

Cabinet side

Cup hinge

Metal slide

Pivot door on hinges to open.

Push door into pocket.

Allow 3 in. for door knobs.

A

Pocket-Door Hardware

Pocket and flipper doors are perfect for those times when you want the doors in a cabinet to stay open without intruding into the room, such as on an entertainment center that houses a TV. The hardware for pocket doors also works for lift-up or flipper doors, which open upward, perhaps for a stereo cabinet. In both applications, the door is hinged on cup-style hinges and opens like an ordinary door. But with a pocket door, like this one built by cabinetmaker Hector Rodriguez, you can slide the door straight back into the cabinet to get it out of the way (**A**).

Buy the hardware before you construct the cabinet; then size the case and doors so you leave enough depth in the case for the doors to retract. The best strategy is to plan on leaving 2 in. to 3 in. of the door protruding from the case so door knobs remain accessible. Once the doors are built, install the hinges as you would ordinary cup hinges (**B**).

Attach the pocket-door mechanism into the case by referring to the manufacturer's instructions. The mechanism consists of upper and lower metal slides, with either a metal or wood follower or a tension wire that attaches between the slides. The follower prevents the door from racking as it's pulled or pushed into the case. Once the case hardware is in place, slide the door and its hinges onto the hinge baseplates that come secured to the slides (**C**).

To make the "pocket" for each door, install wire supports in the case and mount a vertical divider on the wires. The wire supports allow you to remove the divider and get at the hardware should it ever need adjustment.

The door should slide smoothly into the cabinet between the divider and the case (**D**). To close the door, pull it straight out of its pocket and pivot the door on its hinges (**E**).

B

C

D

E

Door Pulls
and Hardware

Pulls and Handles

➤ Pocket Pulls (p. 165)

➤ Shopmade Applied
  Handles (p. 166)

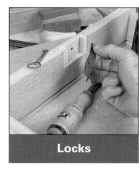

Locks

➤ Cylinder Locks
  (p. 167)

➤ Mortised Locks
  (p. 168)

➤ Escutcheons
  (p. 169)

➤ Door Bolts (p. 170)

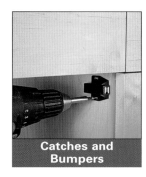

**Catches and
Bumpers**

➤ Bullet Catches
  (p. 171)

➤ Double-Ball Catches
  (p. 171)

➤ Touch Latches
  (p. 172)

➤ Adjustable Magnet
  Catches (p. 173)

➤ Hidden Magnets
  (p. 174)

➤ Stops and Bumpers
  (p. 175)

ONCE YOUR DOOR IS SWINGING on well-oiled hinges, you'll need to add pulls and latches to complete the job. Like hinges, there's a pull for every need. Luckily, commercial pulls are easy to install. Your biggest concern is choosing a pull that complements the style of the door and cabinet you've made. Or you can set your own design standards and construct your pulls from wood or other materials.

Although hinges and pulls will allow you to swing a door closed, chances are the door won't stay there. You can build ledges into your cabinets so the door has something to stop against; but to keep it in the closed position, you'll need some form of catch hardware. If security is a concern, the catch can come in the form of a lock with a supplied key to open it or it can be a simple latch that grips the door.

Commercial Pulls

Like pulls and handles for drawers, commercial door pulls are available for practically every application and style of cabinet.

➤ See *"Drawer Hardware"* on p. 119.

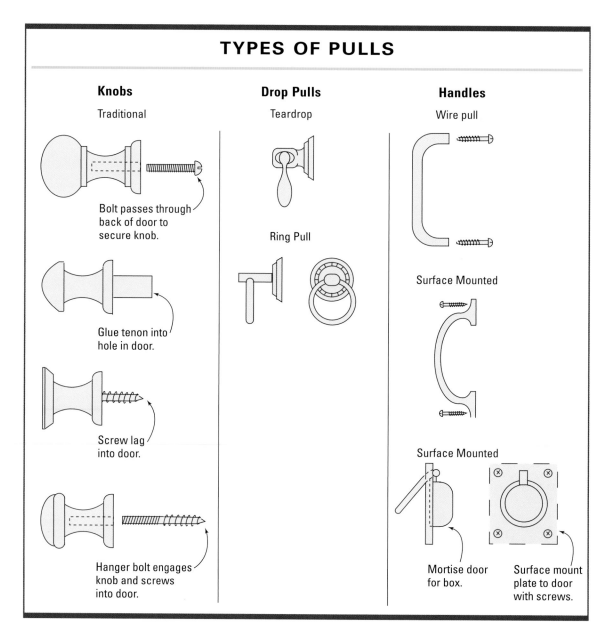

TYPES OF PULLS

Knobs	Drop Pulls	Handles
Traditional	Teardrop	Wire pull

Bolt passes through back of door to secure knob.

Ring Pull

Glue tenon into hole in door.

Surface Mounted

Screw lag into door.

Surface Mounted

Hanger bolt engages knob and screws into door.

Mortise door for box.

Surface mount plate to door with screws.

The drawing above shows some of the more typical varieties on the market and the various methods for attaching them. If you shop around, you can even find some that are far from ordinary, such as pulls made from natural materials like stone and one-of-a-kind pulls made by jewelers and metal artisans. Expect to pay extra for more elaborate, fanciful pulls and handles.

It's wise to buy all your pulls for a project at the same time, for consistency's sake, and before building your furniture. If one of the pulls doesn't match or a tapped hole or mounting bolt is faulty, now is the time to return it for a new one. Once you've inspected your hardware, store it in a cool, dry place such as a drawer until you need it.

Handmade Pulls

If you'd prefer to make your own wood pulls or handles, you'll take a satisfying detour that will reflect your craftsmanship where store-bought hardware can't. There's nothing quite like the look and feel of a unique, hand-crafted pull. And the design possibilities are endless. Like other homemade hardware such as hinges, save your best stock for your pulls. Hard and dense woods, such as ebony, rosewood, and many of the tropical timbers, are perfect for pulls because they have the necessary strength to hold up to use and abuse when fashioned as relatively small parts.

Catches, Latches, Stops, and Bumpers

Keeping a door closed can be a challenge if you haven't installed locks or self-closing hinges. In a perfect world, a perfectly hung door would just stay put when closed. But prying hands, drafts of air, or—more likely—the vagaries of furniture making all contribute to allowing a door to creep open, especially when you're not looking. Fortunately, there are many ways to secure a wayward door, from commercial catches to shopmade devices. Your choice depends on your taste and the style of the project.

Locks

For most of the doors we make, we needn't bother with locks. A simple catch will suffice to keep the door closed. Of course, certain period pieces of furniture had mortise locks, and we can use these types of locks to duplicate faithfully our forebears' work. But when security is a premium or when you want to keep a door out of bounds for children and general safe-keeping, choosing the right lock is important.

Locks for doors and drawers consist of two main parts: the lock itself, usually housed in a metal box or a cylinder that you install in the door, and a mortise or a strike plate, which becomes part of the cabinet. The lock engages the strike plate via a pin or bolt to lock the door in place. Generally, it's best to install the lock after assembling the door but before hanging it in the case. Once the door is on its hinges, you can easily locate and install the strike plate, or cut a small mortise in the case, by using the door lock as a reference.

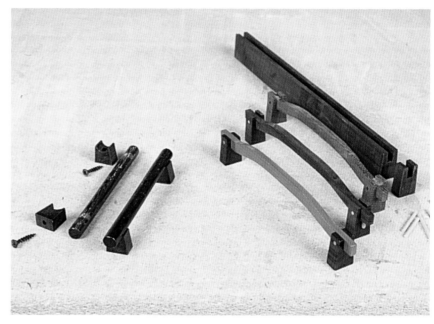

The pulls shown here, made by furniture maker Edward Schoen, connect to a door via posts screwed from the back of the door. The rod is either pinned to the posts (right) or the screws pierce the post and grasp the back of the rod (left).

► PIVOTING PULL

Woodworker Ellis Walentine devised this beautiful and ingenious pull. It works particularly well on large cabinet doors or on passage doors. Most of the parts are turned on the lathe, and assembly consists of drilling a series of holes and attaching the pull with two carriage bolts.

When at rest, the handle remains vertical and the strike protrudes from the edge of the door, locking it into the strike plate or mortise cut in the case.

When you pivot the handle to the side, the strike pulls out of the mortise and retracts into the door stile, releasing the door.

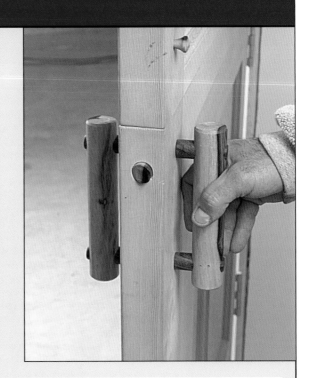

PIVOT PULL PARTS

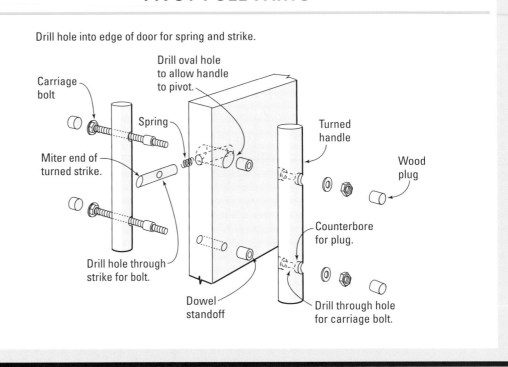

Drill hole into edge of door for spring and strike.

Drill oval hole to allow handle to pivot.

Carriage bolt

Spring

Turned handle

Wood plug

Miter end of turned strike.

Counterbore for plug.

Drill hole through strike for bolt.

Dowel standoff

Drill through hole for carriage bolt.

Pocket Pulls

The pull shown here lends an air of clean sophistication and works particularly well where you want flush surfaces without visible hardware (**A**). The design works with door stock ⅞ in. or thicker. You can create the pull after assembling the door if you wish, but I find it easier to make the cuts before assembly.

Start by drilling a half hole with a 1½-in. Forstner bit into a scrap fence clamped to the drill press table. Center the bit about 1/16 in. in from the edge of the fence. Lay out the location of the pull on your stile stock; then align the stock to the hole in the fence and clamp the stile firmly to the table. Drill to a depth that leaves about 3/16 in. of wood on the back side of the stile (**B**).

With a ½-in. mortising bit in a plunge router, rout a 1¼-in.-deep mortise into the pocket to create an undercut for fingers to grasp. To make the cut safely and accurately, clamp a block to the bench to support the router and use an edge guide to steer the router (**C**).

The finished pull can be used alone or in pairs where stile meets stile (**D**).

This pull works with stock ⅞ in. or thicker.

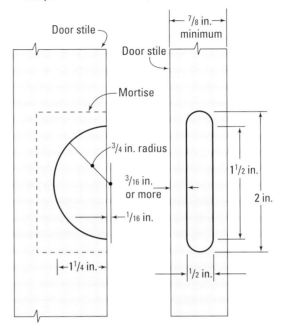

Door stile

Door stile

⅞ in. minimum

Mortise

¾ in. radius

3/16 in. or more

1/16 in.

1¼ in.

1½ in.

2 in.

½ in.

A

B

C

D

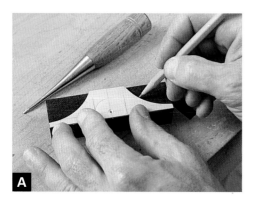

Shopmade Applied Handles

The handle shown here is made by cutting curves in two planes, which makes for interesting lines. Lay out the shape of the pull using two templates made from thin plywood. The first template outlines the side of the pull onto the blank and lets you mark a center point for a half hole (**A**). Use the second template to trace the contours of the top of the handle (**B**).

At the drill press, use a Forstner bit to cut the half hole through the blank by aligning the spur of the bit with your mark. An L-shaped fence prevents the work from spinning away from the bit as you drill (**C**).

Make two bandsaw cuts: The first cut follows the top of the blank, slicing off each side (**D**). Tape the marked side back onto the blank, turn the blank 90 degrees, and make the second cut by following the marks on the side of the blank (**E**). Remove the saw marks and refine the shape by hand or with a light touch at the spindle sander (**F**).

Spread some glue on the underside of the pull and use small screws to attach the pull to the face of the door (**G**).

Cylinder Locks

Perfect for utility drawers or doors—or wherever you need a sturdy, simple-to-install lock—the cylinder, or cam, lock can be mounted by drilling a single hole through the workpiece (**A**). A cam lever engages the back of the cabinet's frame or a wooden block attached inside the cabinet.

It's easier if you drill and install the lock before hanging the door. Choose a lock matched to the thickness of your work and use the supplied template to lay out the hole location (**B**). Then drill a ¾-in.-diameter hole through the face of the door (**C**).

Install the decorative ring and the cylinder through the front of the door; then add the cam lever and the parts that secure the lock from behind (**D**).

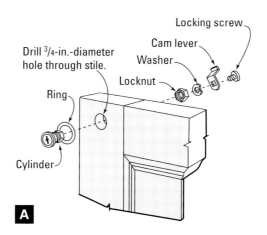

Drill ¾-in.-diameter hole through stile. Locking screw. Cam lever. Washer. Locknut. Ring. Cylinder.

A

B

C

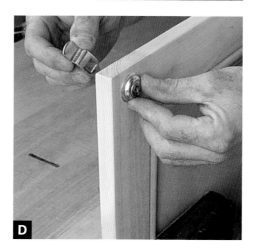

D

With its sliding bolt, this half-mortise lock will secure flush-mounted drawers or doors.

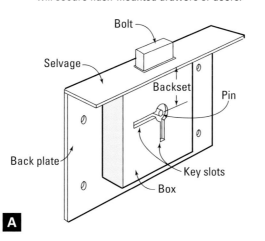

A

Mortised Locks

Half-mortise locks, so named because they require only a pocket or half mortise for fitting, work equally well on doors or drawers (**A**). Once fitted, the lock is discreet, since all you see is a key hole or escutcheon. Half-mortise locks come in a variety of styles. In all cases, though, installation of the lock body is the same.

The lock shown here is used for flush-mounted drawers and doors; a key turns a bolt into a mortise that you cut in the case. If you use this lock on a door, be sure to specify whether the lock is for a left-hand or right-hand door. Start by laying out the keyhole location on the front of the door or drawer. Measure the backset on the lock and transfer this measurement onto the work. Drill a hole through the workpiece the same size as the hole in the lock. *Note:* If you're going to install an inset escutcheon, do it now before installing the lock.

A half-mortise lock requires three mortises. Cut the first mortise by positioning the lock on the back of the workpiece and scribing around the box. Use a router and a small straight bit to remove the waste inside your scribed lines; then finish up by chiseling the shoulders to the layout lines (**B**).

B

C

Turning the lock around, hold it with the back plate against the work and the selvage flush with the top edge; then scribe and cut the second mortise for the back plate. Next, transfer the selvage measurements to the edge of the work and chisel the third mortise. The lock should fit securely in all three mortises (**C**).

D

Finish up by laying out the wedged-shaped, lower half of the keyhole on the face of the work and saw out the opening with a coping saw (**D**). Install the lock with screws driven into the back side of the door or drawer.

Escutcheons

An inset escutcheon protects the keyhole-shaped opening for a lock, and it dresses up an otherwise plain door front or drawer. It's important that you install the escutcheon before fitting a lock mortise. The first step is to drill a hole to accept the escutcheon's circular head. Use a brad-point bit or a Forstner bit for this operation, drilling to the same depth as the escutcheon (**A**). Then drill a second, smaller hole through the first hole for the key, sized to the lock you'll install.

Next, place the escutcheon onto the workpiece. If your escutcheon is tapered, place the smaller side down. Insert a dowel the same size as the keyhole through the hole and through the escutcheon to aid in positioning the escutcheon. Then scribe around the lower half of the escutcheon (**B**).

At this point, you'll need to cut out the rest of the keyhole with a coping saw.

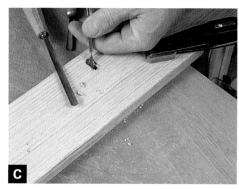

Then use chisels and small gouges of the appropriate sweep to cut a recess into the workpiece, chiseling up to your scribed lines. Chisel to the same depth as the large hole (**C**).

To install the escutcheon, mix some sanding dust with epoxy, line the recess with the mix, and tap the escutcheon into the recess (**D**). If you're installing an escutcheon that's been colored or coated with a finish, gently tap the escutcheon until it sits flush with the surface and wipe off any glue residue. For new, bright-brass escutcheons, level the surface with a file once the adhesive has cured; then smooth the metal and the wood with successively finer grits of sandpaper wrapped around a felt block (**E**).

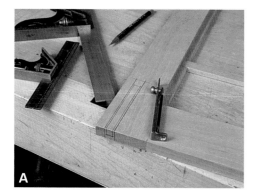

A

B

C

D

E

Door Bolts

When two doors meet, you can lock them together with a mortise lock but you'll need to provide a catch on one of the doors so both doors stay secure.

▶ See *"Mortised Locks"* on p. 168.

A door bolt fits the bill and works with inset doors. Installed on the back of one door, the bolt holds that door and prevents the adjoining door from being opened until the mortise lock is released. I like to install the bolt on the left door, so the door on the right becomes the primary, or "keyed," door. The catch works best if installed at the top of the door, with a corresponding hole in the top frame for the sliding bolt. This way, the hole for the bolt won't accumulate debris.

The key to successful installation is to accurately lay out for the three mortises that are needed to fit the catch. Draw the outline of the catch on the back and edge of the door; then draw the inner mortise for the bolt mechanism (**A**). Rout the inner, deep mortise freehand, staying inside your layout lines. It doesn't matter if the walls of the mortise are rough. The aim is simply to provide free space for the sliding bolt to operate (**B**).

Next, rout the two shallow mortises, one on the back of the stile and one on the top edge. Stay inside your layout lines and use a chisel to pare up to the walls of the mortise (**C**). The mortise depth should equal the thickness of the catch's plate (**D**).

Install the catch into the mortises and secure it with two screws: one at the top and one at the lower part of the catch (**E**). Hang the door; then transfer the bolt location to the case frame by tapping the bolt into the frame, which will leave a telltale mark. Finally, drill a hole on your mark for the bolt.

Bullet Catches

Hidden at the bottom or top of a door, the small bullet catch works on inset doors, where there's a frame above or below the door. The catch consists of two parts: a bullet-shaped cylinder, which contains a small, spring-loaded ball, and a strike plate, into which the ball catches. Tension from the ball holds the door in position when it's closed.

Install the bullet in a stepped hole in the bottom of the door. First, drill a shallow ⁵⁄₁₆-in.-diameter hole for the flange; then drill a deeper ¼-in.-diameter hole for the cylinder. Tap the bullet into the hole, adding a drop of cyanoacrylate adhesive (one brand is Super Glue) to secure it (**A**). The flange should be flush with the surface of the door.

Hang the door and mark the cabinet for the strike plate by transferring the center point of the bullet. Install the strike with small pins onto the surface of the frame (**B**).

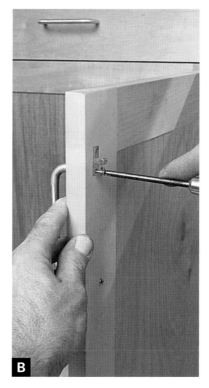

Double-Ball Catches

A double-ball catch is easy to install and allows for adjustment after the door is hung. Secure the ball part of the catch to the case, either on the side, top, or bottom. If necessary, you can shim the catch into the correct position relative to the door by mounting it onto a block screwed to the case. This is a good technique to use whenever off-the-shelf hardware doesn't fit into what you've built (**A**).

Transfer the center measurement of the catch in the case to the back of the door and install the finger, or strike, onto the door (**B**). Check the fit. If the catch grabs the door too tightly or too loosely, you can adjust the tension of the balls by turning small screws located on the top and bottom of the catch (**C**).

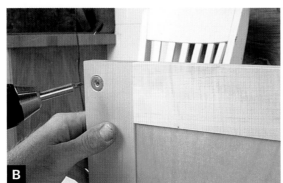

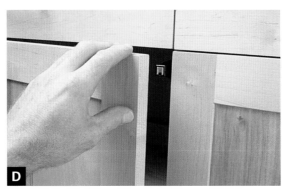

Touch Latches

When you want the sleek lines of a door without hardware—including no handles or pulls—a touch latch is the answer. There are two parts to the latch, a magnetized push-arm mechanism and a steel contact washer. First screw the arm mechanism inside the cabinet, either on the top or on the case side. When locating the mechanism, be sure to allow clearance for the arm to move inward about ⅛ in. without the door contacting the face of the cabinet. Position the screws in the elongated holes first, so you can adjust the final fit of the hardware before installing the remaining screws (**A**).

Once the push arm is in place, measure its exact center and transfer this measurement to the back of the door; next, install the metal washer on the door. I like to drill a shallow mortise for the plate with a Forstner bit to give the hardware a neater appearance (**B**). The magnet in the cabinet contacts the washer and pulls on it, keeping the door closed.

To open the door, simply push inward about ⅛ in. (**C**). The push-arm springs forward and pushes the door out of the cabinet about ½ in., allowing you to grasp the edge of the door with your fingers (**D**).

Adjustable Magnet Catches

One of my favorite catches is the inexpensive plastic catch that houses an adjustable magnet. Although the style may not suit the finest of cabinets, its greatest attribute is the ability to adjust the magnet into or away from the face of the case by simply turning the magnet with a wide, flat screwdriver. This arrangement lets you fine-tune the fit of the door to the case after it's hung—a great benefit.

To install the catch on paired doors in a frame-style cabinet, glue a spacer block underneath the top of the case and drill a ⅜-in.-diameter hole into it for the stub tenon on each catch (**A**). Install the catch by squeezing the ribbed tenon into the hole with a clamp (**B**).

Drill a small hole in the back of the door for the metal pin and disk that attracts the magnet and, as you did for the catch, install the disk with a clamp (**C**).

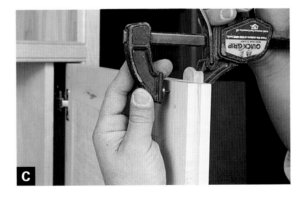

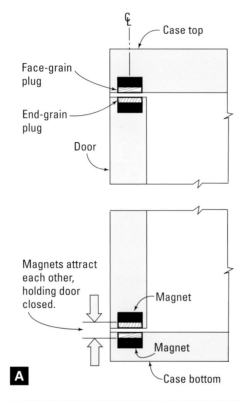

Hidden Magnets

A diabolical way to keep a door closed relies on the attraction of magnets. Magnets installed in the top and bottom of the door attract similar pairs fitted into the cabinet (**A**). By gluing the magnets in holes and covering them with wood plugs, no one will be the wiser.

Use strong, rare-earth magnets for the most pull. The size of the magnets depends on the size and weight of the door. And if you need more magnetic pull, you can increase a magnet's power by adding special thick washers below the magnet.

It's best to drill the holes for the magnets in the case before assembling the cabinet. For a ½-in.-diameter magnet, use a ½-in. Forstner bit on the drill press and drill the hole about ⁵⁄₁₆-in. deep. Then—and this is very important—make sure you set aside pairs of magnets and mark them to designate their "attractive" sides. Place a drop of epoxy or cyanoacrylate glue into the hole and press the marked magnet correct side up in the hole (**B**).

On the drill press using a plug cutter, cut plugs to conceal the magnets. For the grain to match, cut face-grain plugs for the face-grain holes in the case and cut end-grain plugs for the top and bottom of the door (**C**).

Line each hole with glue and install the plug over the magnet, being careful to line up the grain of the plug with the case or door (**D**). When the glue has dried, saw or pare the plug flush, and the hole will virtually disappear. When you close the door, it will gently pull itself into the case.

Stops and Bumpers

Keeping a door closed is the role of the door catch; having the door close quietly without clattering is the job of the bumper. And in cases when there's no door ledge, you'll need to install a stop that halts the door flush with the case.

Attached to the back of the door or to the inside of the cabinet frame, a bumper can be made from any soft yet resilient material to cushion the blow from the wood-to-wood contact when a door is closed. Commercial rubber bumpers come in all shapes and sizes, the most convenient being those with self-stick adhesive on the back. Just press the bumper to the back of the door, in line with the frame of the cabinet (**A**).

When you need a door stop, one option is to use a wood strip faced with leather to cushion the door, similar to how you could stop a drawer.

On cases with face frames, a simple solution is to glue a wood strip to the back of the frame (**B**).

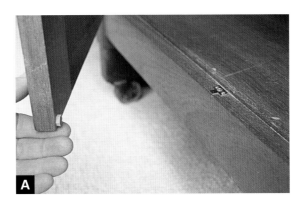

A

B

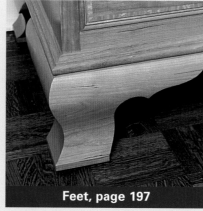

PART FOUR

Bases, Feet, and Stands

T HE BASIC BOX—whether it's a floor-standing case piece, a tabletop cabinet, or small jewelry box—needs a lift now and then. Bases, feet, and stands accomplish that job with aplomb. Even the smallest keepsake box can benefit from the addition of feet or blocks to raise it above the surface it sits on. Or you can wrap the bottom of a cabinet with molding to anchor it visually. In practical terms, a base that's raised on four points of contact is inherently more stable than the underside of a wide, flat box. With large cabinets, it's important to allow room for someone's feet as they access the case so they don't kick the face of the cabinet.

In addition to the visual benefits of bases and feet, a cabinet or piece of furniture should sit solidly on the floor. Tables that tip or rock are usually the result of an irregular floor surface. Although we can't expect our floors to be perfectly level and flat, we can take measures to ensure that the furniture that sits on them stays level.

Bases

Toekicks

Installing Cabinets

BASES ON CABINETS come in two essential forms. The first shape is a recess built in below the case, known as a toekick. It's a practical approach that provides room for your feet, so you can better access the case's contents when you're standing in front of the cabinet. The second variety, a molded base that usually projects beyond the case, is used for more aesthetic reasons. Here, the bottom of the case is defined by moldings or reveals (small gaps or lines) that are attached around the cabinet. The effect visually lifts the case while appearing to anchor the lower section to the floor. The design possibilities for molded bases are endless, whereas the parameters for a kick space are more narrowly defined because of its functional aspect.

Preventing Sag in Cabinets

Bases can also help support long spans or wide cabinets. If you build a box or case with four sides, but no back, you're likely to end up with a cabinet with a serious sagging problem. The case bottom and possibly the top will droop downward over time, especially when you load the cabinet with cargo. Unless you make the top and bottom ridiculously thick, you'll need to secure a back to the case sides, top, and bottom to stiffen the case and prevent sag.

Sometimes, the back itself isn't enough to keep things rigid, especially at the front of the case. This is particularly true on deep or wide pieces, when the case spans 24 in. or more, or when the case must support a heavy top, such as a slab of marble. Often, the quickest remedy is to add a 2-in. or wider rail underneath the case bottom, near the front of the cabinet as shown at right. For cases that have to support very heavy tops, a torsion-box construction solves the drooping dilemma.

▶ See *"Torsion-Box Shelf"* on p. 73.

If your design permits, you can let the back extend to the floor in the center of the cabinet to gain more support or you can secure an L-shaped foot underneath the bottom. To make an L-shaped foot, use plywood for strength and make the foot from two parts. Cut the vertical foot piece to the exact height that the case bottom sits above the floor; then add a 3-in.-wide nailing cleat to the foot. Join the two pieces together with glue and staples, or use screws. Make sure to attach the foot to the cleat—not the other way around—for strength.

Mark the bottom to align the foot with adjacent cleats; then glue and staple the cleat to the underside of the cabinet. You can finish off the base and conceal the foot by adding baseboard around the case or by attaching a kick plate over the foot.

▶ See *"Applied Base with Toekick"* on p. 187.

Traditional Baseboard

A mitered baseboard works well for large case pieces. Keep an eye out for the proportions of the baseboard in relation to the case. In general, as the case gets taller, the baseboard should be wider. This approach will

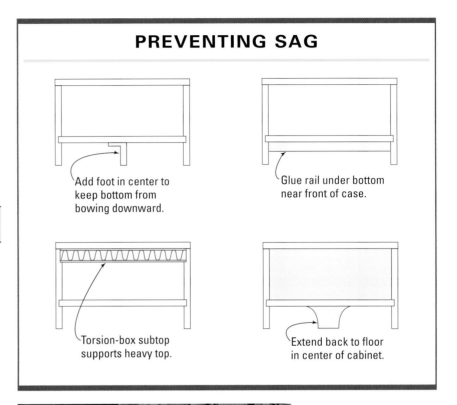

PREVENTING SAG

Add foot in center to keep bottom from bowing downward.

Glue rail under bottom near front of case.

Torsion-box subtop supports heavy top.

Extend back to floor in center of cabinet.

A simple L-shaped foot can be used for extra support under a base cabinet.

Staples and glue secure the foot to the underside of the cabinet.

A mitered base-board is the simplest way to finish off the bottom of large case pieces.

give the case the correct visual weight. A mitered baseboard has the visual effect of grounding the case, but it can also artfully conceal the construction of the bottom of the case from view.

Contemporary Baseboard

The baseboard on the maple cabinet shown below was designed by woodworker Paul Anthony; it's sleek, contemporary looking, and unobtrusive. A small gap or reveal between the case and the base gives the baseboard its distinction. To accentuate the reveal, Anthony inlaid a strip of contrasting purpleheart in the gap.

BASEBOARD ANATOMY

Two-Piece Baseboard

Case side

Molding

Bottom

Flat board

Glue and nail cleat under bottom to provide nailing surface for flat board.

One-Piece Baseboard

Flat board with molding edge

Top of baseboard falls below top edge of bottom to provide reveal on face of cabinet.

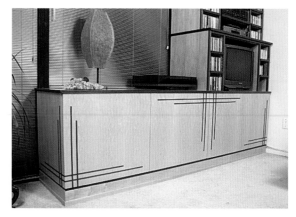

This sleek maple and purpleheart case is defined by flush doors and a flush base-board. (Photo by Paul Anthony.)

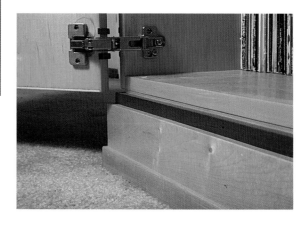

A subtle reveal and a purple-heart accent help give this base-board a distinctive look. (Photo by Paul Anthony.)

The construction is based on an applied base; but instead of standing proud of the cabinet, the base is set back by the thickness of a solid-wood baseboard. With this arrangement, the baseboard is flush with the cabinet on the two exposed sides.

► See *"Applied Base with Toekick"* on p. 187.

Molded-and-Stepped Base

For small or large case pieces, a stepped base adds visual weight to bottom of the cabinet. The flat, rectangular area at the bottom can be thick or thin, depending on how much visual mass you want to create. Mitered

molding above the flat step forms the transition from step to case.

Instead of creating a solid base, make the stepped area at the bottom by mitering a rectangular strip underneath the cabinet. Screw the strip to the underside of the cabinet and plug the screw holes if you wish. A strip of the same thickness at the rear keeps the case level and provides a solid platform

A built-up base provides a classic touch to a small cabinet.

BASEBOARD WITH REVEAL

Cabinet

Applied plywood base

Miter corners.

Glue contrasting strip to baseboard.

Solid-wood baseboard

Reveal

Applied base

Position applied base behind cabinet face by thickness of baseboard.

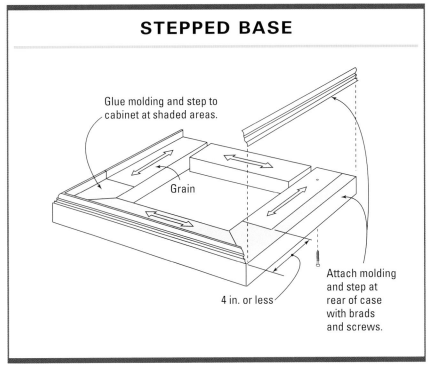

STEPPED BASE

Glue molding and step to cabinet at shaded areas.

Grain

4 in. or less

Attach molding and step at rear of case with brads and screws.

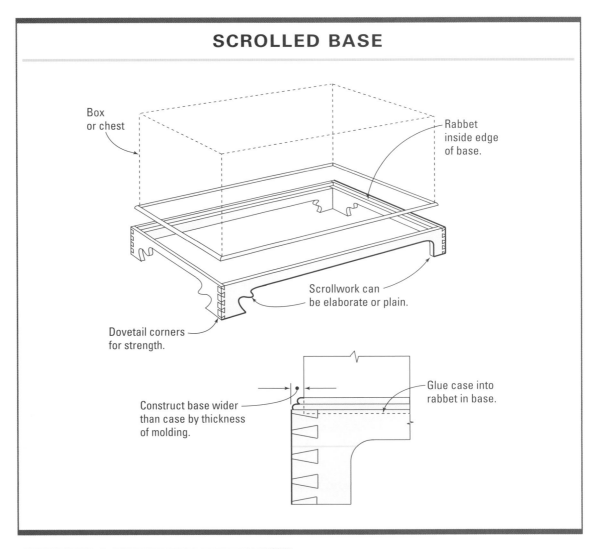

SCROLLED BASE

Box
or chest

Rabbet
inside edge
of base.

Scrollwork can
be elaborate or plain.

Dovetail corners
for strength.

Glue case into
rabbet in base.

Construct base wider
than case by thickness
of molding.

A scrolled base
can be as simple
as a small radius in
each corner.

on which the case stands. Be careful when attaching the molding and the step: If you glue them fully across the case side, the glue will restrict wood movement, and the cabinet sides will likely split or crack. The bottom right drawing on p. 181 shows the areas that are safe to glue.

Scrolled Base

Similar in looks to bracket feet, the scrolled base shown at left has four feet that support the corners of large casework, such as blanket chests and boxes. The scrolled, inner edge profile can be simple or fairly elaborate, depending on your taste.

For strength, dovetail the corners of the frame, as shown in "Scrolled Base" (opposite). After assembling the base, rabbet around the top edge and glue the base to the under-side of the case. Then glue and miter molding around the bottom of the case to make a visual transition from base to case.

➤ See *"Designing Feet"* on p. 197.

➤ TABLE SAW FOOT SWITCH

Keeping your hands and eyes on the sawing action at all times makes it much safer and more accurate when you're working on the table saw. And groping underneath the table to turn off the saw is asking for trouble, especially when you need to make a stopped cut. This foot- or knee-operated switch lets you turn off the saw without losing your concentration. The device, which can be mounted in a matter of minutes, works with all types of saws that have push-button switches.

MAKING THE FOOT SWITCH

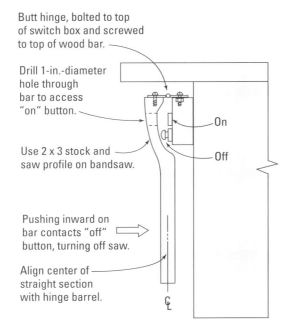

Butt hinge, bolted to top of switch box and screwed to top of wood bar.

Drill 1-in.-diameter hole through bar to access "on" button.

Use 2 x 3 stock and saw profile on bandsaw.

On

Off

Pushing inward on bar contacts "off" button, turning off saw.

Align center of straight section with hinge barrel.

C L

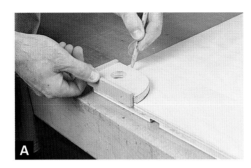

A

Sizing the Toekick

A comfortable size for a kick space is when x = 2¹/₂ in. and y = 4¹/₂ in. You can adjust these measurements up or down by 1 in. to suit your furniture while still leaving room for stray feet.

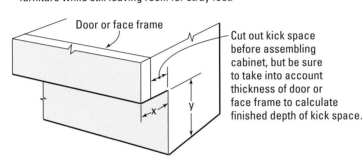

Door or face frame

Cut out kick space before assembling cabinet, but be sure to take into account thickness of door or face frame to calculate finished depth of kick space.

x   y

Finished Toekick

Door or face frame

Case bottom

Case side

Radius equals depth of cutout in case side.

Nail ³/₄-in.-thick subkick to cleat.

Finish-nail ¹/₄-in.-thick kick plate to subkick.

Attach cleat to inside surface of case side.

Unfinished Toekick

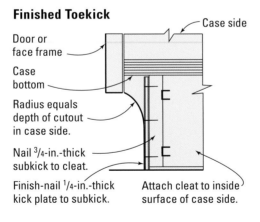

Square cutout

Nail subkick to edge of case side.

Finish-nail plate to subkick.

If necessary, cut kick plate extra-wide and scribe to contour of floor.

B

Integral Base with Toekick

You have two options when incorporating a kick space under a cabinet: Construct the base as a separate assembly and then secure it to the case, or make the base an integral part of the cabinet.

> See *"Applied Base with Toekick"* on p. 187.

For cabinets with finished sides—where you'll see the side of the case when it's installed—you'll need to construct the case sides so they conceal the ends of the kick plate once it's installed.

Once you've cut the case joints, but before assembling the cabinet, use a template to trace the outline of the kick radius onto the side of the case (**A**). Size the template to take into account the thickness of the subkick and finished kick plate, plus any face frame material or doors (**B**). For economy, the example shown here uses a two-part sandwich for the toekick: ¹/₄-in. plywood over particleboard or utility plywood.

Use a jigsaw to cut the profile on the corner of the case side (**C**). Cut on the waste side of your layout line; then clean up and smooth the surface on a spindle sander or with a half-round mill file and sandpaper.

If the case side is plywood, you can cover the raw edge by adding a strip of commercial edge-banding. The thin banding will conform to the curve of the kick with heat and pressure from an iron (**D**).

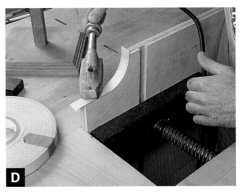

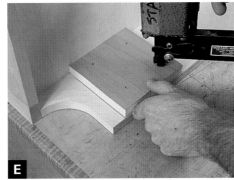

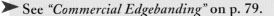

➤ See *"Commercial Edgebanding"* on p. 79.

Mark the inside of the case side, taking into account the combined thickness of the subkick and the kick plate, and then glue and staple a ply-wood nailing cleat to the case (**E**).

Attach the subkick—which can be made from any ¾-in.-thick material, such as plywood or particleboard—to the cleat (**F**). Then attach your finished kick material over the subkick with small brads or finish nails so it's flush with the edge of the case side. Thin ¼-in. hardwood plywood is a great material for the kick plate, since it's backed up by the thicker subkick (**G**).

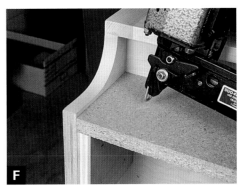

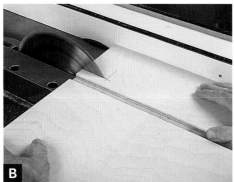

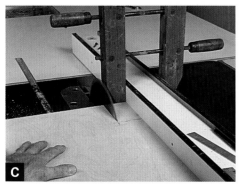

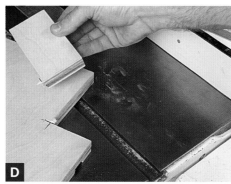

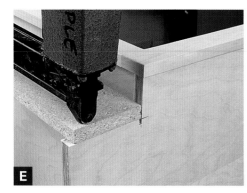

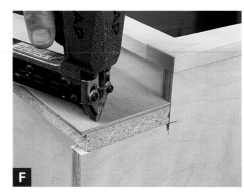

Inside Toekick

When you're faced with an unfinished case side (one that will be covered up by adjoining cases or built into the corner wall of a room), building the kick space is much simpler. Start by laying out the depth and height of the kick on both sides of the case side (**A**). Remember to take into account the thickness of the subkick and kick plate plus any frame or door material.

On the table saw, set the rip fence to the height of the kick, allowing for the blade's thickness, and raise the blade to full height. Be sure to keep your hands clear of the blade and use a blade guard. Position the inside surface of the case so it's facing up on the saw table and make a cross-cut to establish the height of the kick, cutting up to your layout line. Stop when you reach the line; then turn off the saw and let the blade spin to a stop before backing the workpiece out from the blade (**B**).

With the blade still raised, adjust the fence to the depth of the kick. Clamp a stop block to the fence to limit the cut about ¼ in. shy of your lay-out line. Turn the case side over so the outside surface is facing up and push the workpiece into the blade and up to the stop (**C**). Turn off the saw as before, remove the workpiece, and pry away the waste (**D**). A sharp chisel will remove any leftover material.

On an unfinished case side, instead of positioning the subkick on the inside of the case, you secure it directly over the edge of the side (**E**). Then cover the subkick with your finished plywood kick (**F**).

> ⚠ **WARNING** Safe practice on a table saw calls for raising the blade slightly above the work surface—unless a specific operation calls for a higher blade angle.

Applied Base with Toekick

An applied base with a kick space is often easier to construct than an integral base. And it's particularly handy when you're installing a built-in cabinet, because it makes leveling the case a cinch.

▶ See *"Leveling Strategies"* on p. 189.

To make an applied kick for a freestanding case, build the kick base and cabinet as separate assemblies; then join them together with screws (**A**).

To extend the toekick around the corners on a case with finished sides, factor in the overhang of the case on the front and both sides when determining the width and length of the base, as shown. Don't forget to allow for the finished toekick material. Then build the base from strips of ¾-in. plywood ripped to the correct width to raise the case to the necessary height. Glue and nail the parts together, making sure the interior strips are square to the assembly (**B**). Always align the interior strips in the base so they fall directly under any partitions in the case for support. Strips every 2 ft. are sufficient to carry the weight of even large cases.

After the basic frame of the base is assembled, add nailing cleats inside the frame, aligning them flush with the top edges of the base (**C**). Then lay the cabinet on its back and attach the base assembly by driving screws through countersunk holes in the cleats and into the case bottom (**D**).

Complete the base by applying a finished kick plate made from ¼-in. hardwood plywood onto the front and sides of the base. For a seamless look at the corners, miter adjacent kick plates and use glue and brads or finish nails to attach them to the base (**E**).

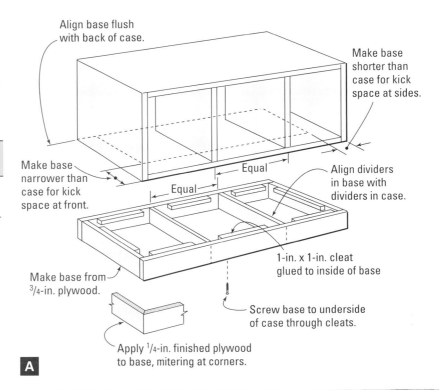

Align base flush with back of case.

Make base shorter than case for kick space at sides.

Make base narrower than case for kick space at front.

Equal

Equal

Align dividers in base with dividers in case.

1-in. x 1-in. cleat glued to inside of base

Make base from ¾-in. plywood.

Screw base to underside of case through cleats.

Apply ¼-in. finished plywood to base, mitering at corners.

A

B

C

D

E

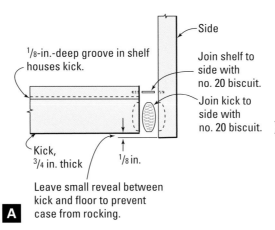

¹/₈-in.-deep groove in shelf houses kick.

Side

Join shelf to side with no. 20 biscuit.

Join kick to side with no. 20 biscuit.

Kick, ³/₄ in. thick

¹/₈ in.

Leave small reveal between kick and floor to prevent case from rocking.

A

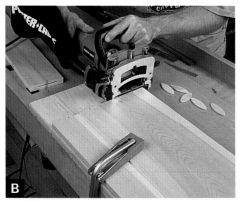

B

C

D

E

Biscuit Toekick

Similar to the integral toekick, the biscuit toekick works well for narrow cases such as a bookcase, where the sides meet square to the floor.

▶ See *"Integral Base with Toekick"* on p. 184.

You can use several types of joints to hold the parts together, but one of the simplest approaches is to use biscuits to join the shelf and the kick to the case sides. To stiffen the connection, house the kick plate in a shallow groove cut in the underside of the case bottom, as shown here (**A**). You can use the case side and bottom to lay out and cut the joints. Once you've grooved the bottom for the kick plate, clamp it square across the case side at the correct toekick height; then cut slots for biscuits into the ends of the bottom. The base of the biscuit joiner registers on the case side (**B**).

Without changing the joiner's setup or the clamped parts, hold the joiner vertically to slot the sides, registering the joiner against the end of the case bottom (**C**).

Insert the biscuits into glued slots in the kick and bottom (**D**) and use clamps to pull the joints tight. To keep the case from rocking on an uneven floor, size the kick so it rises above the floor about ⅛ in., which is enough to keep the sides firmly planted without letting small objects roll underneath. The look is simple and refined (**E**).

Leveling Strategies

Leveling a table or a cabinet—whether it's free-standing or built-in—is the final step before you put it to use. If you don't take the time to do this, your tables can rock or tip because of uneven floors. Heavy cases can rack for the same reason.

If you're planning to attach your furniture or cabinets to the walls or floors of a room, such as a row of kitchen cabinets or a wall-hung case, leveling the work becomes even more important. Before you even build the piece, you'll want to take some logical steps that will ensure the case installation goes smoothly.

The bracket-and-bolt assembly shown here make it a cinch to level a cabinet even after the case is installed. Screw one bracket at each corner of the cabinet and into the case side, directly underneath the case bottom (**A**). Then mark for the adjusting hole through the bracket and onto the bottom (**B**).

Remove the bracket and drill a ⅜-in. clearance hole through the bottom (**C**). Then reinstall the bracket and screw the bolt, or foot, into the bracket. Once the cabinet is in place, you can adjust the foot from inside the cabinet with the turn of a screwdriver (**D**).

(Text continues on p. 190.)

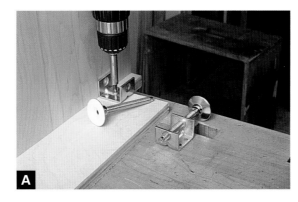

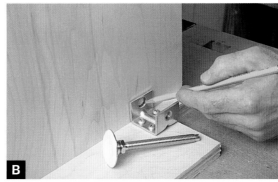

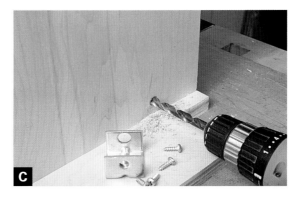

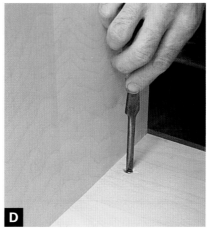

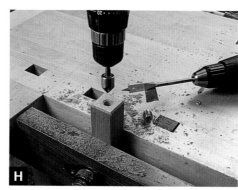

Adjustable feet work fine on cases, boxes, and table legs; and the bearing surface of the feet glide easily over rough surfaces. The hardware consists of nylon-padded bolts and T-nuts. Install the feet by drilling a hole in the bottom of each leg or corner of the case to a depth equal to the length of the bolt (**E**).

Tap the T-nut into the hole. The spurs on the nut grab into the work and keep the nut from spinning or coming loose (**F**). Complete the foot by threading the bolt into the nut. Flats on the end of the bolt allow you to adjust the height of the piece with a small wrench (**G**).

Another technique relies on threaded inserts and carriage bolts and works well under legs or case sides. For ease and accuracy, drill for and install the hardware before assembling the piece. First, in the bottom of each leg drill a hole of the recommended size for the insert and to the depth equal to the length of the carriage bolt. Then lightly countersink around the hole (**H**).

Install the insert into the leg, flush to the surface. Now spin a carriage bolt into the bottom of the leg (**I**). The rounded head of the bolt makes a great surface for the bottom of the leg, and you can adjust the length of the bolt by turning it with a wrench when necessary.

Threaded Inserts

Threaded inserts are notoriously difficult to install. To make installation foolproof, use the drill press. Start by drilling the correct size hole for the insert; then countersink around the hole. The countersink prevents the stock from mushrooming and blowing out around the hole. Next, use a hacksaw to cut off the head of a bolt with the same thread as the insert and chuck the bolt in the drill press. Thread a nut and washer onto the bolt and spin the insert onto the bolt under the washer, hand-tightening the assembly (**A**).

Center the countersunk hole under the insert and clamp the workpiece to the drill press table. With the drill press unplugged, advance the insert into the hole by hand while turning the nut with a wrench (**B**). Keep turning the insert and nut until the washer bottoms out on the workpiece. Then back off the nut with the wrench and spin the chuck in reverse until the bolt comes out of the insert (**C**).

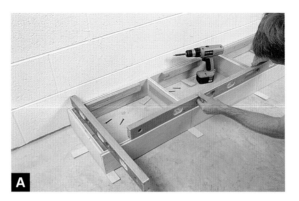

A

B

Leveling a Cabinet with an Applied Base

For wide, built-in cabinets and long case runs, such as a row of kitchen cabinets, it's often easiest to build an independent base and level it before adding the cabinet. Once you've built the base, position it on the floor; use wedges underneath to shim the base level front to back and side to side.

▶ See *"Applied Base with Toekick"* on p. 187.

A single level will let you check when the base is level, but a pair of levels is a little easier, because it lets you read both planes at once (**A**).

Once the base is level, secure it to the wall or the floor and cut any protruding shims flush to the outside of the base. Then install the cabinet by placing it on top of the base and driving screws through the inside of the case into the base (**B**). Secure the cabinet permanently by driving screws through the back of the case at the top and into the wall. Then wrap the base on three sides with finished kick material.

Built-In Cabinets

When you're installing a cabinet, it pays to plan the job carefully before installing or even building your piece. Also, make a scale drawing of the cabinetwork and the room it goes in, including doors, windows, and any other permanent features of the room (for example, switch and outlet locations) (**A**).

If the piece is going onto a wall, you'll want to secure it to something more substantial than just the wall sheathing, especially if it's a panel of drywall. Use wood screws and plan on screwing through the cabinet and into the studs behind the sheathing. If the wall or floor is masonry, use masonry anchors and a masonry drill bit (**B**).

[**TIP**] **Locating masonry screws when hanging wall cabinets can be difficult unless you follow a specific procedure. First, drill clearance holes through the work; then position the cabinet and drill pilot holes with a carbide-tipped bit through the holes in the case and into the masonry. Without repositioning the cabinet, drive the screws and you're done.**

Once you've selected the right hardware, you'll need a reliable level to mark the wall and to read the cabinet for level as you install it. Start by marking a horizontal level line on the wall to indicate the finished height of the case (**C**).

Then, still working with the level, find the high spot on the floor and run another level line from the high spot all along the wall, providing a reference line for the rise of the floor. The installation is then shimmed to the high spot.

If you're working with a stud wall, locate the centerline of the studs (**D**) and transfer the stud locations to the case. Then drill clearance holes through the hanging strips on the case for the screws. Use wedges to shim the case level and plumb.

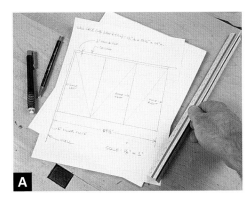

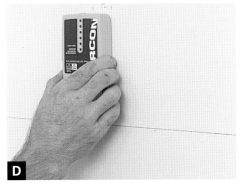

Wall Cabinets

When hanging a wall cabinet of considerable size, first remove all doors, drawers, and shelves to lighten the case as much as possible. If helping hands are hard to come by, make a set of adjustable supports. Wedges driven under the blocks raise the cabinet in small, measurable increments (**A**).

Before attaching the cabinet permanently, use your level to check that the case is level with the floor and, for wall-hung units, plumb with (parallel to) the wall. Don't cheat here. A case that's not installed plumb and level will invariably rack, twisting the case opening and making doors misalign and drawers stick. Use the level to read two planes: the case's top (or bottom) and its face (or front) (**B**).

When both planes read level and plumb, drive screws through the holes in the case and into the studs in the wall. Make sure to secure the top (**C**) and bottom of the case (**D**). Note that when you are installing multiples of cabinets, you'll want to drive screws to join the individual cabinets together before securing the run of cabinets to the wall. Otherwise, it'll be difficult to get the face frames flush.

Fillers for Frameless Cabinets

On built-in cabinets without face frames, you often need to create a dead space between the case and the wall or ceiling so that doors or drawers can operate freely without obstruction.

▶ See *"Built-In Cabinets"* p. 193.

Instead of leaving a gap, the best approach is to fill the space with a strip of wood that matches the front of the case. To make the strip, build a two-piece, L-shaped assembly, called a filler. The face of the assembly should be made from the same material as your cabinet. You can make the face piece any width, but a 1-in.-wide piece usually provides enough clearance between the case and the wall as long as the wall itself has no obstructions. Make the filler by gluing the face piece at right angles to a backing piece (**A**). Let the face piece extend beyond the backer by at least ¼ in. so you have some extra material to scribe to the wall if necessary.

Attach the filler with screws to the side of the cabinet (or the top, depending on the installation) so the face of the filler aligns flush with the door or drawer fronts (**B**). If you discover that the filler needs scribing after leveling the case, mark the amount of scribe, unscrew the filler from the cabinet, and cut it to the contours of the wall on the bandsaw. Then reattach the filler and install the cabinet.

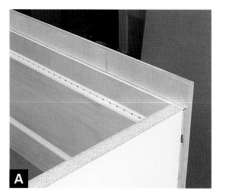

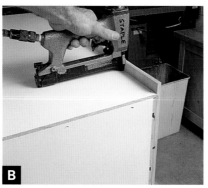

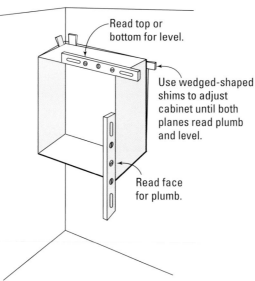

Read top or
bottom for level.

Use wedged-shaped
shims to adjust
cabinet until both
planes read plumb
and level.

Read face
for plumb.

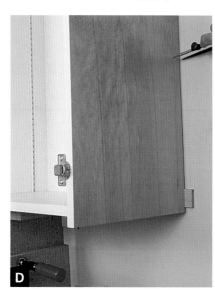

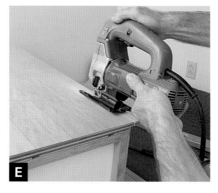

Scribing a Cabinet to a Wall

Attaching a cabinet to a wall sometimes leaves you with one or more exposed ends, where the side and the wall are in plain view for all to see. Because walls are rarely dead flat, you often end up with small unsightly gaps between the case side and the wall due to small dips and bumps in the wall. Scribing makes the cabinet fit the uneven contour.

When you build the cabinet for scribing, it's important to allow an extra 1 in. of material for the exposed or finished side; then mill a rabbet for the back that's 1 in. wider than all the other rabbets in the case (**A**). When you attach the back to the cabinet, you should have 1 in. of scribe material extending past the back (**B**).

Position the cabinet on the wall and use shims at key points to shift the case until it's plumb and level (**C**). Then use a compass set to the width of the scribe (roughly 1 in, but adjusted to leave the correct finished cabinet depth) and run it evenly down the cabinet side, following the contours of the wall (**D**).

Remove the cabinet from the wall, lay it on its side, and use a jigsaw to cut to the scribed line. Make an angled cut to the waste side so you create a slight back bevel, which will fit the wall better. I find it easier to simply tilt the saw rather than the baseplate. The 1-in.-wide scribe supports the jigsaw as it's tilted, and angling the saw to the waste side avoids marring the finished surface (**E**). Clean up any rough spots with a block plane. After cutting the scribe, you're ready to install the cabinet permanently with screws.

Feet

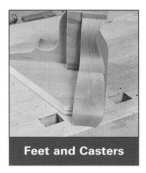

Feet and Casters

ADDING FEET TO FURNITURE is a good method for getting cases off the floor, and it's an effective way to personalize an otherwise ordinary leg. The feet you build can be contemporary looking or have a traditional feel. Or, for simplicity's sake, you can add small buttons under a case to create a reveal or gap. If mobility is your goal, feet with wheels is the way to go. Casters and other rolling devices can help move furniture from spot to spot.

Designing Feet

If the piece you're building is based on frame construction, where there are extended legs that meet the floor, you can leave them as they are or give them a flourish by wrapping moldings around them. Case pieces that don't have bases need feet of some sort—and the options here are plenty. Traditional chests and bureaus often have some form of bracket foot to elevate the case itself and give the piece a unique style. Simpler designs, such as turned or scrolled feet, can be just as effective.

The most basic approach is just to let the leg of the piece run straight to the floor. The only structural problem with this approach is that the sharp edges of the feet tend to snag carpets and other floor coverings. And if the piece is ever moved, you're likely to chip the feet. You can easily overcome this by planing a small chamfer around the bottom of the leg. The chamfer not only

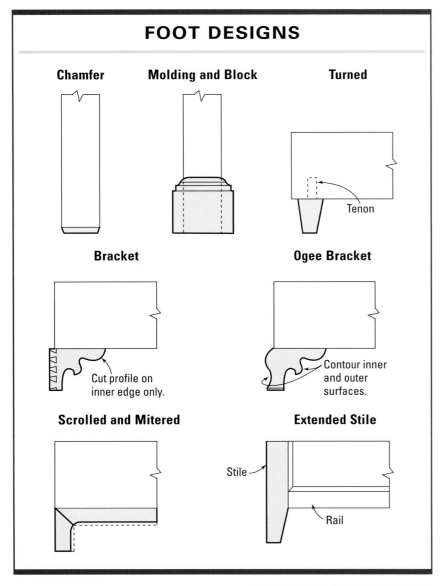

FOOT DESIGNS

Chamfer

Molding and Block

Turned

Tenon

Bracket

Cut profile on inner edge only.

Ogee Bracket

Contour inner and outer surfaces.

Scrolled and Mitered

Extended Stile

Stile

Rail

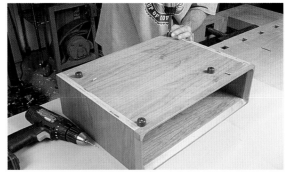

Blocks installed on the outside corners are a simple way to elevate a small case.

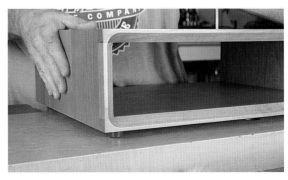

When the case is turned right side up, a slight rise creates an attractive shadow line.

reduces the chances of splitting or chipping but also looks much better than leaving the edges sharp.

A simple solution to lifting a leg or raising a box is to add plastic or rubber blocks underneath. The blocks provide a no-slip grip, and they're quick to install. Simply screw them to the underside of your project. On a case, position the blocks at the outside corners for stability. Once they're installed, the blocks are inconspicuous from above. The result is a slight lift to the box and an elegant dark line, or reveal, below.

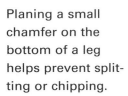

Planing a small chamfer on the bottom of a leg helps prevent splitting or chipping.

TYPES OF WHEELS

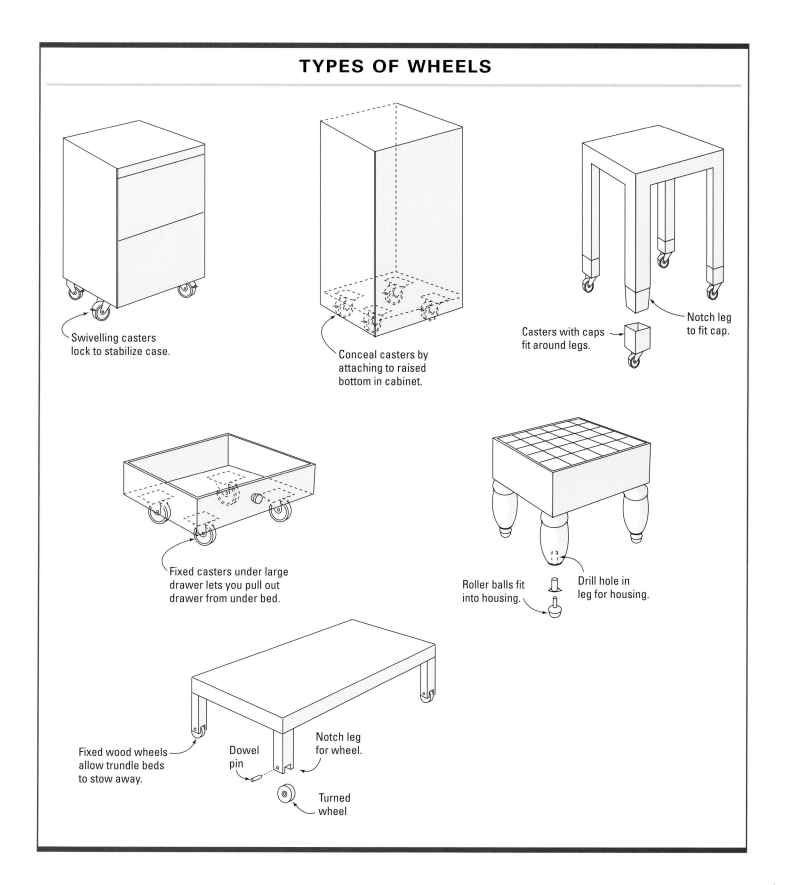

Swivelling casters lock to stabilize case.

Conceal casters by attaching to raised bottom in cabinet.

Casters with caps fit around legs.

Notch leg to fit cap.

Fixed casters under large drawer lets you pull out drawer from under bed.

Roller balls fit into housing.

Drill hole in leg for housing.

Fixed wood wheels allow trundle beds to stow away.

Dowel pin

Notch leg for wheel.

Turned wheel

Caps, Casters, and Wheels

If you need to move your furniture often, consider adding wheels (see the drawing on p. 199). Wheels are a boon for heavy cases, such as loaded filing cabinets, making them easy to move without straining your back or gouging your floors. Wheels don't have to be seen, either. You can conceal them underneath a large cabinet, yet they're ready to be pressed into service when you need them.

On smaller pieces, such as tea trays and serving tables, you can introduce some flair by adding brass wheels to the bottoms of legs while making them more practical to move around. Wood wheels have a traditional look and feel, and you can turn them yourself on the lathe.

When making your furniture mobile, consider whether you want the wheels to swivel and whether they should lock. Swiveling casters make it easier to maneuver a large piece in a tight space. If the piece is heavy or large, look for locking casters that keep the piece stationary when you don't want it to move.

Furniture Glides

Making furniture that slides or glides over floors prevents scratches and dings. But wood furniture won't glide naturally. Adding a low-friction material to the underside of your pieces, such as a high-density plastic, is one solution. The other approach is to place the legs of your furniture onto protective pads or coasters.

If a piece is going to be moved often, it's best to install furniture glides to the bottom of the piece. There are many types of glides available in different materials, and some can be screwed to the underside of a piece or simply nailed in place. These plastic glides move smoothly over rough surfaces, wear well, and can be installed by tapping them into the bottom of a case side or leg.

For heavy pieces that don't need to be moved frequently, a plastic or rubber coaster placed under a leg is a painless solution that protects floors.

Small plastic furniture glides are simply nailed in place.

Plastic and rubber coasters come in a variety of sizes and shapes and protect the floor as well as the furniture.

Scrolled and Mitered Feet

The mitered foot design shown here is very simple in form and is reminiscent of the bare-bones approach used by Shaker furniture makers of the past (**A**). Construction is uncomplicated (**B**).

Use the jigsaw or bandsaw to cut a scrolled profile on the case sides before assembling the cabinet. For the front scrollwork, it's easiest to glue the mitered feet and rail to the case after the joints are cut but while the stock is still square (**C**). Once the glue has dried, trace the profile on the assembly and use the jigsaw to cut to your outline (**D**). Clean up and smooth the sawn contours with a round-bottomed spokeshave or a sanding drum chucked in a portable drill.

A

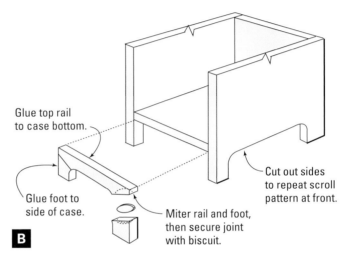

Glue top rail to case bottom.

Glue foot to side of case.

Miter rail and foot, then secure joint with biscuit.

Cut out sides to repeat scroll pattern at front.

B

C

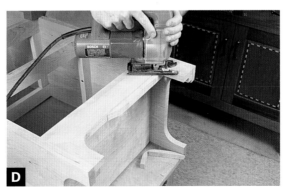

D

A

Ogee Bracket Feet

Bracket feet are appropriate for traditional case pieces, such as eighteenth-century secretaries and the like (**A**). This type of foot seems to defy gravity. With its swooping ogee, it appears to have insufficient strength to support a cabinet. But don't be fooled: The bracket foot is very strong.

Construction is straightforward for the front feet. (**B**). First, miter two feet blanks on the table saw. A crosscutting sled helps control the cut and guide the work (**C**). With the blade still angled to 45 degrees, slot each miter for a plywood spline to reinforce the joint. Then lay out the scrolled bracket profile on each blank. Using a plywood template makes the job easy and accurate when you're making multiple feet (**D**). Saw the bracket contours on the bandsaw, following the lines as closely as possible to keep cleanup to a minimum (**E**). Smooth the sawn contours with a drum sander or by hand, but don't get too fussy—most of the underside of the scrollwork won't be seen. Glue up the two halves, gluing in the spline to keep the joint strong and checking that the blanks are square to each other.

Once you've glued the blanks together, lay out the ogee profile on one face, and saw out that profile on the bandsaw. You'll need a box-type

Front Foot

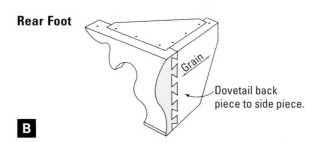

Plywood spline reinforces miter joint.

Glue plywood gusset into rabbeted edge; screw through gusset into cabinet.

Cut profile on each outside face on bandsaw.

Nail or screw foot to case here.

Grain

Glue stacked block to inside corner for support.

Rear Foot

Grain

Dovetail back piece to side piece.

B

C

D

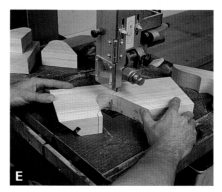

E

jig to support the foot as you saw, as shown (**F**). As before, follow the layout line as closely as you can (**G**). Once you've sawn the first face, cut the second face. No layout is necessary; the outline is revealed by the first cut (**H**). Simply follow the outline to saw the second face (**I**).

To further strengthen the foot, glue a stacked block of wood—the grain oriented with the feet—into the inside corner. The stack strengthens the miter and helps support the weight of the cabinet above. Then add a plywood gusset to provide a means of screwing the foot to the cabinet (**J**).

Constructing the rear feet is similar to the front, except for the back of the foot, which remains flat so the foot and case can be placed against a wall. After sawing the bracket profile on the inner edge of the side piece, join the two pieces with large dovetails. Then bandsaw the ogee profile on the side piece only, using the same technique you used for sawing the profiles on the front feet. (For more on making a bracket foot, see *The Complete Illustrated Guide to Shaping Wood*, by Lonnie Bird, The Taunton Press.)

[**TIP**] **Relying on your machine's angle or bevel gauge to provide you with an accurate 45-degree setting will often disappoint you, especially when cutting large miters. A better way is to cut miters in two blanks, then hold the miter joint together and check that the combined angle equals 90 degrees. If the joint is off, adjust the angle of the blade by half that amount and check again with the square. Keep checking and adjusting the blade until the joint is dead on.**

Clamp the foot securely to this box jig when sawing the ogee contour.

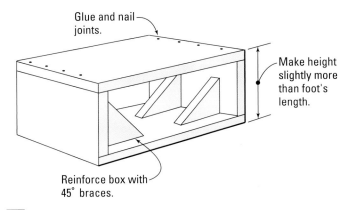

Glue and nail joints.

Make height slightly more than foot's length.

Reinforce box with 45° braces.

F

G

H

I

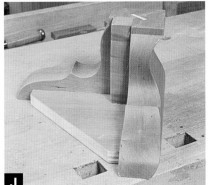

J

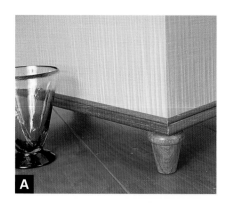

Turned Feet

Simple, tapered feet are great for small boxes and chests (**A**). Turn the feet between centers on the lathe, forming a tenon at one end of each foot. Cutting the shoulder dead flat with a parting tool ensures the foot will sit tight to the base (**B**). Then drill holes into the underside of the box to accept the tenons and glue and clamp the feet to the box (**C**).

Great for larger boxes or chests, bun feet have a wonderful, bulged feeling to them if you get their shape just right (**D**). The secret is to leave a small flat and a pad on the bottom of each foot where it touches the floor, and another flat or shoulder at the top, where it comes in contact with the case. The flats make the foot appear to swell attractively under the weight of the piece it supports. You can screw the foot to the underside of the piece or turn a tenon on one end and glue it into a hole drilled in the case.

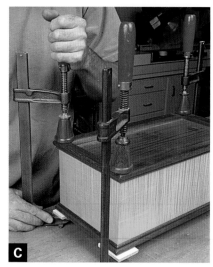

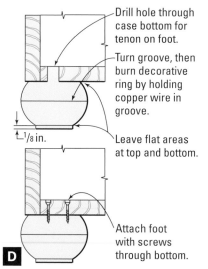

Drill hole through case bottom for tenon on foot.

Turn groove, then burn decorative ring by holding copper wire in groove.

1/8 in.

Leave flat areas at top and bottom.

Attach foot with screws through bottom.

Brass Casters

The refined-looking casters shown here are smooth running and made of solid brass. They can add an elegant touch to small tables and bases (**A**).

Installation is a snap: Drill for the lag screw, centering the hole on the bottom of each leg. A masking tape flag gauges the correct hole depth (**B**). Install the lag screw, using a nail or awl to coax the plate tight to the bottom of the leg (**C**). Secure the caster by driving pan-head screws through the plate and into the leg (**D**).

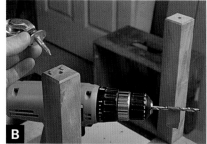

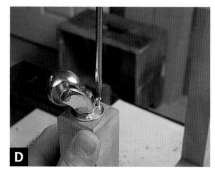

Roller Balls

A roller ball, housed in a metal sleeve, is heavy duty and great for roll-around carts and butcher blocks. It's easiest to drill for the rollers before assembling the piece. For the neatest appearance, counterbore the bottom of each leg to conceal the majority of the hardware. To drill the counterbore, turn the drill press table 90 degrees and chuck a 1⅛-in. Forstner bit into the press. Clamp the workpiece square to the bit, which is made easy by drawing parallel lines on the table. Now drill a ½-in.-deep hole (**A**).

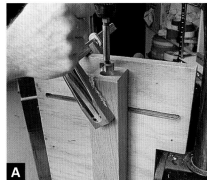

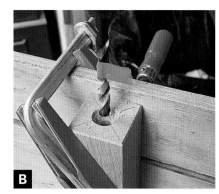

Without moving the work or the drill press setup, bore a ½-in. hole in the center of the counterbore for the ball pin and housing. A piece of masking tape tells you when you've reached the correct depth (**B**).

The housing has serrated teeth that bite into the end grain of the leg (**C**). Use a stout stick to tap the housing into the hole inside the counterbore (**D**).

Slip the pin and ball into the housing and get ready to roll (**E**).

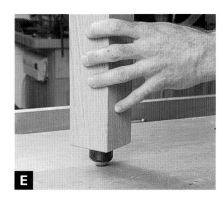

Stands

Making Stands

S TANDS CAN HAVE A DRAMATIC EFFECT on furniture by elevating a piece to eye level. They can display art objects or hold plants and other items on their top surfaces. Even small chests or special containers can benefit from being placed on a stand. A more sophisticated approach is to build a stand for holding and displaying a cabinet, incorporating a framework of shelves or drawers as part of its design, as seen in Ming's Cabinet opposite.

You can use solid wood, plywood, or a combination of the two for stand construction. There are two basic methods for building stands. One approach is to use wide, solid panels joined at the corners, creating lots of mass and visual weight. Frame-type stands rely on more delicate-looking frame members and are usually constructed with mortise-and-tenon joinery. These types of stands elevate a piece and provide a light overall texture and feel.

Designing Stands

Stands can hold all sorts of work, from small boxes, chests, and artwork to larger items such as cabinets. You'll need to decide between carcase or frame construction, the later having a lighter feel with its open framework. On tall stands with relatively thin frames, be sure to add lower rails to the construction to strengthen the assembly and to keep the frame from racking.

Stands made from wide panels offer more solidity and can be made from solid wood or hardwood plywood. The former can be butted and glued together at the corners, although chances are you'll see contrasting grain at the joints. A better-looking solution with solid wood and plywood is to miter all four corners. Plywood, with its thin and delicate face veneers, must be mitered very accurately and then glued at the corners to conceal the inner plies.

Ming's Cabinet, by Yeung Chan, is made from kwila and spalted maple and incorporates a framework for drawers into the stand design.

TYPES OF STANDS

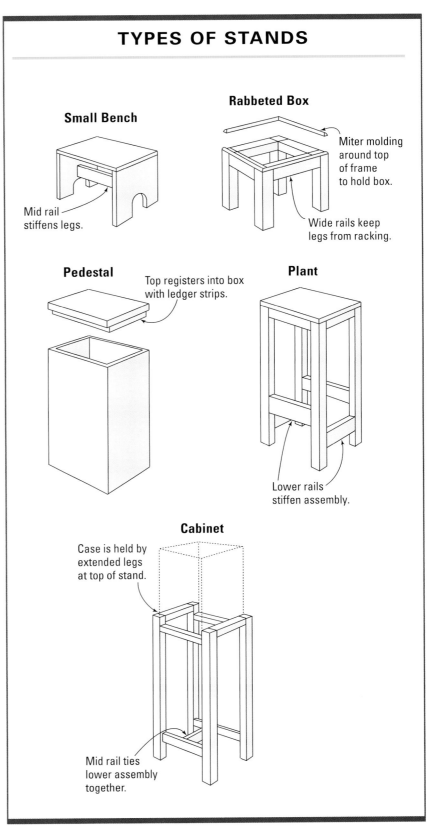

Small Bench

Mid rail stiffens legs.

Rabbeted Box

Miter molding around top of frame to hold box.

Wide rails keep legs from racking.

Pedestal

Top registers into box with ledger strips.

Plant

Lower rails stiffen assembly.

Cabinet

Case is held by extended legs at top of stand.

Mid rail ties lower assembly together.

A

Chest Stand

The small frame-type stand shown here can hold boxes or small chests (**A**). Make the stand from 1½-in. or thicker stock to provide support for the chest on the top of the frame (**B**). Wide 3-in. or 4-in. rails keep the joints strong and prevent racking.

Adding molding around the perimeter on the top of the frame keeps the chest from shifting, without having to secure it with screws or other hardware. Center the container on the frame and mark for the miters in succession by wrapping the molding around the container (**C**). Then use glue and brads to secure the molding to the top of the frame (**D**).

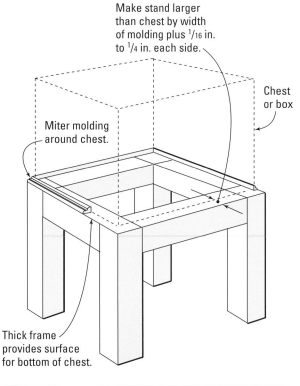

Make stand larger than chest by width of molding plus ¹⁄₁₆ in. to ¹⁄₄ in. each side.

Chest or box

Miter molding around chest.

Thick frame provides surface for bottom of chest.

B

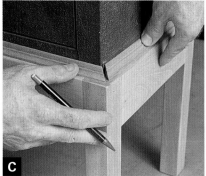

C

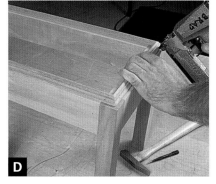

D

Pedestal Stand

The pedestal stand in this example has a heavier, more solid feel than typical frame-type designs. Its height makes it ideal for displaying objects (**A**). The removable top fits into the case via ledger strips secured to its underside, which makes fitting the top easy (**B**). You can add a bottom if you wish, so you can remove the top and fill the base with weight for stability.

The key to building a pedestal is to miter and spline the long edges of the sides. The splines help position the joints and prevent slippage when you glue up the case. First rip 45-degree bevels on the panel edges, using a board clamped to the fence to close the gap at the table to prevent the tip of the miter from slipping under the fence. Exert downward pressure near the blade to maintain an accurate cut (**C**). With the blade still at 45 degrees, turn each panel over and ride its mitered edges against the rip fence to groove the opposite miter for a spline (**D**). Then rip some long-grain strips of wood for splines, making sure to size them so they slide into the grooves easily without binding.

Gluing up the pedestal can be frantic, because you have to glue all four panels at the same time. It's wise to get help from a friend. At the very least, make sure to rehearse the assembly procedure first and check that you have enough clamps. Then spread glue on all joints, slip the splines into the grooves, and stand the panels upright. Use cauls and deep-throat clamps to pull the joints tight (**E**).

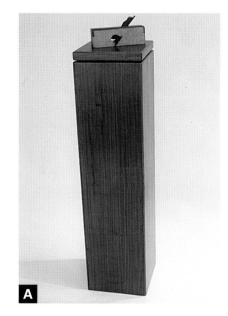

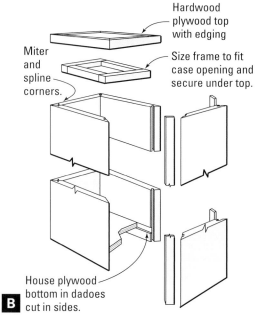

Hardwood plywood top with edging

Miter and spline corners.

Size frame to fit case opening and secure under top.

House plywood bottom in dadoes cut in sides.

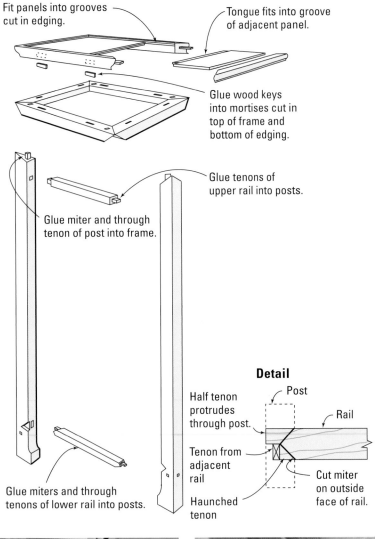

Fit panels into grooves cut in edging.

Tongue fits into groove of adjacent panel.

Glue wood keys into mortises cut in top of frame and bottom of edging.

Glue tenons of upper rail into posts.

Glue miter and through tenon of post into frame.

Detail

Post

Rail

Half tenon protrudes through post.

Tenon from adjacent rail

Haunched tenon

Cut miter on outside face of rail.

Glue miters and through tenons of lower rail into posts.

A

Plant Stand

The delicate plant stand shown here was made by woodworker Yeung Chan. It's constructed of relatively thin and narrow frame members, joined with miters and mortise and tenons (**A**). With so many interconnecting joints, the assembled stand is incredibly strong (**B**).

Although you can use power tools to cut the miters and most of the mortises and the tenons, it's best to make the final fitting cuts by hand, especially with the mitered and through-tenoned joints, such as on the tops of the posts. To finish the joint, Chan uses a homemade, $\frac{1}{16}$-in.-wide chisel to clean up some of the inner waste material in the narrow confines at the tops of the legs (**C**).

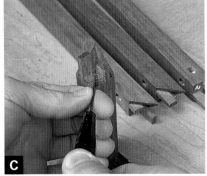

B

C

Once all the joints are cut, it's important to assemble the stand in the correct sequence. First, put together the lower frame by connecting all the rails to the posts (**D**). Then assemble the mitered upper frame and carefully lower it onto the miters and tenons of the posts (**E**).

Next, assemble the top by fitting the tongue-and-groove top boards together and installing them into the edging pieces (**F**). Finally, insert wood keys, or slip tenons, into the mortises in the upper frame; then lower the top assembly onto the keys to secure it in place (**G**).

Legs and Aprons, page 214

Chairs and Stools, page 231

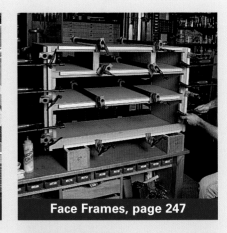
Face Frames, page 247

Frame and Panel, page 256

PART FIVE

Frame Construction

WHEN YOU START TO THINK BEYOND BOXES in woodworking, you quickly discover the world of frame construction. Instead of joining wide panels to construct a box or carcase, frame construction involves connecting relatively narrow members such as stiles, legs, rails, or stretchers to form the basic structure. A table is an obvious example. The frame is composed of legs connected to rails or aprons that support a top.

Frame-and-panel construction also serves to solve a basic woodworking problem. Built in the same fashion as paneled doors, frame-and-panel assemblies solve the problem of wood movement, allowing you to use wide, solid-wood panels without the risk of joints blowing apart. Used to dress up the front of a cabinet, face frames are another form of narrow members joined together.

One of the key elements when building any kind of frame is the use of appropriate joinery to fortify the connection and keep the narrow members free from rack or twist.

Legs and Aprons

Strong Joints

- ➤ Reinforcing an Apron (p. 220)
- ➤ Mitered Wood Brace (p. 220)
- ➤ Metal Brace (p. 221)
- ➤ Scrolled Bracket (p. 222)

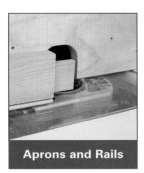

Aprons and Rails

- ➤ Beaded Rail (p. 223)
- ➤ Cutout for a Drawer (p. 224)

Legs

- ➤ Quirk Bead on Square Leg (p. 225)
- ➤ Two-Sided Taper (p. 226)
- ➤ Four-Sided Taper (p. 227)
- ➤ Compound-Curved Leg (p. 228)
- ➤ Turned Leg (p. 229)

Tables, desks, beds, chairs—most of these frame-type constructions require legs that connect to apron or rails. Although chair construction, with its angles and curves, is worthy of a section all its own, learning how to put together a basic leg and apron allows you to build any number of furniture projects that require a framework for support.

➤ See *"Chairs and Stools"* on p. 231.

Using the appropriate joinery is important, because many legs are subject to a lot of sideways stress and narrow aprons won't offer sufficient support to prevent racking. The styling of a leg and apron can affect the piece's structure and will certainly have an effect on the overall feel and look. You'll have many options for leg and apron styles, from simple rectilinear forms to turnings, tapers, and curves.

Designing a Leg and Apron

One of the first questions you face with leg-and-apron assembly is the type of joinery you'll need. While there are many joints that work well for this type of connection, a traditional mortise and tenon is one of the best choices for strength and convenience. (For more on joinery, see *The Complete Illustrated Guide to Joinery*, by Gary Rogowski, The Taunton Press.)

For strength, the tenon on an apron must be long. How long? The answer is the longer the better. At a minimum, make your tenons 1 in. Unless your leg stock is unusually narrow, milling a mortise to this depth poses no problem. But when it comes to the other half of the joint, you're often faced with two tenons from adjacent aprons that meet in the same leg. The tenons interfere with each other, making it impossible to use a long tenon in either piece. There are two solutions to this problem: One is to offset the tenons to the outside of the stock, which provides more room in the leg for the joint. How far can you offset the joint? Let your mortises inform you. Generally, it's best to leave some meat in the leg between the wall of the mortise and the outside of the leg, say ¼ in. or so, as shown above right.

An alternative solution is to leave the tenons centered on the stock's thickness (which generally makes it easier to mill the tenons themselves) and then miter the ends of the tenons where they meet. The result is a significantly longer tenon. Be sure to leave a small gap at the miter joint to ensure that the shoulders of the aprons close fully onto the leg during assembly.

Apron and Rail Styles

Although rails and aprons form an essential structural ingredient to a frame, they don't have to force you into rectilinear boredom. There are plenty of design options to select beyond the basic straight rail. Keep in mind that you'll need to keep the area at the joint, or the shoulders of the rails, as wide as possible for strength—especially for large constructions, such as tables or desks. As a rule of thumb, a minimum width of 4 in. is sufficient for a strong, rack-free joint.

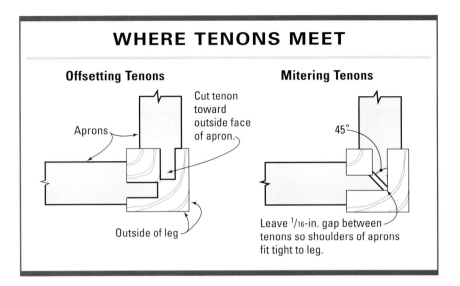

WHERE TENONS MEET

Offsetting Tenons

Aprons

Cut tenon toward outside face of apron.

Outside of leg

Mitering Tenons

45°

Leave ¹/₁₆-in. gap between tenons so shoulders of aprons fit tight to leg.

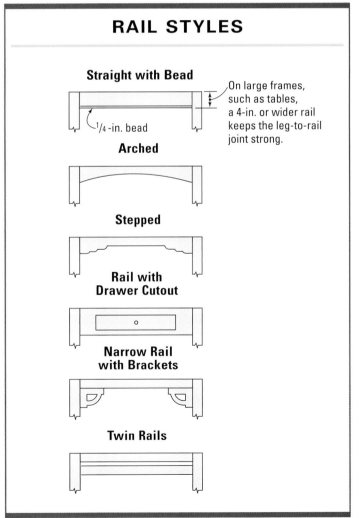

RAIL STYLES

Straight with Bead

¼-in. bead

On large frames, such as tables, a 4-in. or wider rail keeps the leg-to-rail joint strong.

Arched

Stepped

Rail with Drawer Cutout

Narrow Rail with Brackets

Twin Rails

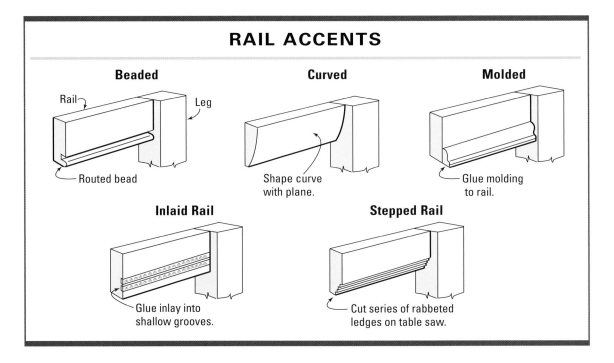

RAIL ACCENTS

Beaded

Rail

Leg

Routed bead

Curved

Shape curve
with plane.

Molded

Glue molding
to rail.

Inlaid Rail

Glue inlay into
shallow grooves.

Stepped Rail

Cut series of rabbeted
ledges on table saw.

Constructing an apron or rail is a straight-forward task, providing you use suitable joinery methods.

▶ See *"Reinforcing an Apron"* on p. 220.

Rails can be straight or curved, depending on your design; or you can introduce details that add a design flair to the work, such as beads, inlays, and grooves.

Leg Options

Beautiful legs are a hallmark of fine furniture, plus they're just great to look at. On utilitarian pieces, a straight-sided leg is fine. Strong and stout, it provides a solid feel to furniture.

But like rails, your tables and other frame furniture can look more vibrant and exciting if you branch out from the basic square leg.

Details such as beads and roundovers can add flair without added work, or you can employ tapers and curves for a distinct signature.

Usually, it makes sense to mill any joints before shaping the leg stock. This lets you set up fences and blades by referencing them to the still-square stock, a much easier task than trying to accomplish joinery once the stock is no longer rectilinear. For turned legs, most styles provide square sections where the aprons and rails intersect. But it's best to lay out the joints before turning and leave the mortising for later.

Assembling a Frame

Gluing up a complicated frame can be a real headache if you don't have time to get all the parts clamped before the glue starts to set. And even if you've milled your stock and cut

Glue up complex frames as subassemblies. Keep checking alignment with an accurate square as you work during the glue-up.

It's also important to check the surface with a straightedge to ensure the parts remain flat and in alignment.

your joints accurately, with flat, straight surfaces and square shoulders, the clamping pressure can twist an assembly out of square.

The first step is to divide a major assembly into subassemblies. Glue up one side of a frame, which will require fewer clamps, and check that the clamps align over the center of the joints. Then use a reliable square to read intersecting parts. If a joint is out of square, shift the clamps and recheck with your square until you're satisfied. Make a second check using a straightedge to read the surface for flat, placing the straightedge at various points across the frame. Any day-

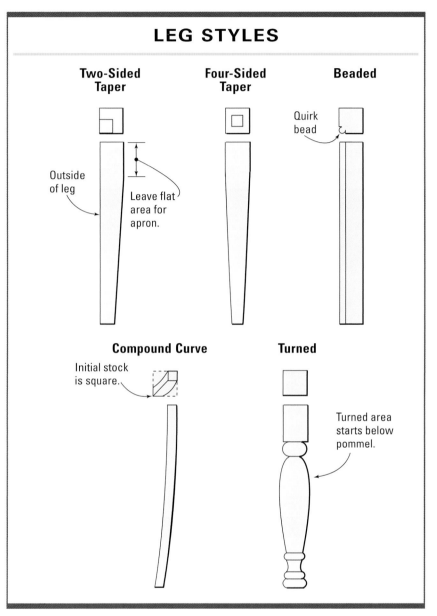

LEG STYLES

Two-Sided Taper

Four-Sided Taper

Beaded

Quirk bead

Outside of leg

Leave flat area for apron.

Compound Curve

Initial stock is square.

Turned

Turned area starts below pommel.

Bring subassemblies together into one final unit. A flat surface, such as a good workbench, is essential for glue-up.

By allowing you to drop the box spring below the rails, bed hangers let you to adapt the look of a traditional bed to modern tastes in mattress foundations.

Bed hangers screw to the frame and support the box spring from underneath.

light between the straightedge and the work means you've introduced twist, and you'll need to reclamp.

Once the subassemblies have dried, join them together to create the final assembly (see the bottom photo on p. 217). Here, it's critical to glue up on a dead-flat surface, such as the top of your table saw or a flat benchtop, to ensure the assembly goes together flat.

Adding Support to Bed Rails

While thick bed rails are strong and can easily resist deflecting under a load, the space between the rails offers no support for a mattress. This arrangement is fine if you're using a mattress atop a box spring, since the frame of the box is stiff enough to support itself and the mattress. You can simply let the rigid box spring rest on ledger strips glued or screwed to the sides of the rails.

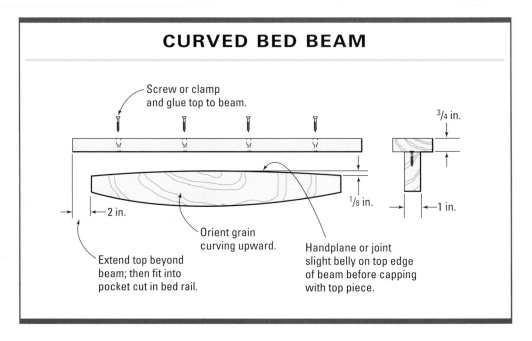

CURVED BED BEAM

Screw or clamp and glue top to beam.

3/4 in.

2 in.

1/8 in.

1 in.

Orient grain curving upward.

Extend top beyond beam; then fit into pocket cut in bed rail.

Handplane or joint slight belly on top edge of beam before capping with top piece.

But for narrow rails, such as in traditional pencil-post beds, there's not enough depth to hold the box without it raising obtrusively above the rails. Here, you'll need to use bed hangers, which are made from thick steel and have a 90-degree bend. Screw the hangers to the insides of the rails, allowing them to drop below the rails so the box spring and mattress are at the correct height.

For "soft" mattresses—futons and mattresses without box springs—you'll need a considerable amount of support between the frame of the bed to keep the mattress flat. Rigid beams can serve to hold the weight. Cut or rout pockets in ledger strips and glue the strips to the insides of the bed rails. Then make a set of curved beams to fit the pockets.

Install the beams into the pockets; then place sheets of plywood or particleboard over the beams. Cutting the sheets into thirds allows for easier assembly, and a cutout in each sheet helps you drop them in place and avoid pinched fingers.

Ribs that are notched into ledger strips glued to the rails provide a sturdy foundation for a mattress.

Three panels with cutouts for your hands make assembling and disassembling a bed platform quick and easy.

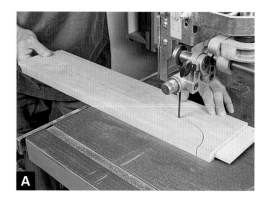

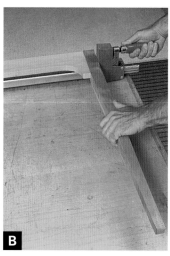

Reinforcing an Apron

To keep a frame strong, you need a solid connection between the legs and rails. You can achieve this by keeping the joint relatively wide and using a strong joint, such as a long and deep mortise and tenon.

If you want to use a fairly narrow apron in a piece, you can still make a joint of sufficient width where the apron joins the legs or posts. Start with wide stock and mill the joints while the stock is still square. Lay out a curve in the center portion of the rail, leaving the shoulders full width; use the bandsaw to cut to your lines (**A**).

When you assemble the frame, the wide shoulder supports the connection, making the joint strong and resistant to racking (**B**).

Mitered Wood Brace

One of the simplest methods for strengthening a rail joint is to brace it from the inside. Chairmakers use this method on seat frames to keep the legs of the chair securely joined to the frame, but it works equally well on large pieces, such as tables and desks. Using 2-in. or thicker stock, cut 45-degree miters on each end (**A**).

Chuck a countersink bit into the drill press and bore a hole in the center of the block. Also drill two holes through each miter by holding the stock at 45 degrees to the bit (**B**).

Spread some glue on the miters; then secure the block to the inside of the frame by screwing through the block and into the leg and both aprons (**C**).

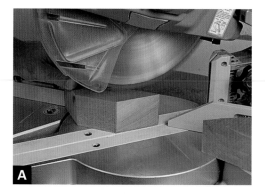

Metal Brace

Identical in function to a wood brace, a commercial metal brace has the added advantage of letting you use biscuits or dowels to connect the aprons to the legs. The brace is useful for knockdown frames; it lets you assemble the parts without glue, if you need to, relying on the brace itself to hold the joints tight. Once you've cut the joints, cut a narrow groove across the inside face of the rails with a standard sawblade (**A**).

With the rails dry-fitted to the leg, position the brace into the grooves in the rails and drill through the brace and into the leg for a hanger bolt (**B**). A masking tape flag notes the correct hole depth. Disassemble the frame and install the bolt into the leg. Lock a pair of nuts on the threaded end of the bolt to help with driving the lag screw portion into the leg (**C**).

Assemble the leg and rails; then install the brace by bolting it to the leg and screwing it to the inside of the rails (**D**).

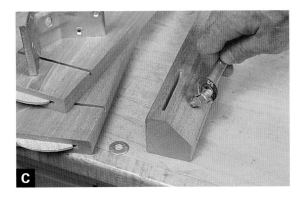

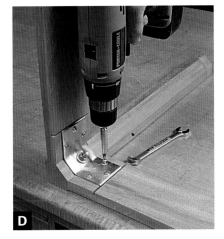

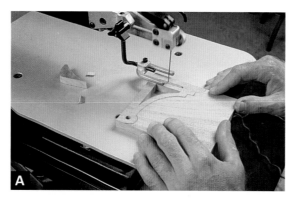

Scrolled Bracket

If your aprons must be narrow, you can beef them up and add some visual interest at the same time by adding a wood bracket between the leg and rail connection. Crosscut some brace stock with one dead-square corner; then trace the desired pattern onto the stock. You can saw the shape on the bandsaw, but for really intricate cuts—especially inside cuts—it's best to use a scrollsaw (**A**).

Spread glue on the inner edges of the leg and apron and on the mating surfaces of the bracket; then clamp in place (**B**). The finished bracket adds strength to the joint while embellishing the frame (**C**).

[**TIP**] **Getting into nooks and crannies to clean up tool marks can be a challenge. Save your kids' Popsicle sticks and use contact cement to stick a piece of sandpaper to the surface. Then shape the stick to the job at hand. For circular openings, try wrapping a dowel of the appropriate diameter with sandpaper.**

Beaded Rail

Simple to make, but eye-catching in detail, a bead routed along the bottom edge of a rail adds a nice touch (**A**). You can buy piloted beading bits in sizes ranging from ⅛ in. to ½ in. or larger. The size refers to the diameter of the bead itself (**B**). It's important to set the height of the cutter so the bit cuts the full bead in the stock or you'll end up with flat spots. A nice trick is to raise the bit a few thousandths of an inch above the table, which leaves a small fillet on the edge of the rail. A few swipes with a handplane brings the edge flush to the bead. Try the setup on some scrap first; then rout the workpiece on the router table for maximum control (**C**).

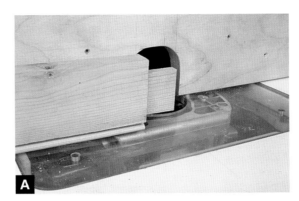

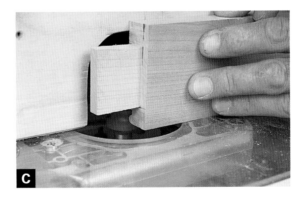

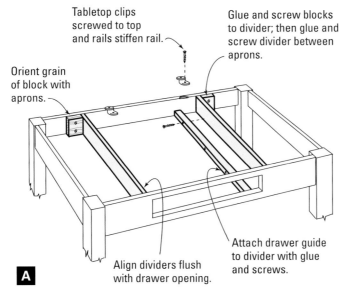

Tabletop clips screwed to top and rails stiffen rail.

Glue and screw blocks to divider; then glue and screw divider between aprons.

Orient grain of block with aprons.

Attach drawer guide to divider with glue and screws.

Align dividers flush with drawer opening.

A

Cutout for a Drawer

Placing a drawer in the middle of an apron is a great way to use what is often wasted space, especially if the apron is part of a work surface such as a kitchen table. Just make sure to re-inforce the apron as shown (**A**), so the drawer opening doesn't compromise the frame's strength. You can cut out the apron and fit the opening with an overlay drawer; but a slicker way to go is to build a flush-fit drawer using the apron itself as the drawer front. The idea is to rip the apron into three pieces and reassemble it without the section for the drawer opening, which you save for the drawer front. The result is a drawer that blends seamlessly with the grain of the apron.

> See *"Full-Overlay Drawer"* on p. 110 and
> *"Flush-Fit Drawer"* on p. 111.

Start by squaring lines across the face of the rail, using double lines at one end. The lines will help you reassemble the parts later in the correct orientation (**B**).

Once you've decided on the finished height of the drawer front, rip a strip from both edges of the rail stock on the table saw. The center strip will equal your drawer height (**C**).

On the center piece, lay out the location and length of the drawer and crosscut it from the blank. Then reassemble the pieces with glue and clamps, using the freed drawer front as a guide. Adjust the opening in the apron so the drawer front barely fits from end to end (**D**). Once you've made the drawer, you can plane it to fit the opening exactly.

Once the glue has dried, pass the apron through a thickness planer to clean up both sides of the rail (**E**). The finished apron and drawer front should match very closely in grain pattern and color, and nobody but you will know how it was done (**F**).

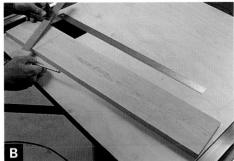

B

C

D

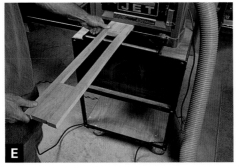

E

F

Quirk Bead on Square Leg

A bead centered on the sharp edge, or arris, of a leg adds a nice touch (**A**). You can use a conventional piloted beading bit for this operation, but the setup is somewhat different from when routing a bead in one face.

> See *"Beaded Rail"* on p. 223.

See *"Beaded Rail"* on p. 223.

On the router table, instead of positioning the fence flush with the bearing on the bit, you need to move it *away* from the bearing by half the diameter of the bead, or its radius. Rout one side of the leg stock, pushing the stock at an even feed speed past the bit (**B**).

Then turn the workpiece end for end and rotate the stock 90 degrees; make a second pass to complete the cut (**C**).

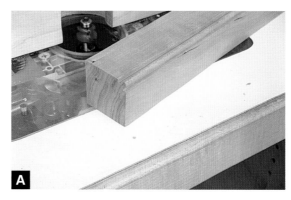

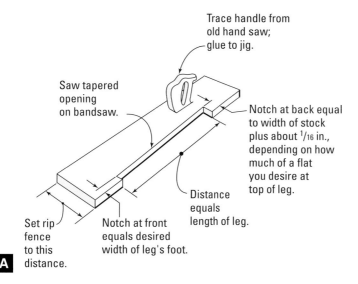

Trace handle from old hand saw; glue to jig.

Saw tapered opening on bandsaw.

Notch at back equal to width of stock plus about 1/16 in., depending on how much of a flat you desire at top of leg.

Distance equals length of leg.

Set rip fence to this distance.

Notch at front equals desired width of leg's foot.

A

Two-Sided Taper

Legs that taper on two faces or sides work well with all sorts of furniture designs, from traditional to contemporary. To cut the tapers effortlessly and safely, use a dedicated jig to push the stock past the sawblade on the table saw (**A**). The jig produces a specific size taper in a predetermined size of leg. I have several of these jigs for a variety of styles and leg sizes. By varying the depth of the rear notch, you can alter how much flat area you'll leave at the top of the leg for the apron joint. Once you've made the jig, mark it permanently with important setup information, such as the width and length of the leg stock and the distance you need to set the rip fence from the blade.

Place the square leg stock between the notches in the jig and raise the blade slightly higher than is customary. The tall blade helps keep the stock firmly on the table as you push it past the blade. Make the first cut on one face of the stock (**B**). Then turn the leg 90 degrees and make the second cut in the same manner as the first (**C**).

Finish the leg by handplaning the sawn surfaces. As you plane, pay attention to the transition between the taper and the flat area at the top of the leg. The goal is to leave a crisp line at this point (**D**).

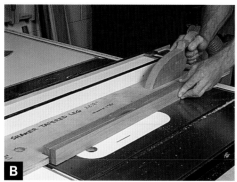

B

C

D

Four-Sided Taper

A leg that tapers on four sides seems to dance on its toes and is suited for small tables and delicate frames. Like the two-sided taper, you can leave flat areas at the top of the leg to facilitate joining the leg to aprons or taper the leg the full length. Be warned: tapering full length will require some tricky fitting, since the shoulder of the rail has to angle to match the taper of the leg.

Taper the leg on the jointer, which is a safe procedure as long as you follow some common-sense guidelines. Set the depth of cut $\frac{1}{16}$ in. or less, never place your hands directly above the cutterhead, and use a push block whenever possible. Mark a line with masking tape on the jointer's fence to indicate where you'll start the leg. Then position the top of the leg to your mark; edge the cutterhead guard out of the way; and slowly drop the leg onto the spinning cutterhead, keeping your hands well in front of the spinning knives (**A**).

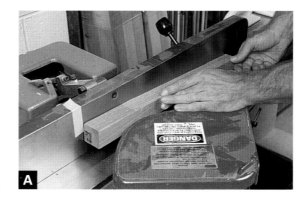

Make several passes on one face of the leg until you have the desired amount of taper and note the total number of passes. On the last pass, don't drop the leg onto the jointer. Instead, start with the tapered face held firmly on the infeed table and make a full-length pass (**B**).

Taper the remaining three faces by turning the stock 90 degrees for each side, repeating the tapering procedure and taking the same number of passes. Using this technique will leave a crisp transition between the flat at the top of the leg and the taper below (**C**).

> ⚠️ **WARNING** Never place your hands directly over the spinning cutter when operating a jointer. Apply pressure before and after the cutter when hand-feeding the workpiece.

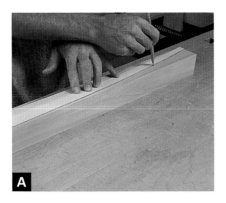

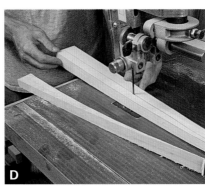

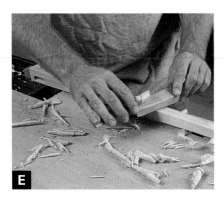

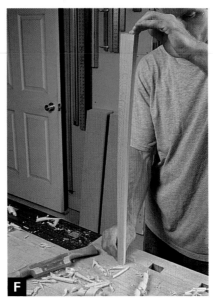

Compound-Curved Leg

There are all sorts of complex curves you can introduce into your leg-making repertoire; but one of the simplest is a shallow compound curve in which the two adjacent faces of the leg curve gently away from each other in separate planes. (For more on curves, see *The Complete Illustrated Guide to Shaping Wood,* by Lonnie Bird, The Taunton Press.)

The first order of business is to cut all the joinery while the stock is still square. Then use a thin template of your desired shape to lay out the curve on one face (**A**).

Use a narrow blade in the bandsaw to cut to your layout lines (**B**). Then flip the stock 90 degrees and draw the curve again by bending the template onto the sawn outer surface of the leg. Be sure to orient the joints correctly before positioning the template (**C**). Saw the adjacent side as you did the first, this time keeping the work in contact with the saw table directly below the blade to prevent the stock from rocking (**D**).

Finish the sawn surface by cleaning up the saw marks and fairing the curves with a flat-bottom spokeshave (**E**). For more severe curves, use a round-bottom shave. The finished leg curves gracefully outward in two planes (**F**).

Turned Leg

The design possibilities are endless when it comes to turning legs for furniture. However, you should follow some basic guidelines to ensure success. Generally, it's best to leave the top section of legs square, as woodturner Mike Callihan has done here. This flat transition area, or pommel, makes fitting the legs to the aprons or rails much easier, since you can reference square rails and cut more conventional joinery, such as square-shouldered tenons. You can lay out for these joints in the square stock and cut them after you complete the turning work.

Start by squaring lines around the blank at the shoulder; then mount the blank between centers. Begin by using a roughing gouge to round the stock, stopping about 2 in. below the marked pommel (**A**).

To keep the junction between the pommel and the turned area crisp, use a backsaw to saw about ⅛ in. deep around the blank, just below your marks. Note that you can cut deeper at the corners (**B**).

With the blank spinning, use the long point of a skew on the waste side to relieve the rough shoulder of the pommel (**C**). Then use the corner of the roughing gouge to round the stock up to the shoulder (**D**).

Next, use a parting tool and calipers to establish the finished round below the pommel (**E**). Finish the pommel by using the long point of the skew to refine the shoulder, taking light cuts up to your marked line (**F**).

(Text continues on p. 230.)

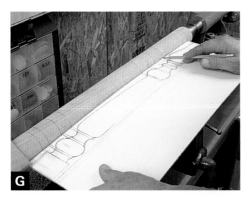

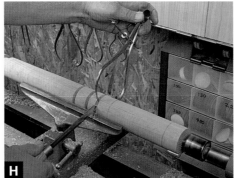

A turning pattern comes in handy for making multiples, and it's practical for laying out the major diameters of the leg. Once you've roughed out the leg to round, hold the pattern up to the shoulder of the blank and transfer the important diameters (**G**). Use a parting tool to cut a series of grooves in the leg on your marks, widening each cut as you go to prevent binding. To gauge the correct depth, use calipers set to the correct diameters shown on your pattern. To avoid catching, make sure the tips of the calipers are rounded and hold them *only* on the side opposite the cutting tool (**H**).

Once you've defined the diameters, work the large diameters before turning the smaller ones to prevent flexing. Use a gouge or the skew to cut the straight sections and roundovers, referring to your pattern by eye. The skew takes some skill to master but leaves the smoothest surface. To cut a bead, draw a centerline on the stock and try rolling the skew over with the long point up (**I**). Use the tip of a small gouge to turn the hollows, keeping the bevel rubbing on the stock to prevent catches. Judge the fairness of the curve as you turn by eyeballing the profile at the top, not at the cut (**J**).

Finish up by removing the tool rest and sanding the leg while it's spinning, starting with 180-grit and working up to 220-grit sandpaper.

Chairs and Stools

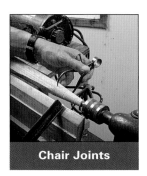

Chair Joints

➤ Shaved Round
   Tenons (p. 237)

➤ Turned Round
   Tenons (p. 238)

➤ Round Mortises
   (p. 239)

➤ Angled Mortises
   and Tenons (p. 240)

Chair Backs

➤ Curved and
   Bandsawn Back
   (p. 241)

Chair Seats

➤ Sculpted Seat
   (p. 242)

➤ Woven Seat (p. 243)

➤ Upholstered Slip
   Seat (p. 244)

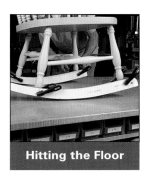

Hitting the Floor

➤ Leveling Chairs and
   Stools (p. 245)

➤ Adding Rockers
   (p. 246)

S EATING IS AN ESSENTIAL form of furniture; and while chairs and stools are known for their complex angled joinery, you shouldn't let this aspect of chairmaking intimidate you. Finding the necessary angles and cutting them to fit are easier than you might think. Some of the tools and methods you'll use have been around for centuries. Most are simple to use, yet very effective.

Chair types generally fall into two categories: plank chairs, in which the upper and lower carriage of the chair emerges from the seat plank, and frame chairs, in which the legs, rails, and stretchers form the basic structural unit and the seat becomes secondary to the construction.

For comfort, most chairs will have curved planes and surfaces so they cradle the body. And when it comes to curves, the seat and back are the two essential forms. You can carve these parts by hand, shape them on the bandsaw, or use laminating techniques. For added comfort, you can consider upholstering the chair seat or back or weaving a pliable seat from fabric, rush, splints, or other materials.

Once a chair is built, it should sit firm and solid on the floor. The chairmaking process often leaves one leg short or long, so leveling a chair is the final step before putting it to use. You can also add rockers to a chair for the ultimate in sitting pleasure.

Designing for Comfort and Strength

Chair design involves three basic goals: comfort, durability, and good looks. Although the aesthetics of a chair involves some universal design principles and personal choices, building for comfort and strength requires more stringent guidelines.

While there are no precise numbers, a chair's dimensions and the angle of the back to the seat play vital roles in comfort. The drawing below shows average dimensions based on a dining chair. You can use these numbers as a starting point for other styles of chairs, such as task chairs and lounge chairs.

Building for strength involves using appropriate joinery as well as choosing and selecting your wood carefully. (For more on joinery, see *The Complete Illustrated Guide to Joinery*, by Gary Rogowski, The Taunton Press.) Keep in mind that chair parts are generally quite thin, so taking the time to select straight-grained wood adds to a chair's ability to withstand use and abuse over time. An important and often neglected touch is to nail furniture glides to the bottom of a chair's legs. Glides can cushion the blow that legs receive from the weight of the sitter, and they allow the chair to be dragged across a floor without damaging the legs or the floor.

➤ See *"Furniture Glides"* on p. 200.

Plank Chairs

The overall structure of a plank-type chair revolves around the seat itself. Windsor chairs best describe this arrangement. Seat blanks must be thick—about 2 in.—so that the posts that connect to them have enough depth for a strong union. The strongest seat joint is when the post is tapered and then wedged in a tapered hole or mortise cut in the seat. Adding stretchers below the seat can significantly increase the overall strength of the chair.

Frame Chairs

The frame-type chair relies on its frame members—not the seat—for its structural integrity. This type of chair can have a plank seat, or you can drop in a slip seat or a traditional upholstered seat inside the seat frame. While legs, posts, and rails can be round, a

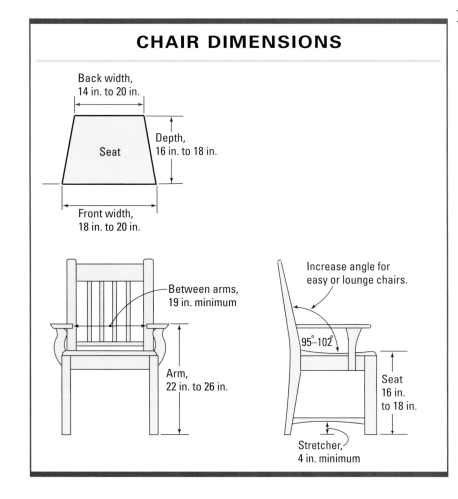

CHAIR DIMENSIONS

Back width, 14 in. to 20 in.

Seat

Depth, 16 in. to 18 in.

Front width, 18 in. to 20 in.

Between arms, 19 in. minimum

Arm, 22 in. to 26 in.

Increase angle for easy or lounge chairs.

95°–102°

Seat 16 in. to 18 in.

Stretcher, 4 in. minimum

frame chair generally consists of many rectangular rails and posts joined at a variety of angles.

Seats and Backs

Ultimately, the acid test of a successful chair is whether the seat and back are comfortable to the sitter. Once you've defined the right dimensions of the seat and back, you'll want to add some contours to these surfaces. For backs, you can use a series of curved slats tenoned into the chair seat or frame or you can make a solid panel sawn to the appropriate curve. Seats can be deeply scooped or woven from pliable materials that give and conform under the weight of the sitter. Upholstered seats add a look of refinement while providing a cushioned surface for the most delicate of derrieres. (For more exacting curves, including laminated seats and backs, see *The Complete Illustrated Guide to Shaping Wood,* by Lonnie Bird, The Taunton Press.)

Anti-Tip Feet

Realizing that everyone at some point in his seated life will rock back on a chair—often with disastrous, leg-breaking results—the Shakers devised a clever wood mechanism that installed on the two rear legs. Called a tilter, it consists of a pivoting, wooden ball captured inside each leg. Its modern counterpart, a metal tilter that slips over the rear legs, can be seen next to the original in the top photo on p. 234.

If you examine the anatomy of the original wood tilter, you can see how to make it. Use a modified spade bit to drill the concave holes in the legs. You'll get good results if you drill

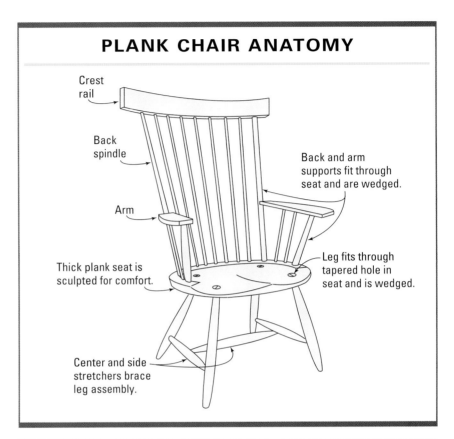

PLANK CHAIR ANATOMY

Crest rail

Back spindle

Back and arm supports fit through seat and are wedged.

Arm

Leg fits through tapered hole in seat and is wedged.

Thick plank seat is sculpted for comfort.

Center and side stretchers brace leg assembly.

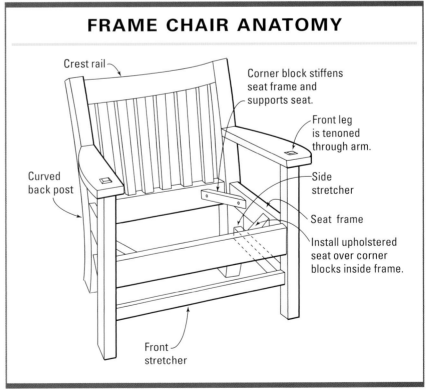

FRAME CHAIR ANATOMY

Crest rail

Corner block stiffens seat frame and supports seat.

Front leg is tenoned through arm.

Curved back post

Side stretcher

Seat frame

Install upholstered seat over corner blocks inside frame.

Front stretcher

The Shakers used wood ball-and-socket chair tilters, while modern furniture makers may use metal ones. (Collection of the United Society of Shakers, Sabbathday Lake, Maine. Photo by John Sheldon.)

Riving stock begins with laying out a grid and splitting the log into regular segments with an ax.

The sections are split into smaller sections with a froe and mallet. The froe handle provides leverage that allows you to control the splitting action and get straight billets.

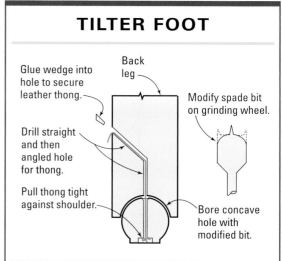

TILTER FOOT

Glue wedge into hole to secure leather thong.

Back leg

Modify spade bit on grinding wheel.

Drill straight and then angled hole for thong.

Pull thong tight against shoulder.

Bore concave hole with modified bit.

the hole on the drill press, tilting the press table to 90 degrees and clamping the leg parallel to the bit. Match the concave hole by turning the tilter ball on the lathe. Before securing the tilter with the leather thong, rub the tilter and the inside of the leg hole with paste wax to reduce friction.

Using Rived Stock

Incorporating rived stock into your chairmaking, when the blank has been cleft from a billet of wood rather than sawn, can add strength to a leg or spindle. And rived stock is much easier to work with hand tools because the grain runs straight without runout. Chairmaker Drew Langsner of Country Workshops in Marshall, North Carolina, starts by laying out squares on the end grain of a freshly sawn billet; then he splits to one of the lines using an ax and a big wooden club.

The next step is to section the split billet into individual squares, using a froe and a froe club, which is a smaller wooden mallet. Position the blade of the froe roughly center on the stock; then give it a hard

➤ HOMEMADE BENCH STOP

I first spied a variation of this stop on a workbench in the shop of friend and cabinetmaker Frank Klausz. If you screw a fixed, horizontal piece to the end of the bench and then attach a flip-up stop at both ends, you can use the stops for holding work while you plane or saw. The two stops accommodate two styles of saws, one for traditional European saws, which cut on the push stroke, and the other for Japanese saws, which cut on the pull stroke.

The two top pieces swivel and butt against the bottom section for a simple but effective stop system. You can use either stop, depending on the direction of cut.

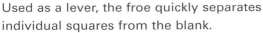

Used as a lever, the froe quickly separates individual squares from the blank.

A shaving horse provides a quick way to hold the squares as you work them. Firm foot pressure tightens the head on the workpiece.

Once two adjacent faces are worked square, Langsner uses a simple shopmade gauge to mark out the width of the piece.

blow with the club. Once split, use the froe as a lever to separate the halves. Continue splitting and separating until you have individual squares.

To bring the rived square to round, clamp the stock in a bench vise, or on a shaving horse, and use a drawknife to shave two adjacent faces roughly straight and square. With two faces square, use a shopmade gauge to mark the width of the stock. Continue shaving with the knife to square the blank, cutting to your layout lines.

Use the drawknife to trim the billet to the layout lines, creating a square workpiece ready for final shaping into a round.

Start rounding over the square billet by first knocking off the corners to make an octagon.

A plywood top protects your chopping block from dirt, helping your axes stay sharp.

Once the stock is square and to width, use the drawknife to shape the blank into an octagon by shaving off the corners. Then switch to a flat-bottom spokeshave to refine the eight facets. Finish the leg or spindle by knocking off the facets with the spoke-shave, checking by feel and eye to see that the leg is round.

Switch to a spoke-shave while working on the octagon to ensure smooth, even facets.

Cover Your Chopping Block

A chopping block or stump is a versatile work surface for all sorts of woodshop tasks, from chopping billets and slicing blanks to hammering hardware on its hard end-grain surface. But a shop block likely suffers one major drawback: The porous grain of the block will collect all sorts of edge-dulling fragments, including dust particles, sanding grit, and dirt from the casual passerby who mistakes the block as a ready-made seat. Chop on this stuff and you can kiss your keen knife and hatchet edges good-bye. To keep the block clean and ready for use—and to dissuade sitters—chairmaker Langsner keeps a lid on it, cobbled together from plywood and scrap wood.

Finish rounding by knocking off the high points with the spokeshave; use your fingers to feel for subtle bumps and hollows.

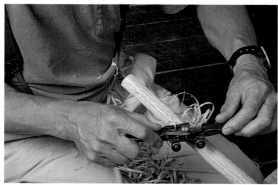

Shaved Round Tenons

The oldest, and often the best, method of making round tenons is to shave them by hand with edge tools. Using a gauge block will help you determine the correct tenon diameter. Once the stock has been rounded with a drawknife and spokeshave, chamfer the end of the blank with a mill file (**A**).

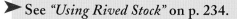

➤ See *"Using Rived Stock"* on p. 234.

After chamfering, rotate the end of the blank to check its fit in a simple graphite-filled gauge block with a hole drilled to the correct diameter (**B**). Drill three holes in your gauge, reserving one for the final fitting.

Use a spokeshave to round the stock, taking off the areas that are marked with graphite (**C**). Concentrate on keeping the tenon straight as you shave and keep checking the fit of the tenon in the gauge block. When the tenon almost fits into the block, use a strip of cloth-backed 80-grit sandpaper to round fully and reduce the diameter, wrapping the strip around the tenon and pulling back and forth (**D**).

When the tenon fits snug and firm in the tenon gauge, you're there (**E**).

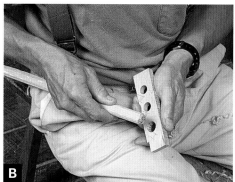

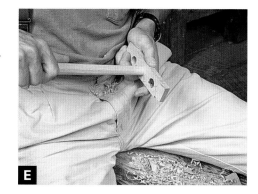

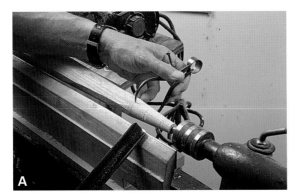

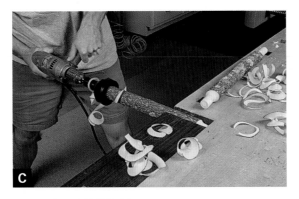

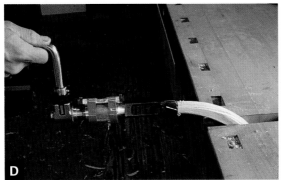

(Photo by Drew Langsner.)

Turned Round Tenons

The most straightforward approach, and arguably the fastest and most economical, is to turn your tenons between centers on the lathe. For a simple tenon, mark the shoulder and use calipers to check your work frequently as you turn. The calipers should just slip over the tenon.

If you're making a tapered tenon to fit a tapered hole the lathe is the way to go. You can gauge the correct amount of taper by cutting two grooves in the stock to the depth of the major and minor diameters of the tenon. Then check your depth frequently as you rough out the tenon (**A**).

Taper the tenon using a ¾-in. roughing gouge. Work at the tailstock end of the lathe to prevent the tool edge from accidentally hitting the lathe's drive spur (**B**).

For long or large-diameter tenons, a commercial tenon cutter chucked in a drill works fast and can make tenons up to 4¼ in. long, depending on the model. The trick to keeping tenons straight is to clamp the work horizontally; then hold the drill level and in line with the axis of the work (**C**). The tool works well in green or dry wood and is best suited for rustic-type work for which the stock is irregular and you don't mind the look of a rounded shoulder.

There are also several specialized tools you can use for making round tenons. One of the simplest is to cut a shouldered tenon using a plug or dowel cutter chucked in an electric drill or brace. A bubble level taped to the drill helps align the bit to the work (**D**). Tenon length is limited with this type of tool.

Round Mortises

Making a tapered hole to fit a tapered tenon is one of the strongest methods for connecting legs to a seat.

► See "*Shaved Round Tenons*" on p. 237.

The joint naturally locks together as the chair is used, since the weight of the sitter—and gravity—forces the tapered parts together (**A**). Chairmaker Drew Langsner starts by laying out the holes in a seat blank using a full-size pattern (**B**).

Once the holes are laid out, drill them at the correct angle using an auger bit chucked in a brace. Homemade gauges—one square and one beveled to the slope of the leg—help you eyeball the correct angle of the bit as you drill (**C**). Stop drilling when the lead screw of the bit just pokes through the bottom of the seat blank; then flip the seat over and finish the hole from the bottom to minimize tearout.

Still working from the bottom of the seat, taper the straight walls of the mortise with a reamer chucked in a drill or brace. As before, gauge the angle with a bevel gauge and square (**D**). A dummy leg allows you to check when the reaming is deep enough (**E**). Test the final fit with the real leg until the major diameter of the tenon meets the bottom of the seat.

Compound angles for mortises in legs and stretchers are another problem. A solution is to build an angled platform on the drill press (**F**). But drilling through round stock at a compound angle can also be done with the legs in place. Using a Powerbore bit and an extension, you can drill through adjoining legs in one operation (**G**). Guide cleats clamped to the legs stiffen the assembly and help visually guide the bit.

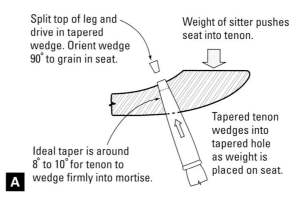

Split top of leg and drive in tapered wedge. Orient wedge 90° to grain in seat.

Weight of sitter pushes seat into tenon.

Ideal taper is around 8° to 10° for tenon to wedge firmly into mortise.

Tapered tenon wedges into tapered hole as weight is placed on seat.

A

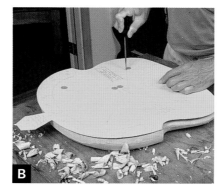

B

C

D

E

F

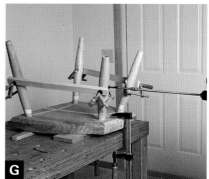

G

(Photo by Drew Langsner.)

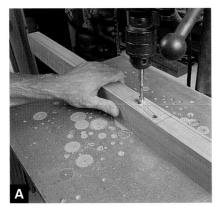

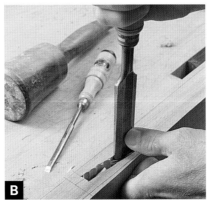

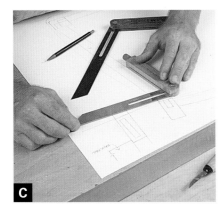

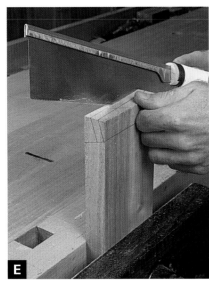

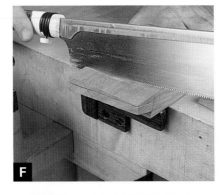

Angled Mortises and Tenons

The mortise-and-tenon joint is the essential joint for chairmaking, and in chairs you often have to cut these joints at one or more angles. It's always best to cut the mortises first, so you can fit the tenons accurately to them. When the mortise angles from the face of the work, lay it out and cut it on the drill press. Use a Forstner bit with a diameter equal to the mortise's width and drill a hole at each end of the mortise; then drill a series of overlapping holes to drill out the waste in the center (**A**).

Square the drilled mortise by hand with bench chisels. Use a narrow chisel to cut the ends flat and square and then pare the walls with a wide chisel (**B**).

When it comes to the angled tenons, you're best off laying them out with the aid of a full-size drawing of the chair and the joints. Instead of calculating the angles mathematically, use bevel gauges to find the necessary angles by laying them directly over your drawing (**C**).

Once you've set the gauges, use them to transfer the angles to the stock. Square off an angled shoulder to mark the cheeks using a flat square held against the gauge (**D**).

With the stock clamped vertically, use a backsaw to rip the cheeks by sawing to your layout lines (**E**). Then crosscut the angled shoulders by tilting the saw and holding the stock flat on the bench against a bench stop (**F**). Clean up any irregularities on the cheeks with a shoulder plane, making sure to keep the cheeks flat and parallel to each other (**G**).

Curved and Bandsawn Back

You can make a wide, curved chair back by sawing the curve on the bandsaw, even on a relatively small bandsaw. Start by ripping separate boards that, once glued together, will make up the desired width of the back. Joint their mating edges. Then lay out the desired curve on the edge of each board using a plywood template nailed to the stock (**A**).

Carefully square your bandsaw blade to the stock (which is more accurate than squaring the table to the blade) and saw out the curves in each board, cutting right to your layout lines (**B**). After sawing, glue and clamp the boards edge to edge, being careful to line up the curves as much as possible (**C**).

Finish by smoothing the back on both faces, using flat- and round-bottom spokeshaves, a scraper, and minimal sanding (**D**). Periodically check the surface with a straightedge to maintain a flat surface across the face.

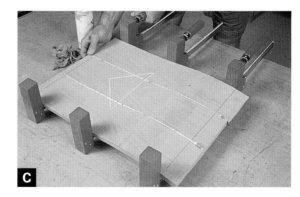

(Photo by Drew Langsner.)

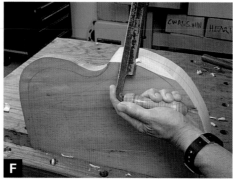

Sculpted Seat

Making a seat from a solid blank isn't difficult, but it requires a fair amount of elbow grease, especially when trying to contour deep areas like the seat of a Windsor-style chair. Chairmaker Drew Langsner starts on the top of the seat by sculpting the deepest areas with an inshave, taking quick, short strokes and working diagonal to the grain. For more control, use an inshave with radiused corners and a flat in the center of the blade (**A**). You can shave freehand to the desired depth or drill two small holes at what will be the most deeply scooped-out areas of the seat. Then shave until you reach the depth of the holes.

Quicker than an inshave but a little trickier to control is an adze, which removes a lot of stock in a hurry. Hold the seat blank against a scrap block nailed to the floor and clamp it with your foot. Swing the adze toward you and between your legs, taking chopping cuts across the grain (**B**).

To refine the surface and even out the tracks left by the inshave or adze, use a fenced tool called a bottoming shave, or travisher. The blade and the bottom of the travisher body curves in two planes, affording great precision and control of the cut (**C**). Set the blade for a light cut and push or pull the shave downhill or with the grain. You'll get shavings similar to those made by a hand-plane (**D**). Use your eyes and fingers to check when the surface is smooth and fair. Final smoothing with a pad sander completes the contours.

To shape the edge of the seat, tilt the bandsaw table and saw around the perimeter of the blank to create a bevel, or undercut (**E**). Then refine the beveled edge with a drawknife. For best control, skew the knife and take slicing cuts (**F**). Smooth and refine the bevel and round it slightly with a flat-bottomed spokeshave (**G**).

Woven Seat

Weaving a seat or chair back is a fast way to make a comfortable surface for post-and-rung chairs, whether the chair is new or old. The technique is similar for many types of seat materials, from fabric tape and nylon webbing to cane, rush, and wood splint. Seat weaver Pat Boggs of Berea, Kentucky, starts with splints, or strips, of hickory, cut from the inner bark of the tree.

After soaking the strips in hot water for about ½ hr., begin with the *warp,* tying or tacking a strip to a side seat rung and wrapping it around the rungs from front to back, keeping it taut (**A, B**). When you near the end of a strip, start a new strip by tying it to the previous one. When you've filled the opening, wrap the strip around the back rung; then turn the corner and tack it to the adjacent side rung.

For the *weft,* or woven cross strips, start at the back of the chair and wrap around the side rungs, weaving over and under the warp strips (**C**). Depending on the look you want, you can arrange the weft across single strips, or weave over and under pairs or multiples of front-to-back strips (**D**). Use a block of wood to tap the edge of the splints, keeping them tightly together (**E**). Finish the final loose end by weaving under several cross strips underneath the seat. As the bark dries, it will shrink and pull the weave tight, leaving a tough and resilient seating surface.

A

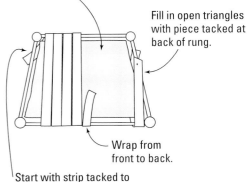

With webbing or tape, insert foam or cloth bag filled with shavings between strips.

Fill in open triangles with piece tacked at back of rung.

Wrap from front to back.

Start with strip tacked to underside of side rung. Strips can be nylon webbing, fabric tape, rush, or wood splints.

B

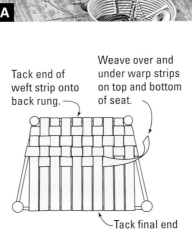

Tack end of weft strip onto back rung.

Weave over and under warp strips on top and bottom of seat.

Tack final end to front rung.

C

D

E

A

B

C

D

E

Upholstered Slip Seat

Making a padded slip seat is a simple way to provide cushioned support for your chairs. Start with a seat blank, which can be a piece of solid wood contoured to shape, or use a flat piece of plywood fit to the chair. Then gather a piece of 1-in.-thick foam, some cotton or polyester batting (cotton produces a more "natural" feel), some fabric, and a few upholstery tacks, all available from fabric stores. Cut the foam just inside the outlines of the seat and lay it on top; cut the batting to fit over the foam (**A**). You can saw the foam to size on the bandsaw, tilting the saw table to bevel the edges slightly.

Cut the fabric, leaving a 3- to 4-in. margin all around. Place the foam and batting on the seat, center the fabric over them, and turn the pile over. Use a couple of upholstery tacks to temporarily tack, or "baste," the fabric to the underside of the seat, working at the center of the front and back edges. Concentrate on stretching the fabric tightly as you work and check that the pattern or weave is straight and even (**B**). Then tack the sides in the same manner, stretching the fabric from side to side and tacking the fabric in the center (**C**).

Use a staple gun to secure the fabric permanently to the seat. Start at the center of the front and back edges and then work toward the corners (**D**).

Staple the sides as you did the front and back, working from the center out to the corners. As you progress, constantly flip the seat over to check that the fabric pattern is even. Keep a pair of nail pullers handy to remove staples if you need to realign the fabric; then restaple. At the corners, you'll have to fold and tuck the fabric to keep it stretched tight to the seat, especially if the seat blank is severely curved (**E**).

Leveling Chairs and Stools

Most chairs and stools won't sit solidly once you've made them. You usually end up with at least one leg that's a hair too long, and the result is a slight wobble to the chair or stool. The fix is an easy one. Place the chair on a dead-flat surface, such as a large square of medium-density fiberboard (MDF) or the table saw, and let the offending leg hang over the edge. Make sure each of the remaining legs sits firmly on the surface. Mark a line around the leg, using the edge of the table to guide your pencil (**A**).

Use a backsaw to saw to your marked line (**B**). As a final check, place the chair back on the flat surface. It should sit square and firm.

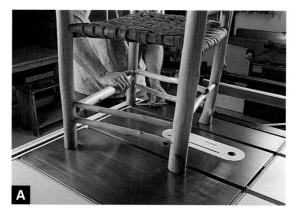

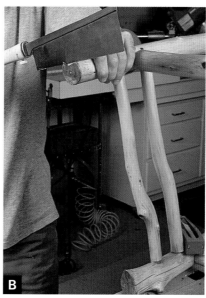

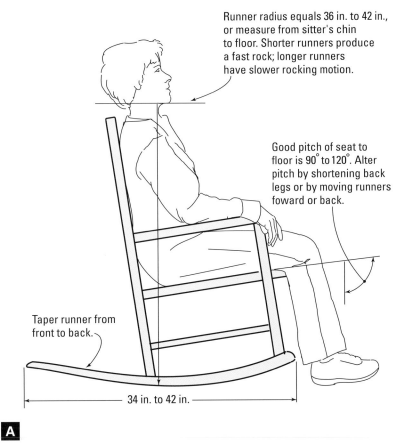

Runner radius equals 36 in. to 42 in., or measure from sitter's chin to floor. Shorter runners produce a fast rock; longer runners have slower rocking motion.

Good pitch of seat to floor is 90° to 120°. Alter pitch by shortening back legs or by moving runners foward or back.

Taper runner from front to back.

— 34 in. to 42 in. —

A

B

C

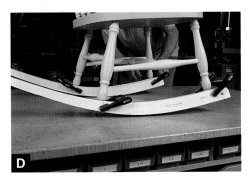

D

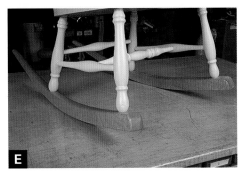

E

Adding Rockers

There are no hard-and-fast rules for the shape of runners, but the drawing (**A**) shows some general guidelines that work for a variety of rocker styles.

To test a proposed curve, draw a full-size runner on scrap and cut it to shape. For the runner to rock properly, it's important that it be a perfect arc with a fair curve—no flats, hills, or valleys. Paper-faced foam board, about 1½ in. thick, is an inexpensive material to use for the mock-up and saws easily on the bandsaw (**B**). Test the rocking motion on your pattern by rocking it back and forth on a flat surface. The bigger the radii, the longer the rocking action. A smaller curve results in a faster, harder rock (**C**).

Once you're satisfied with the rocking movement, saw a second pattern that's identical to the first and temporarily clamp both to the chair legs to judge the resting angle, or pitch, of the seat and back and to recheck the rocking action. You can change the angle by shortening or lengthening the back legs or by moving the rockers forward or backward in relation to the legs. Once you have the appropriate pitch, mark the location of the leg joints on the runner patterns (**D**).

Use the patterns to make the runners, sawing them out on the bandsaw and fairing the curves with spokeshaves and sandpaper. Join the runners to the legs by referring to your marked pattern, using mortise and tenons, dowels, or slip joints, depending on your chair design. The finished rockers can be shaped however you like, but rounding the edges and gradually tapering the rockers from front to back give the chair a more refined appearance (**E**).

Face Frames

Making Face Frames

Corner units

B UILT FROM NARROW STILES and rails joined together and glued to the face of a cabinet, a face frame can stiffen a case opening to help prevent racking. It also provides a handy surface for installing hinges or other hardware for doors and drawers.

There are several styles of frames you can choose from, and various methods of joinery to consider, from simple biscuits and screws to more elaborate mortise-and-tenon joints. And you can use a frame on practically any type of cabinet, from conventional kitchen casework to curved or angled boxes such as corner cabinets.

Designing Face Frames

Face frame stock can be as wide and thick as you wish, but generally a stile and rail that are 1¼ in. to 2 in. wide are sufficient for stiffening the carcase without encroaching on valuable space inside the case. Frames ¾ in. to 1 in. thick provide plenty of support for attaching hardware. Joinery can be down and dirty, such as screws or biscuits, or more exacting, such as dowels or mortises and tenons. Your choice of joints can be tailored to your tooling and style of woodworking. One important consideration: Make sure to size the rails so the assembled frame

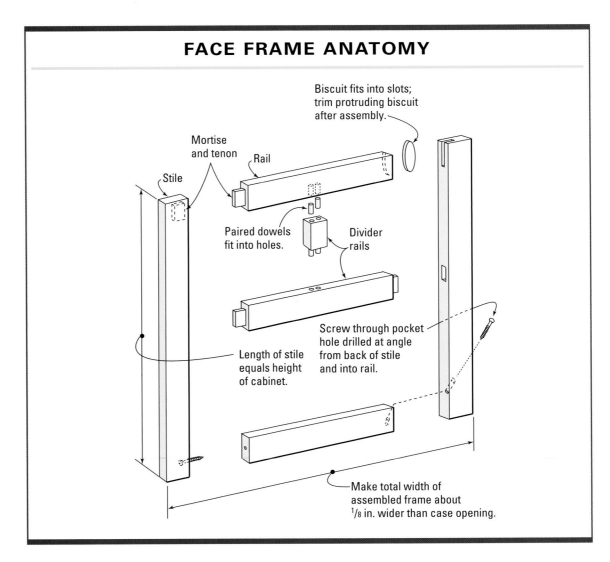

FACE FRAME ANATOMY

Biscuit fits into slots; trim protruding biscuit after assembly.

Mortise and tenon

Rail

Stile

Paired dowels fit into holes.

Divider rails

Screw through pocket hole drilled at angle from back of stile and into rail.

Length of stile equals height of cabinet.

Make total width of assembled frame about 1/8 in. wider than case opening.

is slightly wider than the case. This leaves some material for trimming the frame flush to the sides of the case after gluing it in place.

When designing a cabinet that will be built into a room, you'll want to leave some scribe material in the frame so you can fit the cabinet tight to a wall or ceiling.

➤ See *"Scribing a Cabinet to a Wall"* on p. 196.

Keeping Biscuits Fresh

Biscuit, or plate, joinery is a very simple method for face frame construction.

➤ See *"Simple Square Frame"* on p. 251.

But a common problem is that the biscuits swell up over time as they absorb moisture and then fail to fit as designed when needed. They need to be kept dry, since

EXTENDING A FACE FRAME

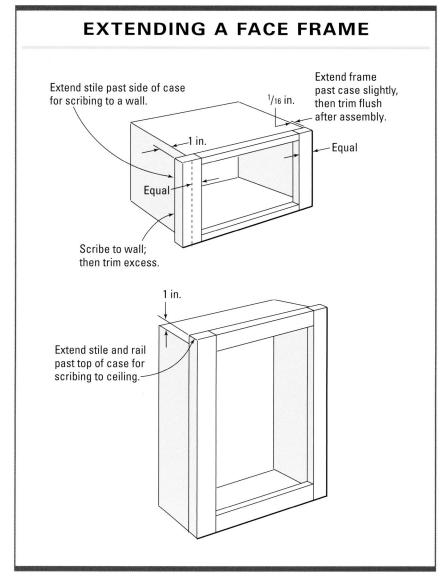

Extend stile past side of case for scribing to a wall.

Extend frame past case slightly, then trim flush after assembly.

1/16 in.

1 in.

Equal

Equal

Scribe to wall; then trim excess.

1 in.

Extend stile and rail past top of case for scribing to ceiling.

Drop a bag or two of desiccant into a jar filled with plate biscuits to keep them dry.

they're compressed during manufacture and want to swell in the slots once glue is applied. Leaving your biscuits lying around the shop will encourage them to pick up ambient moisture, making for a too-tight fit when you try to install them in their slots.

You can overcome the tendency for biscuits to swell before their time by keeping them in a jar with a tight-fitting lid. Drop a packet or two of silica, a natural desiccant, into the jar along with the biscuits. You can collect little bags of silica from all sorts of commercially packaged products, such as kitchenware and tools, or any item that's prone to rust. Place the bags in the oven on a regular basis to remove excess moisture.

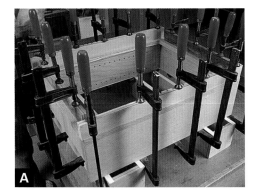

Attaching Face Frames

Although you can certainly nail a face frame to the front of a case, gluing the frame with clamps is a cleaner alternative. Because of the frame's relatively thin and narrow members, it can be difficult to apply sufficient clamping pressure over the frame for tight joints. The trick is to use some scrap cauls, about 2 in. wide, between the clamps and the frame to distribute the pressure. Spread glue on the edges of the case and carefully align the frame to the case. There should be about 1/16 in. of overhang on either side. Now position the cauls and apply clamps every 6 in. or so (**A**). If you see any gaps at the joint line, add more clamps.

Once the glue has dried, clamp the case on its side and use a bench plane to trim the small overhang (**B**). By keeping the body of the plane on the work and skewing the plane so the cutter is over the frame only, you avoid planing into the side of the case. Smooth any difficult spots and remove plane tracks with a hand scraper (**C**).

Finish by sanding the edge with 180-grit sandpaper wrapped around a felt block. If you're careful with your grain selection when picking the stiles of the frame, you can make the joint almost disappear (**D**).

Simple Square Frame

One of the easiest ways for constructing a frame is to mill square stock; then join it using biscuits. This technique works well when the case won't be seen at the top and the bottom, such as a base cabinet that will be covered with a counter-top or a wall cabinet hung at eye level. Cut all the stiles and rails to length; then dry-fit the parts and use a biscuit to lay out the joints. If you draw a centerline on the biscuit, you can mark the stiles and rails by eye if you position the bis-cuit so it won't protrude inside the frame (**A**).

Cut half slots for the biscuits with a plate joiner. On such narrow pieces, use a shopmade fixture to secure the stock so your hands are out of the way (**B**). Slot all the stiles and rails using the fix-ture, aligning the center mark on the joiner with the marks you made on the stock (**C**).

Spread glue in the half slots, insert the biscuits, and clamp the frame together (**D**). Then saw the protruding biscuits flush with a backsaw (**E**).

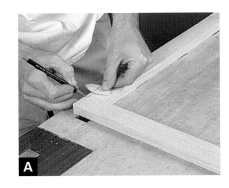

Slotting Stiles

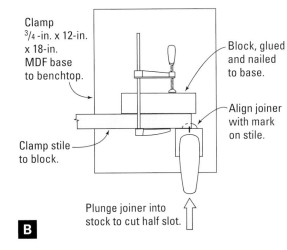

Clamp ³/₄-in. x 12-in. x 18-in. MDF base to benchtop.

Block, glued and nailed to base.

Clamp stile to block.

Align joiner with mark on stile.

Plunge joiner into stock to cut half slot.

Slotting Rails

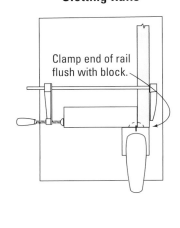

Clamp end of rail flush with block.

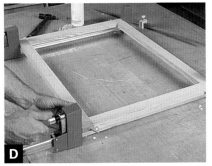

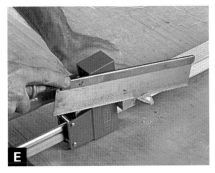

Rail length = opening between stiles + combined mortise
depth + combined width of beads and fillet.

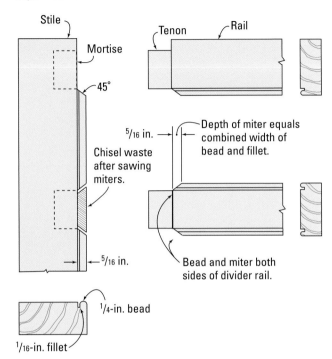

Stile

Mortise

45°

Tenon   Rail

5/16 in.

Chisel waste
after sawing
miters.

Depth of miter equals
combined width of
bead and fillet.

5/16 in.

Bead and miter both
sides of divider rail.

1/4-in. bead

1/16-in. fillet

A

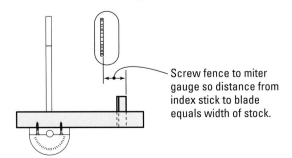

Fence, 3/4-in. x 2-in. x 14-in.
hardwood plywood

4 in.

Kerf, 45° miter in
plywood with saw-
blade on table saw.

5/16 in.

Plane bottom of stick
flush with bottom
of fence.

Glue 1/8-in. x 1/4-in. x 1 3/4-in.
hardwood indexing
stick into kerf.

Screw fence to miter
gauge so distance from
index stick to blade
equals width of stock.

B

Beaded Frame

Introducing a bead on the inner edge of a face
frame can add some extra spice, especially if
you're reproducing traditional cabinets on which
beads were often a common detail. The key to a
successful beaded frame is to miter the beads
where they meet in a corner (**A**).

Instead of cutting the miters by hand, I use a
table saw and a simple mitering jig that indexes
the tricky inside miters (**B**). Start by cutting the
stock to length; then bead all the rails and stiles
on the router table with a beading bit. A 1/4-in.
beading bit gives a nice proportion to most
frames about 1 1/2 in. wide. Be sure to rout double
beads on interior divider members (**C**).

After beading the stock, cut all the joints, making
sure to take into account the depth of the combined miters on the ends of the rails. Then crank
the sawblade to 45 degrees and use the rip
fence to register the work as you miter the ends
of the rails (**D**). If you need to cut very large
miters—when the blade is high above the table—
then play it safe and clamp a block to the rip
fence well before the blade. Use the block as
your reference surface instead of the fence.

Once you've sawn the rail miters, use the same setup to cut the miters at the ends of the stiles as well as to cut one side of each area that receives a divider rail. For accuracy and safety, always work with the short end of the stile against the fence (**E**).

Use the mitering jig attached to the miter gauge to cut the opposite side of each interior, or divider, miter. Move the rip fence out of the way and register the opposing miter cut on the indexing stick in the jig. Then hold the work against the jig and push it through the tilted blade (**F**).

Once you've cut all the miters, chisel out the waste in between the divider miters and at the ends of the stiles, and dry-fit the frame. Then assemble the frame with glue, clamping across all the joints and checking for square (**G**).

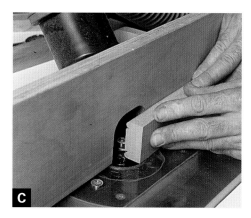

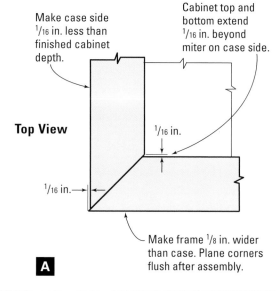

Make case side ¹/₁₆ in. less than finished cabinet depth.

Cabinet top and bottom extend ¹/₁₆ in. beyond miter on case side.

Top View

¹/₁₆ in.

¹/₁₆ in.

Make frame ¹/₈ in. wider than case. Plane corners flush after assembly.

A

Mitered Frame and Case

When you want the joint between a face frame and case to disappear, miter the edges of both the case and the frame, join the two with clamps, and glue (**A**). This eliminates the butt joint on the side of the cabinet and fools the eye into thinking the cabinet is constructed from extra-thick sides. Before assembling the case, miter the case sides to 45 degrees on the table saw with the panel face side down (**B**). Make sure to size the sides as shown.

Assemble the case; then glue up the face frame, holding it with pipe clamps and quick clamps (**C**). Check to see that the width of the frame is about ¹/₈ in. wider overall than the case, protruding ¹/₁₆ in. on each side. Once the glue dries, saw the miter along the face frame to a knife edge. Stabilize the work with a tall fence secured to the rip fence and use featherboards (**D**).

Glue the frame to the cabinet, using cauls beneath the clamps to distribute pressure. To prevent slippage at the miter joints, place clamps both side to side and front to back (**E**).

Trim the overhanging frame with a plane or with a sanding block (**F**). Then ease the sharp corners by rounding them over gently with some 220-grit sandpaper.

B

C

D

E

F

Angled Frame

Angled frames, such as you find in corner cabinets, are usually mitered at the edges to fit the case—and gluing the joint together can be tricky. To build the frame for a corner cabinet, construct the frame as you would a conventional face frame; then rip 22½-degree miters on both sides of the frame on the table saw to correspond to the angled sides of the cabinet (**A**). A board clamped to the rip fence closes the gap at the table to prevent the long point of the miter from binding under the fence. To help in ripping such a large frame, use a featherboard or hold-in to keep the frame firmly against the fence (**B**).

Even with a good-quality rip blade, chances are you'll get some scoring or burning making this bevel cut. Before gluing the joints, clean up any irregularities in the miters with a block plane (**C**).

The challenge when attaching angled frames is gluing them to the case sides, because the parts want to slip as you apply clamp pressure. The shopmade cauls shown here give purchase to the clamps so they apply pressure at 90 degrees across the center of the joint. Position the cauls around the frame and use opposing cauls around the mitered case side; then draw the joint together with quick clamps (**D**).

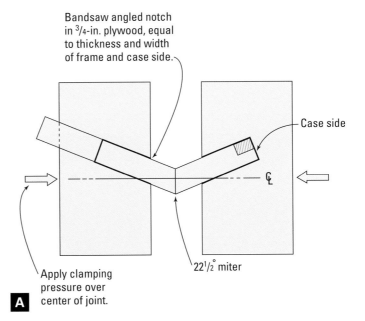

Bandsaw angled notch in ¾-in. plywood, equal to thickness and width of frame and case side.

Case side

$22\frac{1}{2}°$ miter

Apply clamping pressure over center of joint.

A

B

C

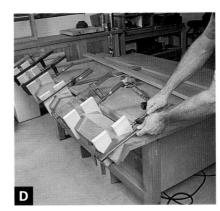

D

Frame and Panel

Making Panels

➤ Flat Panel with
Reveal (p. 261)

➤ Solid-Wood Raised
Panel (p. 262)

➤ Veneered Raised
Panel (p. 264)

Back Strategies

➤ Removable Plywood
Back (p. 265)

➤ Grooved-and-
Splined Back
(p. 266)

➤ Frame-and-Panel
Back (p. 267)

THE FRAME AND PANEL is a brilliant design solution for solid-wood furniture, because it so aptly solves the problem of wood movement. Take a wide, solid-wood panel and house it in grooves cut in a frame so it can expand and contract freely and yet be restrained flat. That's the essence of a frame and panel. And yet the design goes so much further, since the look of a panel in a frame has a broad visual appeal for many different styles of furniture. Used for making frame-and-panel doors, case sides and backs, chest lids, dividers, dust panels, and even wall paneling, the frame and panel is indispensable for general furniture making.

➤ See *"Building Doors"* on p. 132.

Frame-and-panel construction is, for the most part, identical to making paneled doors. If you're going to attach the panel directly over a case surface, such as a cabinet side, you won't have to pay much attention to the back surfaces of the frame and the panel—since tool and machine marks won't be seen. And the construction isn't limited to solid-wood affairs: A frame and panel can just as well be incorporated into plywood or other sheet-good constructions when you want to impart the look and feel of solid wood. Best of all, a frame and panel adds detail and depth, because the offset surfaces offer facets of light and shadow.

Frame-and-Panel Construction

Like doors, frame-and-panel assemblies for cabinets can be constructed in a variety of ways, as shown below. Design choices include the style of panel, from flat or molded to raised. When your design requires a wide or tall panel, it's better to divide the frame to accept two or more panels. This keeps the assembly more stable and adds stiffness to the frame. You can add visual appeal by off-setting the stiles and rails, using different thicknesses of stock. Or add "legs" to a frame by simply extending the stiles beyond the bottom rail and then using the legs in your furniture design.

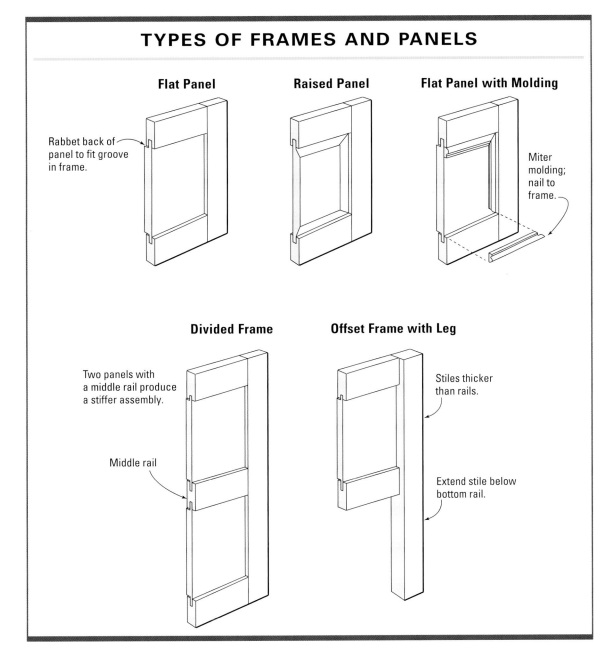

TYPES OF FRAMES AND PANELS

Flat Panel

Rabbet back of panel to fit groove in frame.

Raised Panel

Flat Panel with Molding

Miter molding; nail to frame.

Divided Frame

Two panels with a middle rail produce a stiffer assembly.

Middle rail

Offset Frame with Leg

Stiles thicker than rails.

Extend stile below bottom rail.

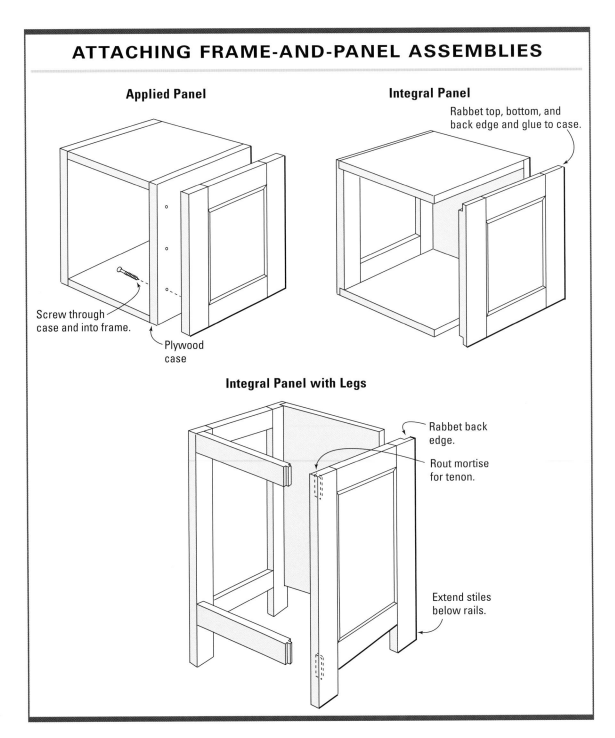

ATTACHING FRAME-AND-PANEL ASSEMBLIES

Applied Panel

Screw through case and into frame.

Plywood case

Integral Panel

Rabbet top, bottom, and back edge and glue to case.

Integral Panel with Legs

Rabbet back edge.

Rout mortise for tenon.

Extend stiles below rails.

Attaching Panels

A frame-and-panel assembly can be used as a conventional panel in casework, as shown above. You can use standard joinery to attach the panel to the case, including mortises and tenons, dadoes, biscuits, grooves, and dovetails. When designing a frame and panel, be sure to orient the stiles and rails so they align with the connecting members of the case to avoid cutting joints in the panel.

TYPES OF BACKS

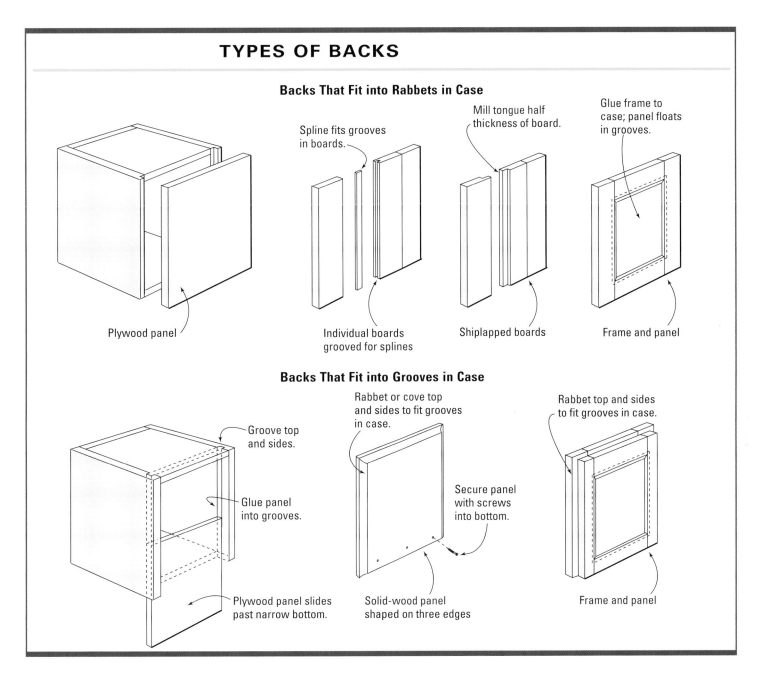

Backs That Fit into Rabbets in Case

Spline fits grooves in boards.

Mill tongue half thickness of board.

Glue frame to case; panel floats in grooves.

Plywood panel

Individual boards grooved for splines

Shiplapped boards

Frame and panel

Backs That Fit into Grooves in Case

Groove top and sides.

Rabbet or cove top and sides to fit grooves in case.

Rabbet top and sides to fit grooves in case.

Glue panel into grooves.

Secure panel with screws into bottom.

Plywood panel slides past narrow bottom.

Solid-wood panel shaped on three edges

Frame and panel

And if you're joining a frame and panel to a plywood panel, glue or screw the frame to the case, not the panel. This approach leaves the panel free to expand and contract.

Backs for Cabinets

Frame-and-panel construction really shines if you want to dress up the back of a cabinet, since it will look good on both the inside and the back of the case. And a frame and panel allows you to use relatively wide solid-wood panels without worrying about wood movement. For special projects, or when the back of the case will be seen, the extra effort required to install a good-looking back is worth it. Many times, we need a back that

▶ DROP-DOWN RABBETING FENCE

A "sacrificial" plywood fence can be used with most box-style rip fences, which lets you make cuts where you need to bury the blade (such as when rabbeting the edge of a board) without cutting into your existing fence. The fence installs in seconds by dropping it over your rip fence—no tools or hardware. To use the fence, lower the blade and move the rip fence until the plywood fence is above the blade; then slowly raise the blade into the plywood. When one side gets too chewed up, you can turn the fence around to use the opposite side.

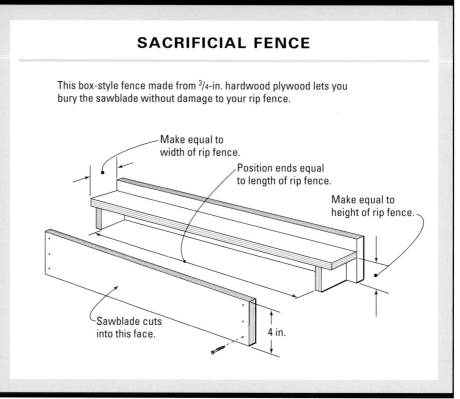

SACRIFICIAL FENCE

This box-style fence made from $^3/_4$-in. hardwood plywood lets you bury the sawblade without damage to your rip fence.

Make equal to width of rip fence.

Position ends equal to length of rip fence.

Make equal to height of rip fence.

Sawblade cuts into this face.

4 in.

looks good from the inside of the case only. Hardwood plywood with a high-quality face veneer on one side is a good choice for these applications.

To avoid seeing the edges of the back panel, you need to recess it into the case sides. The easiest approach is to rabbet the back of the case and then glue and nail the back into the rabbets, as shown on p. 259. Another option is to cut grooves in the case and rabbet the edges of the back to fit the grooves. With this approach, it's best to cut grooves in the top and sides only; then make the case bottom narrower so the back can slide past the bottom and into sides and top. You can groove all the case parts for the back; but this makes assembly tricky, because the back must be installed at the same time as you assemble the case. And if you ever need to remove the back, you're out of luck.

Flat Panel with Reveal

The most basic of all frame-and-panel construction is a flat panel captured in grooves cut in the frame. Instead of using a thin panel that can rattle around in the frame, it's best to use a thicker panel; then rabbet its edges to fit the grooves. Technically, the panel isn't flat at this point, since you've introduced a stepped edge along its perimeter. For a traditional flat panel, you simply orient the rabbet on the inside of the case so the show side displays a flat, uninterrupted surface. However, you can use the rabbeted edge as a design element if you reverse the panel and show the stepped edge on the panel's face. To allow for wood movement, dimension the panel about ¼ in. narrower on its long-grain edges, as shown here (**A**).

Once you've milled a rabbet in the panel to fit the grooves in the frame, bevel the shoulders of the rabbet with a sanding block or a small plane (**B**).

During assembly, insert thin shims between the frame and the panel to keep the panel centered before applying pressure with clamps (**C**). Make sure no glue migrates from the frame joints and onto the edges of the panel or into the grooves.

After the frame is assembled, you're left with a distinctive gap or reveal between the stile and the panel on the long-grain edges. Note that the rail fits tight to the end-grain edges of the panel, since wood movement in this direction is not an issue (**D**).

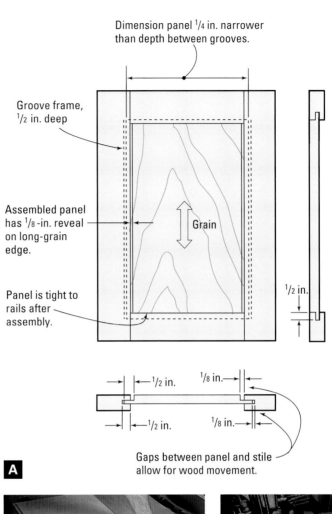

Dimension panel ¼ in. narrower than depth between grooves.

Groove frame, ½ in. deep

Assembled panel has ⅛-in. reveal on long-grain edge.

Grain

Panel is tight to rails after assembly.

½ in.

½ in.

½ in.

½ in.

⅛ in.

⅛ in.

Gaps between panel and stile allow for wood movement.

A

B

C

D

Solid-Wood Raised Panel

The easiest method of raising panels is on the router table, using a panel-raising bit and a sturdy fence. You'll need a powerful (3 hp or more) router with an base opening large enough for the diameter of the cutter. If the cutter exceeds 2 in. in diameter, be sure to use a router with speed control so you can lower the speed of the motor to around 10,000 rpm for safety. To prevent blowing out the edges, make a series of cuts by turning the panel counterclockwise after milling an edge, orienting the next edge against the fence. Rout with the face down on the table, starting with the end-grain edge and then routing the long-grain edge (**A**).

Make successively deeper passes instead of routing the bevels in one shot. The last pass should be a light, skimming cut at an even speed feed to remove any burning or tearout (**B**). The finished edge of the panel should fit snugly into the groove in the frame (**C**).

If you don't have access to a raised-panel cutter, you can raise a panel on the table saw. The first step is to groove the panel to the depth of the desired field, creating a shoulder on all four sides. Raise the table-saw blade to the correct height; then push the stock face side down over the blade (**D**).

Tilt the sawblade to the desired angle of the bevel—15 degrees to 25 degrees is optimum; the smaller the angle, the wider the bevel. Make sure the blade tilts *away* from the fence to avoid trapping the offcut; use a throat plate that fits closely around the blade to support the narrow edge of the work. Attach a tall fence to your rip fence and raise the blade until it barely intersects the depth at which you cut the grooves (**E**).

The surface quality on a sawn bevel is never perfect, particularly in hard or dense woods. You can use a hand scraper to clean up saw marks and remove any burning (**F**). For greater accuracy and a flatter surface, use a shoulder plane. Refine the field's shoulder by holding the plane level with the panel (**G**); then smooth the face of the bevel (**H**).

[**TIP**] **You've raised all the panels and milled the grooves in your frames and now you find one or more panels are slightly too tight to fit into the frames. Instead of going back to reshape the panel, you can fix the thick edge with a few swipes from a plane. Turn the panel face down and use a block plane to shave the offending edge on the back face. By holding the plane at a slight angle, you can shave the edge until it fits the groove, and no one will notice the slight taper on the back of the panel.**

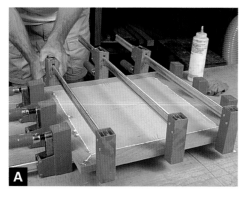

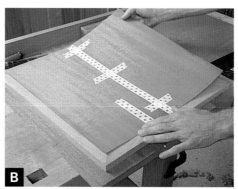

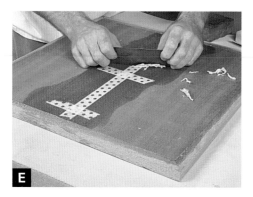

Veneered Raised Panel

Here's a neat trick I picked up from woodworker Paul Sapporito for making raised panels from plywood or MDF combined with narrow strips of solid wood and a couple sheets of veneer. The result is a panel that's stable and bypasses the problem of wood movement. It's a great technique for producing really wide panels or when you want to incorporate fine veneer into your work. First, rip some solid-wood edging about ⅛ in. wider than of the width of the bevel you'll be cutting, using the same species as your veneer. Then miter and glue the edging to the edges of the panel (**A**). When the glue dries, level the banding flush with the surface of the panel.

➤ See *"Flush–Trimmed Lippings"* on p. 75.

Before veneering the panel, make a reference mark on one edge to indicate the show side. Cut your face veneer so that it overlaps the inner edge of the banding by ¼ in. or more. Let the veneer for the back of the panel extend beyond the assembly (**B**). Press the veneer onto both sides of the panel using cauls and clamps, a veneer press, or a vacuum and bag. A vinyl caul over the veneer prevents glue from sticking to the bag (**C**).

Once the veneer has dried, trim the overhang on the back with a flush-trimming bit (**D**). Then scrape and sand the veneer smooth. Wiping the surface with a damp sponge helps loosen any veneer tape (**E**). Raise the panel on the shaper or router table.

➤ See *"Solid–Wood Raised Panel"* on p. 262.

The raised panel differs visually from a conventional, solid-wood panel since there's long grain running around all four edges (**F**).

Removable Plywood Back

Using plywood for a case back has the advantage of stability, allowing you to use a wide panel without the concern for wood movement. And screwing the back into rabbets in the case lets you remove it for applying a finish. Before you assemble the cabinet, rabbet the sides ⅜ in. deep and make the rabbet width equal to the thickness of the back panel. Use a stacked dado blade and attach an auxiliary fence to the rip fence so you can bury the blade (**A**).

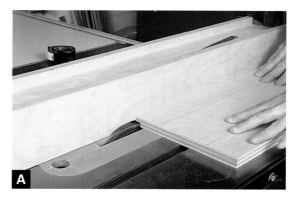

➤ See *"Drop-Down Rabbetting Fence"* on p. 260.

Once you've assembled the case, countersink the back for screws and secure the back without glue into the rabbets and into the top and bottom of the case. Temporarily clamp across the case to keep the sides tight to the back. Then toenail the screws at a slight angle for good purchase into the rabbets (**B**).

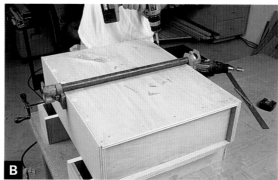

When it comes time for applying a finish, remove the back and lay it horizontally for more control over the finishing process. Finishing the insides of the cabinet without the back in place is much easier, too, since you can reach the very back surfaces without running into abrupt corners (**C**).

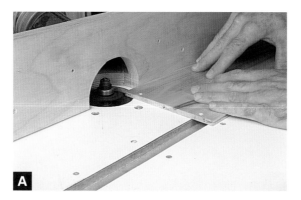

A

Grooved-and-Splined Back

A splined back panel is made from several separate boards fitted edge to edge and then let into rabbets in the case. Grooves along the edges of the boards accept wood splines, which stiffen the assembly and conceal gaps between adjacent boards. Start by routing a narrow groove along the edges of each backboard. You can use a thin ⅟₁₆-in. slotting cutter to rout grooves of any width by simply adjusting the bit height after each pass (**A**).

Rip some splines to fit the grooves. The width of the splines should equal the combined depth of two grooves. Fit the backboards together, slipping the splines between the boards without using glue (**B**).

Install the boards as a discreet panel into rabbets in the back of the case, screwing them in place through countersunk holes. Make sure to leave a small gap between each board for expansion (**C**).

B

C

Frame-and-Panel Back

For a back that looks as good as the front of the cabinet, you can glue a frame-and-panel back into rabbets milled in the case. This is a ton of work, so it's worthwhile only if the piece is really high end or it will be freestanding and seen from the back.

Mill the rabbets slightly deeper than the frame is thick; then assemble the case. The key to a tight-fitting joint is to build the frame slightly larger than the rabbet opening in the case and then plane a very slight back-bevel on the edge of the frame until it just fits the case (**A**).

Grab your bar clamps, because you're going to need all of them to attach the back to the case. Brush glue into the rabbets; then drop the back into them and clamp the sides, top, and bottom of the case to pull the joints tight. Cauls between the case and the clamps help distribute the clamping pressure (**B**).

You'll have some cleanup work to do once the glue has dried. Use a handplane to level the slightly raised rabbeted edges of the case flush to the back panel (**C**).

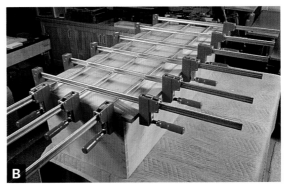

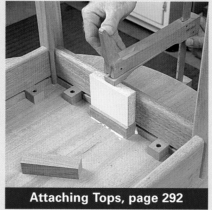

Making Tops, page 270

Attaching Tops, page 292

PART SIX

Tabletops and Work Surfaces

AKING AND ATTACHING a tabletop or counter is the defining point in a cabinet or table's construction. An open framework or case is transformed into a useful work surface, and you're ready to prepare a meal, arrange a reading lamp, or any one of the myriad other daily tasks that a horizontal surface accommodates.

Tabletops and work surfaces share two important construction requirements: They must be flat and provide a usable surface. If the framework that will support the top is flat, then your main concern is in flattening the top itself. This is relatively simple if you're making a plywood or plastic laminate top. Solid wood is more challenging, especially if the top is wide.

Once you've made your top, you'll need to attach it to the base. The easiest approach is to screw into the top from underneath, and this is fine for man-made materials such as plywood and medium-density fiberboard (MDF). Solid-wood tops require a different approach that takes wood movement into account.

Making Tops

Top Construction

- ➤ Wide Solid-Wood Top (p. 276)
- ➤ Wood-Edged Plywood (p. 278)
- ➤ Easing Hard Corners (p. 279)
- ➤ Round Top (p. 279)
- ➤ Filling Holes (p. 280)
- ➤ Laminate Countertop (p. 281)

Top Options

- ➤ Leather Desktop (p. 284)
- ➤ Tooling Leather (p. 285)
- ➤ Lift-Up Lid (p. 286)
- ➤ Using Natural Defects (p. 287)

Leaves and Ends

- ➤ Breadboard Ends (p. 288)
- ➤ Biscuit Breadboard Ends (p. 290)
- ➤ Drop-In Table Leaves (p. 291)

A HORIZONTAL SURFACE OR TOP may be the most useful of all everyday objects. Whether it's a tabletop, a desktop, a countertop, or the lid of a chest, the surface has a vital function: It may close and seal a chest, it may give us a place to work, or it may simply provide a place to spread out our stuff. Tops should be flat, and they should be smooth and well finished so we can enjoy their surfaces comfortably. If you choose a man-made material for your top, such as plywood or plastic laminate, you can construct broad surfaces quite easily and without much labor. If solid wood is your cup of tea, then making a wide top will involve some special considerations, such as wood movement and how to cope with it and finding a way to flatten and smooth such a large expanse of natural material.

Tops come is all shapes and sizes, from round and elliptical to long and wide. The final surface will often depend on your needs. For special work areas, such as an executive desktop, using leather is a great way of embellishing a top with a very refined surface. If you need a durable workstation, such as a kitchen counter, covering a top in plastic laminate makes sense.

When company arrives, you might want to expand a small tabletop into something more accommodating. Tables with drop-in leaves, or leaves that pull out, can quickly transform

TOPS ON FURNITURE

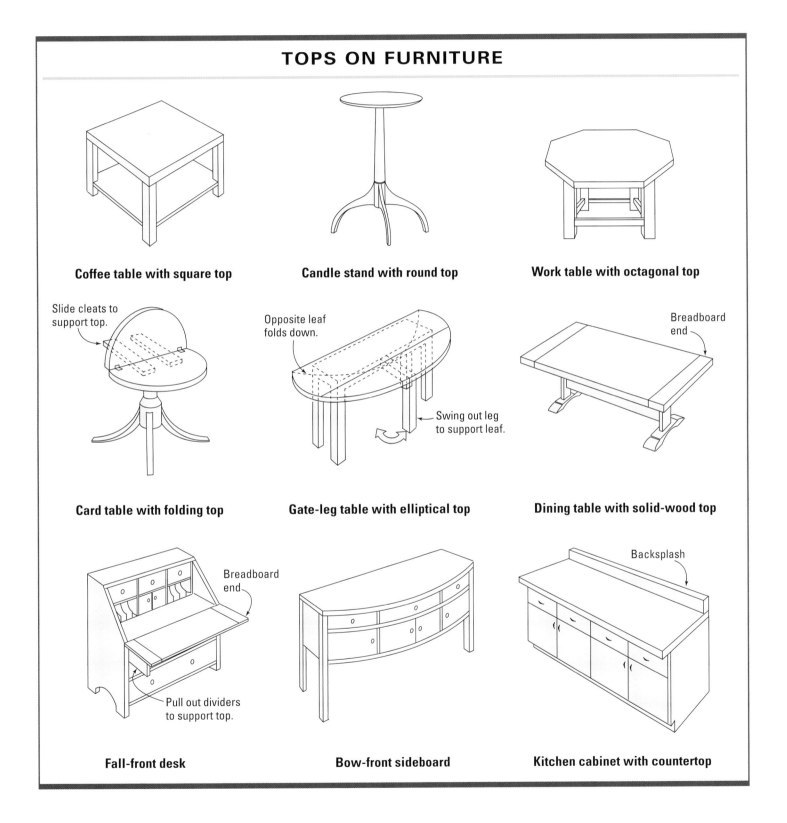

Coffee table with square top

Candle stand with round top

Work table with octagonal top

Slide cleats to support top.

Opposite leaf folds down.

Breadboard end

Swing out leg to support leaf.

Card table with folding top

Gate-leg table with elliptical top

Dining table with solid-wood top

Breadboard end

Backsplash

Pull out dividers to support top.

Fall-front desk

Bow-front sideboard

Kitchen cabinet with countertop

a small utility table into an expansive surface fit for a feast. To keep your guests comfortable, yet still retain a sense of style, you should consider the treatment you give the edge of your tops. A small bevel or roundover along the edge of a tabletop will invite resting arms and add flair to a design; sharp edges are jarring.

Basic Top Design

Tabletops and work surfaces come in many flavors and styles, from utilitarian counters to high-end, inlaid masterpieces covered in rare veneers or exotic materials. The particular furniture's function plays an important role in deciding the style and construction of the top. Low tables, such as a coffee table, need a simple surface for drinks, books, magazines, and other paraphernalia or a pair of feet. More

complex structures, such as a fall-front desk or a gate-leg table, require tops that move or separate to create changing surfaces, depending on each use of the piece.

Grain Up, Down, or Alternating?

How should you orient the annular rings when you edge glue planks to form a top? The correct approach is to arrange your boards so the growth rings all face in the same direction—an easy task by looking at the end-grain pattern on the end of each board. There are two reasons to avoid alternating the grain: The first is that, as individual boards move and cup, the top takes on a washboard-type surface. Second, alternating boards results in a visual light and dark contrast between different boards, most noticeable as strong light rakes across the top. With matched boards, you'll get an overall curve, which will be held flat by the frame or case that supports it. Plus you'll achieve an even reflection or contrast as the light plays over the surface.

Once you've arranged the boards facing the same direction, you need to decide which face to show. Whenever possible, avoid the "outside" of the tree. You'll find it best to display the inside of the tree on all the show faces. This surface has a richer grain pattern and a deeper reflection.

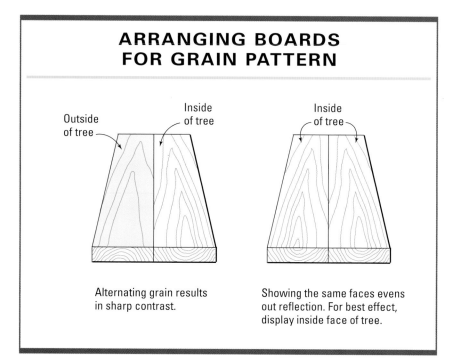

ARRANGING BOARDS FOR GRAIN PATTERN

Outside of tree

Inside of tree

Inside of tree

Alternating grain results in sharp contrast.

Showing the same faces evens out reflection. For best effect, display inside face of tree.

Tabletop Edge Treatments

Treating the edges of your tops with special consideration will add style to your furniture, plus make it more pleasing to the eye and more comfortable to use. Unlike shelving, for which it's usually easiest to rout or shape an edge by bringing the work to the tool, it's generally best to rout a profile on a large top by moving a router and the appropriate bit around the edges. Make sure to use a bit equipped with a ball-bearing pilot to make these freehand cuts. Or mold a separate piece and attach it to the top with tenons or a tongue-and-groove joint.

Two Ways to Generate an Ellipse

Oval or elliptical tops offer and intriguing look and feel unlike any other curve. Based on an accelerating curve, an ellipse seems to flow with a natural rhythm all its own. Cutting and shaping an elliptical top is a simple affair and can be done with handheld power tools, such as a jigsaw, or on the bandsaw. But laying out an ellipse can't be done by hand; you'll need a mechanical method to figure it out. The simplest method is to use a compass, some string, and a pencil to draw the ellipse (see the drawing on p. 274). The downside is that inconsistent tension on the string can create a slightly distorted shape. For a more accurate oval, you can use a trammel and framing square.

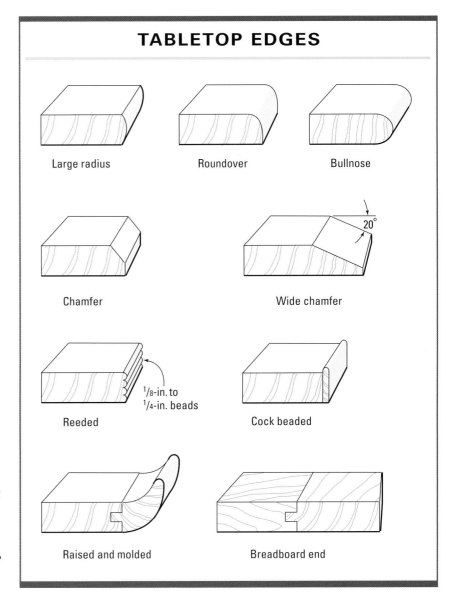

TABLETOP EDGES

Large radius

Roundover

Bullnose

Chamfer

Wide chamfer — 20°

Reeded — 1/8-in. to 1/4-in. beads

Cock beaded

Raised and molded

Breadboard end

TWO WAYS TO GENERATE AN ELLIPSE

String and Pencil

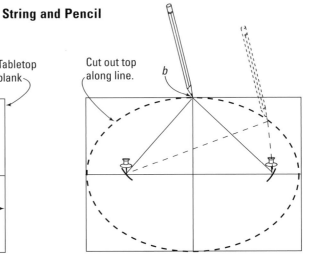

Step 1. Cut a rectangle to outer dimensions of the desired ellipse. Draw *x* and *y* axes through its center.

Step 2. To locate the foci, set compass for a distance *a* and swing two arcs from point *b*.

Step 3. Attach push pins or small brads at each focus; tie a string to pins so that a pencil placed at point *b* pulls string taut.

Step 4. Move pencil around foci while keeping string taut to draw the ellipse.

Trammel and Square

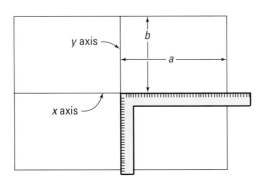

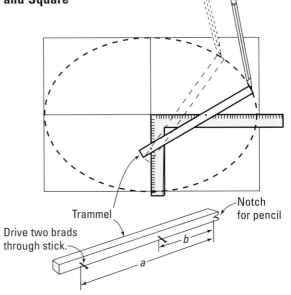

Step 1. Cut a rectangle to outer dimensions of desired ellipse. Draw *x* and *y* axes through its center.

Step 2. Hold framing square or plywood sticks along one quadrant of *x* and *y* axes.

Step 3. Hold pencil in trammel notch, with brads against square, and draw one-quarter of ellipse. Reposition square to draw remaining quarters of ellipse.

Installing Rule Joint Hinges

On drop-leaf tables, where the leaves fold down, a rule joint is one of the best ways of articulating the leaves. Construction of the top and its leaves is straightforward: Use a roundover bit to rout a thumbnail profile on the two long edges of the top, leaving an ⅛-in. shoulder. Then use a matching cove bit to cut a cove on the edge of each leaf. Test your setup first on some scrap of the same thickness as the leaf to ensure a perfect match. Now comes the tricky part: Laying out and cutting for the hinges. You'll need special rule joint hinges, also known as drop-leaf hinges (available at some hardware stores and from common woodworking catalogs).

Lay out for the hinges first, allowing a 1/32-in. offset to avoid binding the leaf as it's rotated over the top. Then rout or chisel the mortises for the hinge leaves and a secondary, deeper channel for the hinge knuckle. Install the hinges and check the action. If any spots rub, adjust the fit with a block plane or some sandpaper.

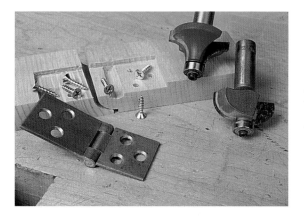

Matched cove and roundover bits create the rule joint used in drop-leaf tables. The joint gets its name from the traditional folding rules that have brass joints of the same design.

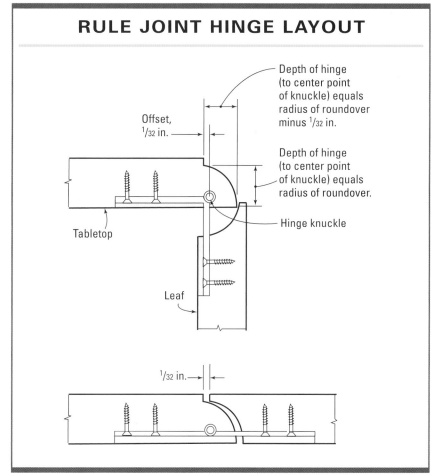

RULE JOINT HINGE LAYOUT

Offset, 1/32 in.

Depth of hinge (to center point of knuckle) equals radius of roundover minus 1/32 in.

Depth of hinge (to center point of knuckle) equals radius of roundover.

Hinge knuckle

Tabletop

Leaf

1/32 in.

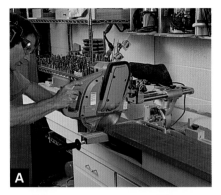

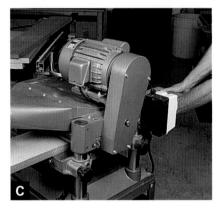
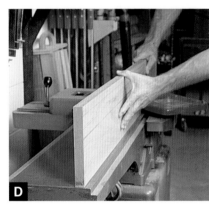

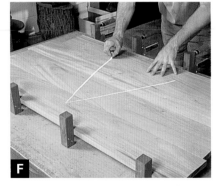

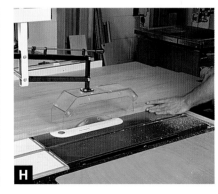

Wide Solid-Wood Top

Constructing a wide, solid-wood top is straight-forward if you follow a few basic steps. The same procedure can be used for making all sorts of wide panels, from case sides, tops, and bottoms to shelves and other horizontal surfaces. Begin by crosscutting rough stock oversize in length by 4 in. or so (**A**).

Flatten one face of each board on the jointer (**B**). Then thickness plane the opposite face (**C**) and continue planing equally on both sides until you've reached the desired thickness. Joint one edge on each board (**D**); then rip the opposite edge on the table saw and joint that edge, too.

Here's a technique that saves time and effort: Before you glue the boards together, handplane the show surfaces to remove any machine marks. This way, all you'll need to do is flush up the joints after glue-up, instead of planing or sanding the entire surface (**E**). Arrange the boards for the best possible grain pattern across the joints and mark a V to help you orient the boards during glue-up (**F**).

To keep the boards flat and aligned with each other during gluing, clamp stout battens across the ends. Wax paper under the battens prevent them from sticking to the glue. First, apply light pressure across the joints with bar clamps. Then clamp the battens to the ends and go back and fully tighten the bar clamps (**G**). Once the glue has dried, rip both long edges to remove any marks or dings and to ensure that the edges are parallel (**H**).

There are a couple of options for squaring the ends of the glued-up panel. The first method involves clamping a straightedge across the end of the panel to act as a fence. One commercial straightedge, available from many woodworking catalogs, has integral clamps; but a stout, straight piece of wood clamped to the workpiece will work just as well. Make sure the fence is square to the long edges by checking with a large square (**I**). Use a circular saw to crosscut the edge square, making sure to account for the width of the saw's baseplate when you position the fence (**J**). To clean up the saw marks, reposition the fence and use a router and a straight bit to rout about $\frac{1}{16}$ in. off the sawn edge. Equipping your router with an oversize baseplate helps stabilize the router and keeps the bit square to the work (**K**).

Another alternative for squaring up the ends of a large panel is to use a sliding table on the table saw. There are many great aftermarket sliders available for relatively low cost, and they work with most types of saws (**L**). Finish up by lightly sanding the top, leveling the edge joints, and smoothing the entire surface. Thanks to your previous efforts with the handplane, there won't be much sanding work at all.

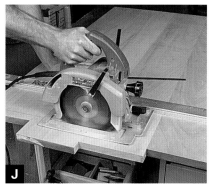

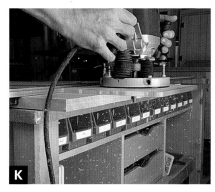

[**TIP**] Machine fences and tables need to be dead square to register the work accurately. Instead of relying on machine stops and screws, it's more accurate to measure the tool at the source. A small 6-in. machinist's square is usually sufficient for the task. Hold the square tight to one surface and look for daylight between the square and the adjacent surface. When you can't see light, the two surfaces are square to each other.

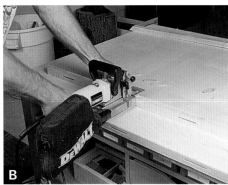

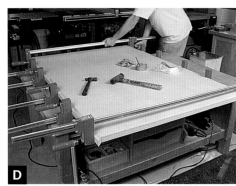

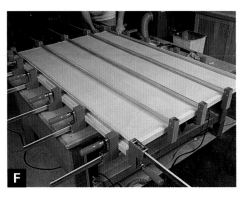

Wood-Edged Plywood

Plywood is an excellent choice for wide tops because you won't have to worry about wood movement and it needs only light sanding.

To conceal the raw edges and add durability, you'll need to edge the panel with solid wood. Mill the edging stock; then miter one end of each strip, keeping all the strips long for now. To locate the opposite miter accurately, hold two mitered corners together, clamp the piece to be marked, and mark for the miter on the free corner (**A**). Mark and cut the long strips to final length in this manner, using the miter saw.

Biscuits will help align the strips when gluing them to the plywood. Mark for the biscuits along the longer plywood edges and on the longer strips, and cut slots every 8 in. or so (**B**).

Glue the two long strips first. Use a dry short piece to help with positioning each long strip by holding its miter against the glued strip (**C**). Use as many clamps as necessary to pull the joints tight along the entire edge (**D**).

As the first strips dry, make the final miter cuts in the shorter strips by holding each strip against the two long strips. Keep mitering one end of the strip until it just fits between the miters (**E**). Then mark and cut for biscuits and glue and clamp the remaining strips in place, clamping the miters to close these joints (**F**). Finish up by leveling the edging flush with the veneered surface.

Easing Hard Corners

The first time you bump into a sharp corner on a tabletop, you won't think kindly of the craftsman who made the piece. Don't let this happen to your furniture. A quick way of softening an edge is to plane a small chamfer on the corner with a block plane (**A**). Then follow by easing the facets to round with 180-grit sandpaper attached to a block (**B**). Your friends will thank you for being so thoughtful.

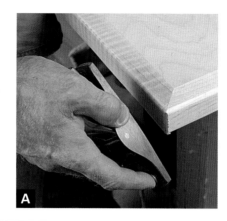

Round Top

Cutting a panel into a circle can be done on the bandsaw or with the jigsaw. But the results are often far from accurate. You can cut a precise circle of practically any diameter using a plunge router, a straight bit, and a trammel made from ¼-in. plywood. Fasten the trammel to the router's base; then measure from the edge of the bit and drive a screw through the trammel to the desired radius. Any bottom-cutting straight bit will work, but I find a four- or six-flute end mill bit makes the cleanest cut, especially when working on end grain (**A**).

Clamp a piece of scrap to the bench, apply strips of carpet tape (double-sided tape) to the top of the workpiece, and flip the work over to adhere it to the scrap (**B**). Screw the trammel to the underside of the top in the center and set the bit depth about ¼ in. deep. Rout in a counterclockwise direction, pivoting the trammel and router around the screw (**C**). Continue making successively deeper passes by lowering the bit with each pass until you've routed through the work and into the scrap (**D**).

Use the dull edge of a putty knife to pry the finished top off the scrap; then remove the carpet tape from the top surface (**E**). Light sanding on the edges is all you need to complete a perfect circle.

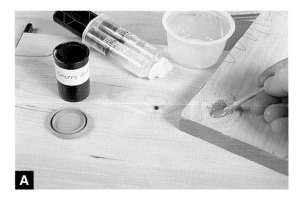

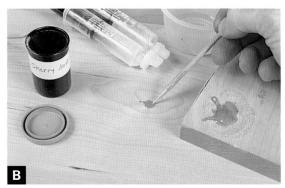

Filling Holes

Making solid-wood tops often involves working with small knots and other minor defects. You can conceal them with epoxy, which makes a great filler for knotholes and other blemishes because it dries hard and, more important, doesn't shrink. For small defects, use a two-part, 5-min. epoxy, which sets up in—you guessed it—5 min. Bigger jobs require an epoxy with a longer open time, letting you fill the crevice completely before it starts to harden. Mix the epoxy thoroughly; then combine it with sanding dust from the project you're working on until you get a creamy consistency (**A**).

With cracks that go right through a board, you'll need to mask the underside of the workpiece with tape to prevent the thin epoxy from flowing out of the crevice. Fill the hole by letting the epoxy mound over (**B**). It may take two or more applications before you completely fill the defect.

When the epoxy mixture has cured hard, level it with a scraper and sanding block (**C**).

Laminate Countertop

Particleboard is the substrate, or core material, of choice for plastic laminate countertops. Particleboard is inexpensive, dimensionally stable, and relatively flat; and its hardness and density are great attributes for withstanding the abuse that countertops receive. Make sure you select industrial-grade particleboard, which is denser and more uniform than builder's sheets, known as flakeboard or chipboard. Typical countertop construction involves using a solid ¾-in.-thick panel for the top of the counter, with narrow, ¾-in.-thick cleats underneath (**A**). The cleats thicken the show edges to 1½ in., stiffen the overall assembly, and provide support for securing the top to a cabinet below.

Begin by cutting the panel about ⅛ in. oversize on the table saw and cut all the cleat stock to width. Glue and staple a cleat to the long front edge, using clamps to help position it flush with the edges of the panel (**B**). Then glue another cleat at the back edge and add short cleats perpendicular to the long cleats, roughly every 12 in (**C**). Once you've attached all the cleats, cut the panel to finished size, trimming the edges perfectly flush and square on the table saw (**D**).

To cover the surface with laminate, you'll need to cut all the laminate pieces about 1 in. oversize; then trim them after gluing to the substrate.

(Text continues on p. 282.)

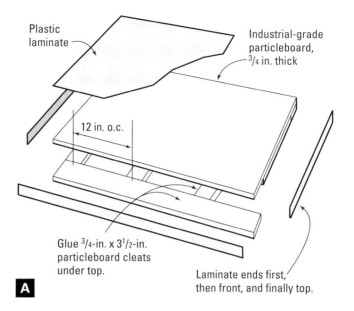

Plastic laminate

Industrial-grade particleboard, ¾ in. thick

12 in. o.c.

Glue ¾-in. x 3½-in. particleboard cleats under top.

Laminate ends first, then front, and finally top.

A

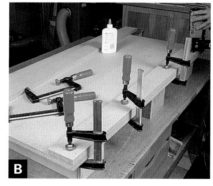

B

C

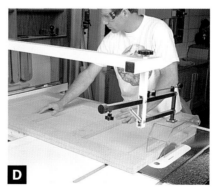

D

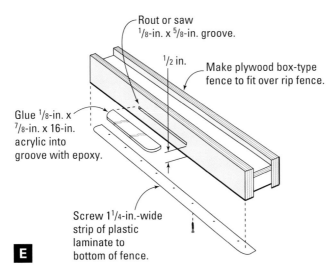

Rout or saw
$1/8$-in. x $5/8$-in. groove.

$1/2$ in.

Make plywood box-type
fence to fit over rip fence.

Glue $1/8$-in. x
$7/8$-in. x 16-in.
acrylic into
groove with epoxy.

Screw $1\,1/4$-in.-wide
strip of plastic
laminate to
bottom of fence.

E

Ordinary carbide-tipped sawblades do a fine job of cutting plastic laminate on the table saw. The problem comes when the thin sheet starts to slip under the rip fence and bind or skew in the cut. To overcome this alarming tendency, make a slip-on fence that closes the gap between the fence and table (**E**). A clear acrylic strip above the laminate helps prevent the sheet from climbing or lifting up and out of the cut, especially when cutting narrow strips. As you feed the sheet into the blade, bow it upward to maintain consistent pressure against the saw table (**F**).

Generally, it's best to cover the edges first; then lay the laminate on the top surface. This way, the glueline won't be exposed on top. Start by brushing the edges of the substrate and the back of the laminate with contact cement (**G**). On porous surfaces, particularly with particleboard, it's best to give the surface a second coat of cement once the first coat has dried. Look for an even, shiny sheen over the entire surface. Let the cement dry for 10 min. to 30 min., or until it doesn't stick to your finger.

Adhering parts with contact cement is a one-shot affair. Once the two surfaces make contact, you won't be able to move them. With relatively narrow pieces, you can simply eyeball the position of the laminate and place it onto the edge, making sure there's an overhang all around (**H**). Then use a rubber roller to press the laminate firmly to the substrate, ensuring a good bond (**I**).

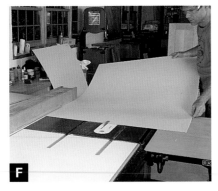

F

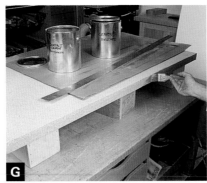

G

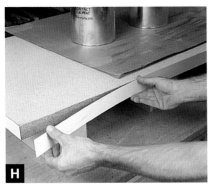

H

I

Trim the overhang with a flush-trimming bit in the router. Flush-trimming routers are great because of their light weight and maneuverability, but any type of router will work for this operation (**J**).

When attaching a big piece of laminate, you'll need to take a slightly different approach. After you've applied the adhesive to both parts and let it dry, position slip sheets of scrap laminate, strips of thin plywood, or any thin material on top of the glued substrate; then position the laminate on top of the sheets (**K**). The slip sheets let you position the laminate for an even overhang without accidentally sticking it to the substrate. Once the laminate is in position, press it to the substrate with your hands, working from the center out. As you progress, remove the slip sheets from beneath (**L**). Then press the laminate with a rubber roller—again working from the center out—using as much pressure as you can muster. A J-type roller makes it easier to tackle large surfaces (**M**).

Once more, trim the overhang with a flush-trimming bit (**N**). This particular bit is designed to cut a very slight chamfer when trimming adjacent laminate surfaces (**O**). Finish up by easing over sharp edges and removing any overhang with a mill file; then soften the edges with a sanding block (**P**).

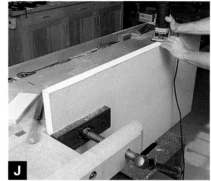

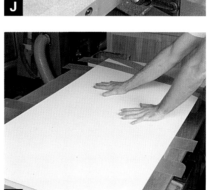

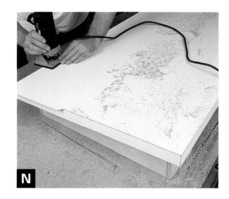

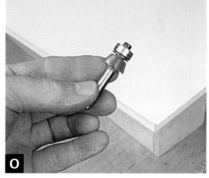

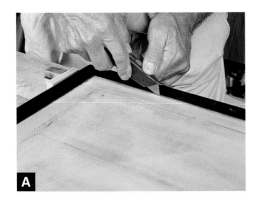

Leather Desktop

For a luxurious writing surface, leather can't be beat. You can lay leather onto practically any substrate, but unfinished plywood is best. When constructing the work surface, make sure to build a perimeter edge that's about 1/16 in. above the surface on which you'll be laying the leather. Begin by cutting the leather 1 in. oversize, using a straightedge and a large square to lay out your cuts. Then trim the leather with scissors. Wet the back of the leather by lightly misting it with water. Then roll it up and let the leather sit for 5 min. to 10 min., allowing the water soak evenly into the fibers.

While you're waiting for the leather to absorb the moisture, use a razor knife to incise all around the raised perimeter of the desk surface (**A**). Blend about 9 parts white glue with 1 part water to make a mixture with the consistency of light cream. Use a small paint roller to apply an even coat of the glue mixture onto the entire surface; then follow by laying a bead of full-strength glue around the edges, flattening and leveling the bead with a brush (**B**). The thinner glue in the center of the panel ensures the leather stays supple.

At this point, your leather should be moist and ready to go. Center the roll over the desk surface and unroll it onto the glue (**C**). Use your palms to flatten the leather from the center out, removing any wrinkles or trapped air pockets (**D**). Then run your fingernail or a blunt stick around the perimeter to crease the leather where you previously made the incision (**E**). Carefully trim the leather at the creased line with the razor knife (**F**). Let the desktop dry overnight before putting it to use. As the moisture in the glue and the leather evaporates, the leather will shrink, pulling tight to the desktop and removing any leftover wrinkles.

Tooling Leather

Tooling, or embossing leather, gives any work surface a classy look (**A**). The technique is straightforward and involves a few simple tools: a small hammer and one or more leather punches in the design of your choice. The tips of leather punches are made from hardened steel with patterns ground into their ends, and you can pick them up from leather suppliers (**B**). Be forewarned: They're expensive!

Tooling must take place during the process of applying the leather, since the glue below should be wet as you work the surface. Start by tapping around the perimeter of the leather with a punch, keeping your hammer pressure firm and consistent (**C**). As you tap, apply slight sideways pressure on the punch to push the leather up against the edge of the border. Use your eye to lay out the pattern as you go, looking to see that the punched designs are evenly spaced. To incorporate a second row of tooling parallel to the first, clamp a straightedge in line with the first pattern and use it to guide your punch (**D**).

Use enamel paint or gold leaf to highlight and emphasize the punched pattern. Gold-colored enamel works well, or you can apply gilder's sizing (a type of glue) and lay gold leaf onto the designs (**E**). Before the paint dries fully, load a pad of 0000 steel wool with paste wax and vigorously rub the painted areas, removing excess paint and giving the tooling an aged look and feel (**F**).

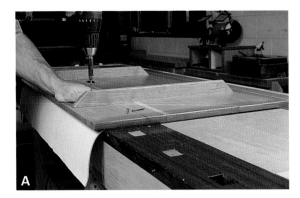

Lift-Up Lid

Hinged lids are great for chests and other low storage boxes, because they make rooting and rummaging inside a chest easier. An important concern when making a wide, unsupported lid is to support and stiffen it, to prevent it from warping. Cleats attached to the lid usually do the trick. Screw—don't glue—the cleats on the bottom side to keep the top flat without restricting wood movement (**A**).

To attach the lid to a rather narrow box side, glue a secondary cleat at a right angle to a top strip; then attach the assembly to the box with glue and screws (**B**). Secure the lid to the strip with cranked strap hinges (**C**).

To prevent the lid from inadvertently closing on the user—particularly for small children—attach a pair of spring-loaded chest hinges inside the case, screwing them to the undersides of the top and to the sides of the box (**D**). Now rooters can safely root to their hearts' content!

Using Natural Defects

Rather than sawing away or concealing certain "defects" in your wood, take the opportunity to highlight them instead. A large knot fell from the cherry board shown here, and the resulting hole is unsightly—not to mention impractical (**A**). With careful sanding around the edges of the hole, you can clean up loose debris and soften any sharp edges. On the underside of the top, attach a small painted panel or a strip of precious wood to seal the hole from the bottom (**B**).

On the top side, what was once a defect is now a focal point that draws and intrigues the eye (**C**).

Another approach is to glue an inlaid dovetailed key, or butterfly, across cracks or splits. The inlay is an appealing element, and it prevents further splitting. Cut the inlay from hard, dense wood on the bandsaw; then mark its outline onto the work (**D**). Make the inlay two-thirds the thickness of the top. Set a small-diameter straight bit to a depth of about 1/16 in. less than the thickness of the inlay and excavate a pocket, routing freehand inside your layout lines. Then shave right to the lines with a chisel (**E**).

Apply glue into the pocket and on the edges of the butterfly and tap it home (**F**). Once the glue has dried, level the inlay flush to the surface with a plane and scraper (**G**).

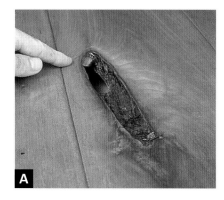

A

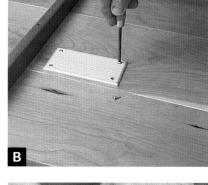

B

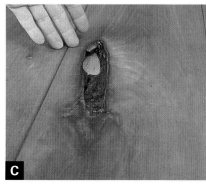

C

D

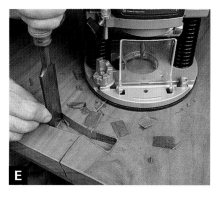

E

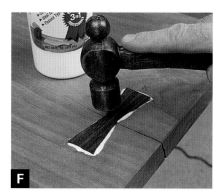

F

G

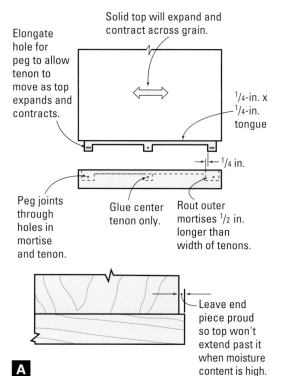

Elongate hole for peg to allow tenon to move as top expands and contracts.

Solid top will expand and contract across grain.

¼-in. x ¼-in. tongue

¼ in.

Peg joints through holes in mortise and tenon.

Glue center tenon only.

Rout outer mortises ½ in. longer than width of tenons.

Leave end piece proud so top won't extend past it when moisture content is high.

A

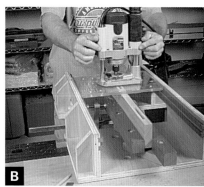
B

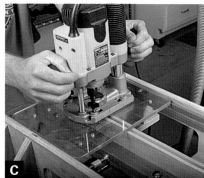
C

D

E

F

G

Breadboard Ends

Breadboard ends add a nice touch to a top, concealing its end-grain edges and offering an air of distinction. It also serves to hold a wide solid-wood surface flat. When constructing a breadboard end, the trick is to attach it in such a manner as to allow the solid top to expand and contract. If you glue the end piece entirely across the top, the top will eventually split due to wood movement. The traditional approach is to cut tenons on the end of the top; then mill mortises into the breadboard end. By gluing only the center tenon, the top is free to expand and contract (**A**). Start by cutting the end piece about 1 in. longer than the width of the top and then mill three mortises in the end, about 1 in. deep by 3 in. to 4 in. wide (**B**). After cutting the mortises, rout or saw a ¼-in.-deep groove between them (**C**).

To ensure a tight fit of the breadboard to the top, plane a few shavings from the center of the piece. This "springs" the breadboard so the ends—which won't be glued—remain tight to the top (**D**).

On the table saw, use a stacked dado blade to mill a 1-in.-long tongue on the tabletop. Make the tongue in two passes on each side of the top. For the first pass, use double-sided tape to attach a subfence to the rip fence and push the panel across the blade (**E**). Then remove the subfence and cut the tongue to full length by running the panel against the rip fence (**F**). This way there's no need to move the rip fence, reducing the chance for error.

Next, lay out the three tenons on the tongue, so that the two outer tenons are about ½ in. narrower than their respective mortises are long. Then lay out the ¼-in.-deep tongue for the groove you milled in the breadboard. Cut the tenons and the tongue with a jigsaw, following your layout lines (**G**). Saw the outer shoulders with a backsaw (**H**). To ease the transition between the breadboard end and the top, plane a slight chamfer on the inner edges of the end and along the shoulders of the top (**I**).

Temporarily fit the breadboard to the top and crosscut it to length. If you suspect the top will expand, depending on its current moisture content, it's best to cut the end about ⅛ in. or so longer than the top is wide. Once you cut the end to length, clamp it to the tabletop and drill for ¼-in. pegs from the underside of the top, through the center of each tenon (**J**). Then remove the breadboard and elongate the two outer peg holes with a coping saw (**K**).

[**TIP**] **A piece of masking tape wrapped around the drill bit makes a quick depth stop. Leave a flap hanging off to serve as a conspicuous flag.**

Brush glue on the center mortise and tenon only (**L**); then attach the breadboard with a single clamp (**M**). Drive the pegs through the tenons and into the top from the underside, adding a drop of glue at the end of the peg to keep it from falling out (**N**). For now, the finished breadboard end, with its nicely chamfered edges, protrudes slightly past the tabletop (**O**). As the top expands, the ends will align flush. With a change in seasons, the ends once again protrude. This is a better-looking solution than having the top extend past the breadboard ends.

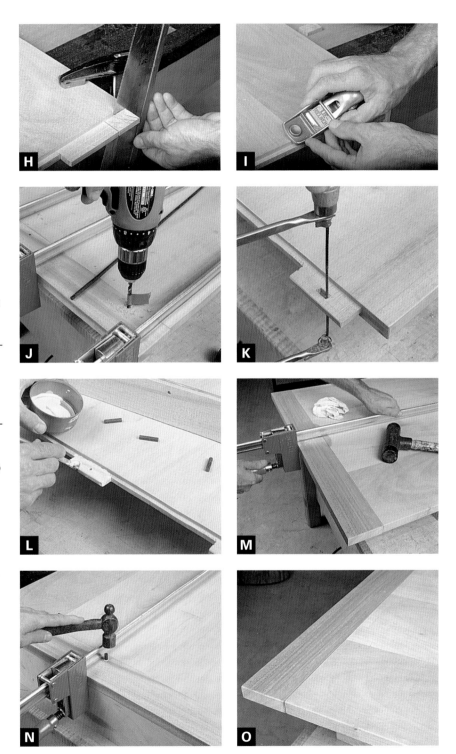

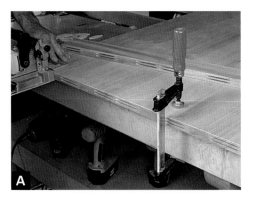

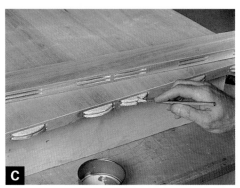

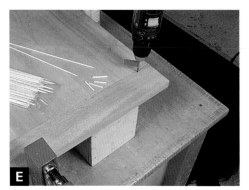

Biscuit Breadboard Ends

Another, more expedient, method for attaching breadboard ends is to use biscuits. This technique is best used on relatively narrow breadboards— say, less than 2 in. to 3 in. wide. Spring the joint by taking a few shavings from the center of the breadboard edge. Slot both the breadboard end and the end of the tabletop for pairs of biscuits. Make sure you reference the biscuit joiner from the same side as you cut the second series of slots and cut the four center slots no longer than 4 in. to 6 in. apart (**A**). Once you've cut the slots, glue all of the biscuits into the top (**B**).

When the biscuits in the top are dry, brush glue in only the four slots in the center of the breadboard (**C**) and then clamp the end to the tabletop (**D**).

Flip the top over and drill ⅛-in.-diameter stopped holes through each pair of unglued biscuits for ⅛-in. pegs in the breadboard. The best pegs are made from bamboo skewers, which you can pick up at the grocery store (**E**). Pin the biscuits with the pegs; then saw them flush to the surface (**F**). As the top expands and contracts, the bamboo pegs will flex without breaking, keeping the joint tight without cracking the top.

Drop-In Table Leaves

Look in common woodworking catalogs and you'll come across *table extension slides*. These clever wood or metal pieces of gear attach to the underside of a tabletop and let you separate the top into two halves. Dropping a table leaf into the gap between the two halves provides you with extra table surface. Table pins or biscuits in the top and leaves serve to line up the parts and keep the surface flat. The pins, available in brass, wood, and plastic, are essentially dowels with rounded ends. Biscuits work just as well when glued on one side only—so that the exposed biscuit can fit into the slot in a leaf. Whether using the table pins or biscuits, the first order of business is to build the table frame as two separate halves, being careful to check the free rails for square as you glue up the frame (**A**).

Next, secure a half top to each frame with tabletop clips. Be sure to brace the free ends of the aprons with plywood gussets (**B**). Glue the table pins or biscuits in only one table half (**C**). Push the two halves together and screw the extension slides to the underside. Pull out each slide by about ¼ in. to ensure the two tabletop halves will fit tightly once they're closed (**D**).

Now make your leaf, or leaves, in a similar manner to the two halves. You can attach aprons to the leaf for a seamless look once it's installed, or keep the leaf flat. Just remember that an apron makes storing the leaf more problematic. Make sure to brace the aprons with corner blocks and slot both ends of the leaf, including the aprons. Glue the pins or biscuits in only one end (**E**).

To add a leaf, spread the table apart and lay the leaf over the extended wood rails, aligning the pins or biscuits into their respective slots (**F**). Now push the table halves together (**G**).

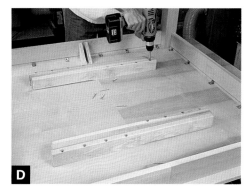

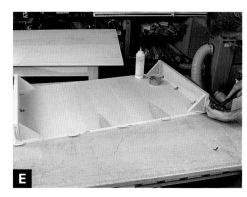

Attaching Tops

Allowing for Movement

➤ Wood Buttons (p. 294)

➤ Splines and Glue (p. 296)

➤ Wood Cleats (p. 296)

Hardware Solutions

➤ Metal Tabletop Fasteners (p. 297)

➤ Deep Screw Holes (p. 298)

➤ Pocket Holes (p. 299)

Some tabletops are nailed to their bases, but there are more elegant solutions for attaching tops to frames or other support structures. All of them offer a secure method of attachment, while concealing the connections underneath the top. And when you're dealing with a solid-wood top, you must allow for expansion and shrinkage across its width. The trick is to hold the top secure to the frame while allowing it to move. Sound impossible? Several strategies accomplish this in simplicity and style.

Strategies for Attaching Tops

The material you choose for your top will affect the way you attach it. With solid wood, you'll have to allow for wood movement. Metal clips and wood buttons fit into slots cut in the aprons and are screwed to the top; they let the top move while holding it tight to the frame. Another option is to use screws driven through the aprons in oversize holes.

Plywood, MDF, and other man-made materials can be screwed from underneath without regard to wood movement. The easiest method is to drill through the aprons themselves; then drive the screws through the aprons and into the underside of the top. Stone and other natural tops must be allowed to move in a similar fashion as solid wood,

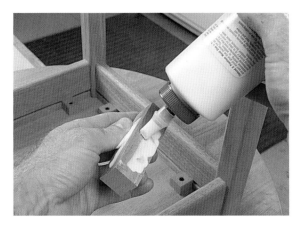

Apply small glue blocks underneath the top to keep it properly aligned as it expands and contracts from season to season.

but screws won't work here. Instead, run a bead of flexible silicone caulk around the frame's perimeter; then gently clamp the top to the frame until the caulk has set.

Glue Blocks

Even when attached with buttons or clips, solid-wood tabletops will often shift on the frame because of wood movement, especially when the top is wide. To keep a large top centered, use wood glue blocks at each end of the frame on the underside of the top. Once you've attached the top with buttons, clips, or screws, run a generous bead of glue on two adjacent faces of a 3-in.-long block and rub it into the tabletop *across the grain*, centered against the apron. Then clamp the block to the top until the glue dries. Follow the same procedure to attach a block at the opposite end of the frame.

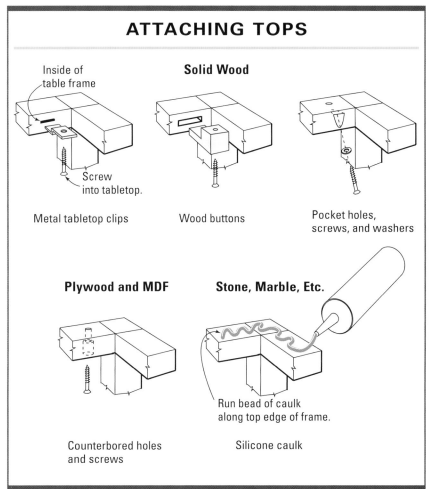

ATTACHING TOPS

Inside of table frame

Solid Wood

Screw into tabletop.

Metal tabletop clips

Wood buttons

Pocket holes, screws, and washers

Plywood and MDF

Stone, Marble, Etc.

Run bead of caulk along top edge of frame.

Counterbored holes and screws

Silicone caulk

Long-reach clamps come in handy for many gluing chores.

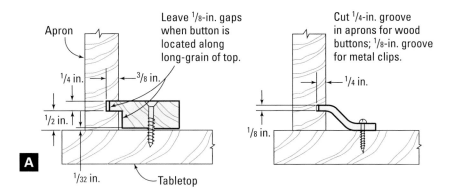

Apron

Leave ⅛-in. gaps when button is located along long-grain of top.

Cut ¼-in. groove in aprons for wood buttons; ⅛-in. groove for metal clips.

¼ in.   ⅜ in.

¼ in.

½ in.

⅛ in.

A

1/32 in.   Tabletop

Wood Buttons

An effective and simple method for attaching a tabletop to a frame is to use wood "buttons" (**A**). I always make a batch of buttons and save the extras for later use. Start by cutting a series of ½-in.-wide notches in a long length of ¾-in. by 1-in.-wide stock on the table saw (**B**). Space the notches about 1 in. apart.

On the miter saw, crosscut individual buttons by aligning the blade with the left shoulder of each notch (**C**). Taking into account the ⅛-in. saw kerf, crosscutting in this manner produces a ⅜-in. tongue on each button. Finish the buttons by countersinking and boring a pilot hole through each button for a screw.

Once you've made the buttons, groove the inside of the aprons before assembling the frame. Use a ¼-in.-wide dado blade and adjust the height to cut a groove ⅜ in. deep. Set your rip fence so the resulting groove will be offset about 1/32 in. with the button's tongue, as shown in the drawing. An arrow drawn on a strip of masking tape indicates the correct edge to run against the fence (**D**).

> **⚠ WARNING** Don't gauge cross-cuts directly from the rip fence. The work can bind and kick back. For safety, clamp a block to the rip fence; then use it to gauge the correct distance of the stock to the blade.

B

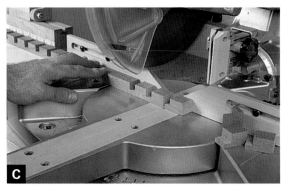

C

D

Assemble the base; then place your tabletop up-side down and center the base over its surface. Position the buttons into the grooves in the aprons, keeping some near the corners to re-inforce the joints. Make sure to leave a gap be-tween each button and apron when they fall on a long-grain surface. Position adjacent buttons tight to the aprons (**E**). Drive a screw through each button and into the underside of the top (**F**). The gaps on the long-grain areas allow the top to expand and contract freely, while the buttons hold the top tight to the aprons.

[**TIP**] **Mistakes happen. You glued up your table frame, but forgot to groove all the aprons for tabletop fasteners. For an easy fix, use a biscuit jointer to cut slots inside the aprons. A standard biscuit cutter will cut a slot the correct width for metal tabletop clips.**

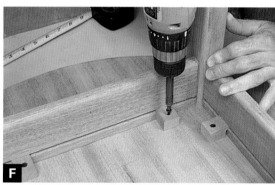

Splines and Glue

On veneered or plywood tabletops—where wood movement is not an issue—you can glue an apron directly to the underside of the top. To stiffen the connection and ensure exact alignment, College of the Redwoods student and furniture maker Konrad Leo Horsch used short plywood splines fitted in both the curved aprons and the top of his Lady's Writing Desk.

Rout grooves in the underside of the top and into the top edges of the aprons; then glue the splines into the aprons every 3 in. or so (**A**).

Assemble the top to the base with glue, using plenty of clamps to draw the joints tight. The result is a perfect fit of base to top with no visible connections (**B**).

Wood Cleats

An effective and elegant way to attach a tabletop is to secure wood cleats to the top of the frame and then screw through the cleats and into the underside of the top. Half notches cut in the tops of the legs and aprons and in the cleats let you lock them flush with the top of the frame. Countersunk screws hold them fast (**A**). The cleats that run along the center of the top can be drilled with an ordinary hole for a screw; cleats along the perimeter of the frame need to have slotted screw holes to allow the top to expand and contract.

With the tabletop upside down, center the base over it and drive screws through the cleats and into the top (**B**).

Metal Tabletop Fasteners

Also called Z-clips because of their shape, metal tabletop fasteners are installed in a similar fashion as are wood buttons.

> ➤ **See the drawing on p. 294.**

Cut all your apron joinery first; then cut a ⅛-in. by ½-in.-deep groove in each rail on its inside face, using a standard sawblade (**A**).

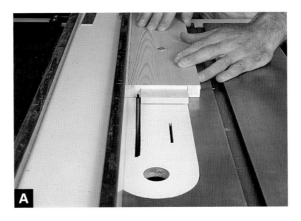

With the tabletop upside down on the bench, center the base over it and carefully arrange the clips. Like wood buttons, be sure to leave room between each clip and the rail when it's positioned across the grain (**B**). Predrill for screws and use pan-head screws to secure the clips to the tabletop (**C**).

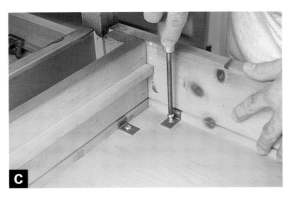

A

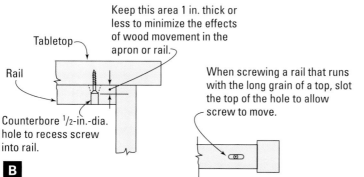

Keep this area 1 in. thick or less to minimize the effects of wood movement in the apron or rail.

Tabletop

Rail

Counterbore ¹/₂-in.-dia. hole to recess screw into rail.

When screwing a rail that runs with the long grain of a top, slot the top of the hole to allow screw to move.

B

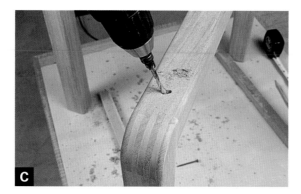

C

D

Deep Screw Holes

Securing a tabletop with screws is a legitimate approach, as long as you follow a few simple guidelines. First, make sure your screws pass through no more than 1 in. of rail or apron width. On rails wider than 1 in., simply counterbore to the correct depth with a Forstner bit (**A**). Then drill a clearance hole through the rail for the screw. Keeping the screw area of the rail rather thin ensures that the screw won't loosen over time as the rail swells or shrinks as a result of wood movement.

Another wood-movement issue is when you're screwing into a solid-wood tops. You must allow the top to move or you risk cracking the top or pulling apart the frame joints. The easiest way to accommodate the top's natural movement is to slot the screw holes in the rails (**B**). On the top side of each rail, angle a drill bit back and forth to enlarge the hole. Make sure to orient the slot in the direction that the top will move (**C**).

Lay the top upside down and center the base over it. Then drive the screws into pilot holes drilled into the top (**D**).

Pocket Holes

When using a pocket hole, you angle the screw slightly, allowing it to start much closer to the surface of the top. There are many excellent commercial pocket-hole jigs that you can use or you can make your own from a hard, dense piece of wood. The idea is to use an angled guide block to drill a ½-in. counterbore into the apron and finish up by extending a shank hole through the apron. The oversize counterbore gives the screw room to move as the top expands and contracts with variations in seasonal moisture content.

Start by sawing a wedge of scrap material to a 20-degree angle on the bandsaw or table saw. Then clamp a 1½-in. by 2-in. square of hardwood to the wedge and to the drill press table. Use a ½-in. Forstner bit to drill an angled hole through the center of the block, allowing the bit to exit on one side (**A**).

After drilling, cut one end off the block so the pocket hole is the correct distance from the end of the block (**B**). Then clamp the block to the inside face of the apron and flush with its top edge. Using the same bit you used on the drill press, drill through the block and into the face of the apron. Use a piece of masking tape to gauge the correct depth (**C**).

Remove the block and extend the hole through the apron, starting with a jobber's bit or any extra-long drill bit (**D**). Then finish by drilling through the apron from the top edge with a ¼-in. bit (**E**). The oversize hole will allow the screw to move as the top expands and contracts. Secure the top to the apron with a #6 pan-head screw, using a washer under the head (**F**).

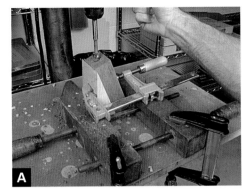

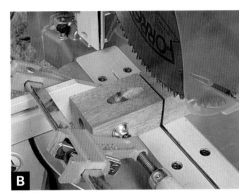

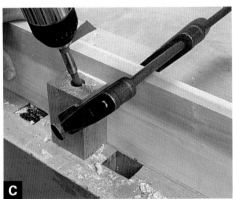

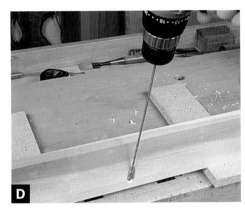

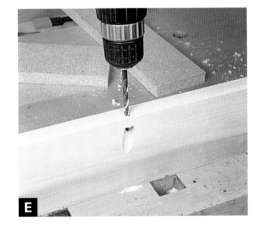

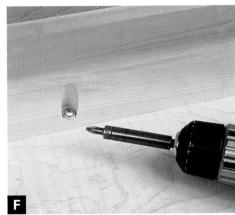

Sources

For technical tool expertise, support, and friendly helpfulness spanning many years, my thanks go to the following tool and material suppliers and manufacturers.

Leonard Lee, president, and Wally Wilson at Lee Valley Tools (800-871-8158)

Todd Langston and Scott Box at Porter-Cable and Delta (800-321-9443)

Tom Lie-Nielsen at Lie-Nielsen Toolworks (800-327-2520)

John Otto at Jet (800-274-6848)

George Delaney at Powermatic (931-473-5551)

Dave Keller at Keller & Co. (800-995-2456)

Carol Reed, The Router Lady (760-789-6612)

Gary Chin at Garrett Wade (800-221-2942)

Harry and Henry at Harris Tools (506-228-8310)

Jim Brewer at Freud (800-334-4107)

Zack Etheridge at Highland Hardware (800-241-6748)

Ann Rockler at Rockler Hardware (800-279-4441)

Kurt Wilke at Wilke Machinery (800-235-2100)

Fred Damsen at The Japan Woodworker (800-537-7820)

Daryl Keil at Vacuum Pressing Systems (207-725-0935)

Vince Barragan at Eagle Tools (626-797-8262)

Mike Peters at Shady Lane Tree Farm (610-965-5612)

Chris Carlson at Bosch (800-815-8665)

Frank Pollaro at Flamingo Veneer (973-672-7600)

Carlo Venditto at Jesada (800-531-5559)

The folks at Woodworker's Supply (800-645-9292)

Bruce Halliburton at Georgia Pacific (404-652-4000)

Ron Snayberger at DeWalt (800-433-9258)

Phil Humfrey at Exaktor (800-387-9789)

Lisa Gazda at American Clamping (800-828-1004)

Cynthia Van Hester at Wetzler Clamp (800-451-1852)

Torbin Helshoji at Laguna Tools (800-234-1976)

Brad Witt at Woodhaven (800-344-6657)

Marcello Tommosini at CMT (800-268-2487)

Darrel Nish at Craft Supplies (800-373-0917)

Jim Forrest at Forrest Mfg. (800-733-7111)

Greta Heimerdinger at Lignomat USA (800-227-2105)

Jim Dumas and Greg Engle at Certainly Wood (716-655-0206)

Ken Grizzley and the lads—even Mark—at Leigh Industries (604-464-2700)

Further Reading

CABINET MAKING

Joyce, Ernest. *Encyclopedia of Furniture Making.* Sterling Publishing.

Krenov, James. *The Fine Art of Cabinetmaking.* Sterling Publishing.

Tolpin, Jim. *Building Traditional Kitchen Cabinets.* The Taunton Press.

WOOD TECHNOLOGY

Forest Products Laboratory. *Wood Handbook: Wood as an Engineering Material.* Forest Products Laboratory.

Hoadley, R. Bruce. *Identifying Wood.* The Taunton Press.

———*Understanding Wood.* The Taunton Press.

DESIGN

Aronson, Joseph. *The Encyclopedia of Furniture.* Crown Publishing.

Editors of *Fine Woodworking. Practical Design.* The Taunton Press.

Graves, Garth. *The Woodworker's Guide to Furniture Design.* Popular Woodworking Books.

Morley, John. *The History of Furniture: Twenty-Five Centuries of Style and Design in the Western Tradition.* Bulfinch Press.

Pye, David. *The Nature and Aesthetics.* Cambium Press.

TOOLS AND MACHINERY

Bird, Lonnie. *The Bandsaw Book.* The Taunton Press.
———*The Shaper Book.* The Taunton Press.

Duginske, Mark. *Mastering Woodworking Machines.* The Taunton Press.

Hack, Garrett. *Classic Hand Tools.* The Taunton Press.
———*The Handplane Book.* The Taunton Press.

Lee, Leonard. *The Complete Guide to Sharpening.* The Taunton Press.

Mehler, Kelly. *The Table Saw Book.* The Taunton Press.

Nagyszalanczy, Sandor. *The Art of Fine Tools.* The Taunton Press.

———*Woodshop Jigs and Fixtures.* The Taunton Press.

WOODSHOPS

Landis, Scott. *The Workbench Book.* The Taunton Press.

———*The Workshop Book.* The Taunton Press.

Nagyszalanczy, Sandor. *Setting Up Shop.* The Taunton Press.

———*Woodshop Dust Control.* The Taunton Press.

Tolpin, Jim. *The Toolbox Book.* The Taunton Press.

WOOD FINISHING

Charron, Andy. *Water-Based Finishes.* The Taunton Press.

Dresdner, Michael. *The New Wood Finishing Book.* The Taunton Press.

Jewitt, Jeff. *Great Wood Finishes.* The Taunton Press.
———*Hand-Applied Finishes.* The Taunton Press.

Index